SPI
EGE
L&G
RAU

WIDE
AWAKE

WIDE AWAKE

A MEMOIR OF INSOMNIA

Patricia Morrisroe

SPIEGEL & GRAU

NEW YORK

2010

Wide Awake is a work of nonfiction. Some names and
identifying details have been changed.

Published in the United States by Spiegel & Grau, an imprint of The Random
House Publishing Group, a division of Random House, Inc., New York.

Spiegel & Grau and Design is a registered trademark of Random House, Inc.

Library of Congress Cataloging-in-Publication Data

Morrisroe, Patricia.
Wide awake: a memoir of insomnia / Patricia Morrisroe.
p. cm.
ISBN 978-0-385-52224-3
eBook ISBN 978-0-679-60363-4
1. Morrisroe, Patricia, 1951—Health.   2. Insomniacs—
New York—Biography.   I. Title.
RC548.M677 2010
362.196'84980092—dc22   2009041660
[B]

Printed in the United States of America on acid-free paper

www.spiegelandgrau.com

2 4 6 8 9 7 5 3 1

First Edition

Book design by Caroline Cunningham

Title page image: *Time,* © Ross C. Brown

For my parents and Bumpa

INTRODUCTION

Sleep broke my heart, and then it tried to kill me.

First, the heartbreak: Picture John Malkovich playing a character called Sleep based on his portrayal of the cruel, seductive Valmont in *Dangerous Liaisons*. He was my nightly visitor—Sleep, the brilliant gamesman, who delighted in torturing me. Though I consecrated my bedroom to him, banishing TV, books, and other distractions, it was never enough. He then demanded goose-down pillows and six-hundred-thread-count sheets and a high-end sound machine to provide the musical score to my sleepless nights, transporting me to the kinds of places he wouldn't be caught dead in, such as a malarial rain forest and an aviary full of screeching cockatoos.

When noise therapy failed, he began pushing sleeping pills and antianxiety medications, along with herbal remedies with deceptively soothing names, such as Beautiful Dreams and Deep Sleep. He sent me to an acupuncturist, who rebalanced my heart and kidneys, and to a pharmacy in Florence for a thirteenth-century sleeping potion that helped the Medici family but didn't help me. He suggested biofeedback and the masseuse Barbra Streisand used for her insomnia. He introduced me to a dozen psychopharmacologists and psychotherapists, including a worldly Jesuit, who was also a gynecologist and who left me wondering if I needed Prozac, estrogen, or an exorcist. Yet Sleep remained an elusive bedmate, lulling me into a state of dreamy ecstasy only to abandon me at 3 A.M. Then there were the hellish evenings when he never showed up at all, deserting me for women whose sleep systems were more "robust" than mine, women who, thanks to his ministrations, slept like logs. But no matter how many times he betrayed me, no matter his incessant lies and indiscriminate bed-hopping, here's the sad truth: I couldn't get enough of him.

I once mentioned to a friend that my insomnia had morphed into Malkovich as Valmont and she said, "You're joking, right?" People who sleep through the night rarely think twice about the mechanics of sleep, let alone envision it as a sadistic French aristocrat, but when you've suffered the miseries of insomnia, the Sandman has a twisted mind. By withholding his affection, he can potentially shorten your life, ruin your concentration, and raise your risk of heart disease, obesity, and cancer. Sleep, in his various dysfunctions, can be one of the most dangerous liaisons of all— a reality that was brought home to me one morning in the winter of 2006, when, after a particularly bad night, I went out for a latte. Not paying adequate attention, I crossed Park Avenue on a red light and, after catching a flash of yellow, steeled myself for the inevitable collision with a speeding cab. The driver slammed on the brakes within inches of hitting me. *"Lady!"* he yelled. *"What's your problem?"*

Up until then, I'd always considered myself a high-functioning insomniac with few compensatory bad habits. I limited my caffeine intake and got plenty of fresh air, taking long, invigorating walks in Central Park. While doctors have linked insomnia to obesity, I watched what I ate and never gained weight. I was so disciplined that I couldn't believe that of all things, I couldn't master the one that required the least amount of effort. What *was* my problem?

A few days after my near collision, I flew to London with my husband, Lee. He was going for business, while I was going on the off chance that changing time zones might shake some sense into my biological clock. (I appreciated the irony that I was now hoping jet lag would help my insomnia, but I likened it to rebooting a computer.) We checked in to the Draycott, a small "country house" hotel in Chelsea, where the rooms are named after famous English personalities. I'd once spent a restless night in the Agatha Christie Suite listening to what I imagined was a murder in the room above, so now I opted for Gertrude Lawrence. That night, while Lee slept, I skimmed the actress's biography, which had been left on the writing desk near the bed. Lawrence had played the title role in *Lady in the Dark,* Moss Hart's "psychoanalytical musical" about a fashion editor who is plagued by turbulent dreams. The character was based on Hart himself, who'd spent much of his life in therapy dealing with his depression and insomnia. It occurred to me that maybe I should write about my own insomnia, a thought that naturally made me less sleepy. I moved from the bed to a wing chair, where the hotel had placed a teddy bear as an homage to Aloysius, the stuffed animal Sebastian Flyte carries in Evelyn Waugh's *Brideshead Revisited.* Waugh had terrible insomnia, which he treated with alcohol and sleeping potions—a regimen that led to his nervous breakdown aboard a cruise ship heading to Ceylon and formed the basis of his novel *The Ordeal of Gilbert Pinfold.*

When I climbed back into bed, I thought of all the other famous people who suffered from insomnia, including my immediate neighbors at the hotel, Vivien Leigh, Lewis Carroll, and Oscar Wilde. I spent the next several hours convincing myself I shouldn't take sleeping pills lest I wind up like Waugh, hallucinating jazz bands and barking dogs. By 4 A.M. I didn't care and reached for the Ambien bottle, swallowing a five-milligram pill. It worked—for forty-five minutes—and the next night I switched to a milligram of Ativan, which gave me a grand total of three hours of sleep.

Given my sleep-deprived state the next morning, I probably should have avoided "Gothic Nightmares," an exhibit at the Tate

Britain that explored the violent and supernatural themes in art and culture from 1770 to 1830. The movie *Frankenstein* had given me nightmares as a child, and one of the paintings in the Tate exhibit—Henry Fuseli's *The Nightmare*—was based on Mary Shelley's original story; it depicted a terrifying image of a young woman prostrate on her bed, a hideous red-eyed incubus perched on her breastbone. In the corner, a leering horse, with milky white orbs for eyes, poked its head through blood-red boudoir curtains. The woman appeared to be heavily sedated, maybe even half-dead, but at least, I noted, she was *sleeping*. I tried listening to the audio guide, but I was starting to crash. I heard a voice cry, *"Sleep, no more! Macbeth has murdered sleep!"* Was it the audio narrator? I followed a woman through parted curtains and sat on a bench in the darkness to watch the "Phantasmagoria," an animated slide show of supernatural images with sound effects. A skeleton flew in front of me. Startled, I screamed and headed for the exit, passing through a series of crimson rooms, where I encountered one of the most unnerving paintings in the show, Fuseli's *Mad Kate*. The portrait depicts a woman insane with grief over the death of her lover. Caught in a tempest, the wind whipping her cloak, she looked at me with the glazed eyes of someone who hadn't slept in weeks.

I went outside to get a cab. The sky had turned threatening and soon it began to pour. The wind, whipping across the Thames, turned my umbrella inside out, breaking its fragile spokes. A rational person would have returned to the Tate and waited for the weather to lift, but I was no longer rational. I was Mad Kate. With no cabs in sight and no sense of direction, I headed off in the downpour, drunk with sleeplessness, crying for poor Kate, for Vivien Leigh, for Moss Hart, for Evelyn Waugh—for all of us sleepless ladies and men in the dark.

Back in New York a week later, I thought I'd left Mad Kate behind, only to find America in the midst of its own Gothic nightmare. People were smashing up cars, pulling towel racks off bathroom walls, picking violent fights with their spouses, engaging in sexual activity, and raiding the refrigerator—all while sleeping. One "sleep eater" claimed she'd gained a hundred pounds, finding clues like half-eaten pork chops and candy bars between the sheets. Another reportedly ripped open a package of hamburger meat, tearing it "like a grizzly bear." Many of these strange behaviors were linked directly to Ambien, but others were not. ABC reported on a couple who had managed to stay married for thirty years, despite the husband's periodic attempts to strangle and stab his wife. "Every night I went to bed, I knew I was going into some kind of hell," explained Ron Voegtli. His terrified wife, Ann, agreed: "During the day he's this fun, caring person, and by night, he's like this monster."

I began to wonder why sleep had seized our imagination in such a primal way. During England's Gothic period, with the British poised between enlightenment and repression, the anxieties of the era had given rise to a macabre aesthetic that prized horror and fantasy. Was it the same with us? Had 9/11, the atrocities in Iraq, the video beheadings, the tsunamis and hurricanes, created a new kind of collective Gothic nightmare? Or did these outrageous stories merely underscore our basic ignorance about the mysteries of sleep? At the same time, I read a startling story in *New Scientist* about the current generation of "wakefulness-promoting" drugs being marketed and developed by pharmaceutical companies. It raised the possibility that in the next decade we might be able to structure sleep around our individual lifestyles, or perhaps do away with it completely.

For years I'd only discussed my insomnia with a few close friends, and I'd certainly never inquired about other people's sleep issues. It seemed too personal, the equivalent of asking about their sex lives or stock portfolios. But at a friend's bridal shower, when I casually mentioned that I was thinking about writing a book on sleep, I was surprised at the passionate reaction it elicited. One woman, a former top-ranked squash player turned high-end matchmaker, confessed that she'd been taking Ambien every night for three years and was worried that she was addicted. Another woman, a public relations executive, had regularly used Ambien, until memory loss and nightly binge eating had forced her to stop. After the shower, she was heading straight to a sleep clinic. The bride-to-be, overhearing the conversation, announced that *she* hadn't slept for two months. "It's probably just pre-wedding jitters," she said. "At least I hope that's all it is."

When I couldn't sleep myself that night, I went on the website Sleepnet.com and began reading the postings on the Insomnia Forum on the Sleep Disorders Information home page. It was positively addictive. Here's just a sampling of topics: *Sleep talking in different languages; Husband sleepwalks—urinates wherever; Boyfriend wakes up with deep scratches on face; Help I'm so tired I can't graduate from school; Screaming while sleeping; Sleeping with one eye open; Restless Groin Syndrome?; Incubus Attack!* On this website and similar ones, the likes of "Perchance Dreamer" and "Need ZZZZs" and "Sleeplady" are all picking one another's brains in a frustrating attempt to reconcile nature with technology, in a desperate attempt to *sleep*. Almost no one, from government workers in Spain, where the traditional siesta has been phased out, to Indian call-center employees, is immune to the madness.

Today, with advances in both neuroscience and sleep medicine, we've entered what sleep researcher Dr. David Dinges has called the "golden age of sleep research." Yet the more we learn about sleep, the less of it we seem to be getting, which raises a lot of vital questions about how we can live in a world where sleep is both devalued and viewed as a luxury. Are we evolving beyond sleep? Or self-destructing? Is sleep deprivation responsible for the obesity epidemic in this country? For the "dumbing down" of America? Have we become a nation of sleep survivors, pushing ourselves to the limits as our waistlines expand and our IQs contract? Or does it all come down to money and marketing? Sleep tends to fall off as we age, and with the baby boomers, pharmaceutical companies are seeing dollar signs in the dark circles of a very large target audience.

Once the recession hit, Americans really had something to lose sleep over. More than one in four complained that the economy was keeping them up nights, and they were turning increasingly to sleep aids. More than ever, sleep had become the Holy Grail. It was out there—but where? At the end of *Indiana Jones and the Last Crusade,* after Indiana loses his grip on the Grail and it plummets into an abyss, he and his father (Sean Connery) commiserate over spending so long searching for something they couldn't hold on to. A dejected Indy asks his father, "What did *you* find?" I've always loved Connery's answer: "Me? Illumination!" After talking to some of the country's leading sleep experts, sampling a host of therapies and pills, and literally traveling to the end of the world, I ultimately found illumination two blocks from home. While it didn't lead to the magic eight hours, it did make the nights a little brighter, the border between wakefulness and sleep easier to navigate. As I write this, I've had seven hours of natural, uninterrupted, drug-free slumber.

Sleep, the John Malkovich look-alike, has left the bedroom. Long live sleep!

1

THE HOUSE OF PUNK SLEEP

When I was a little girl, my grandfather taught me to sing "O Sleep, Why Dost Though Leave Me?" from Handel's oratorio *Semele*. Based on Greek mythology, it tells the story of a beautiful mortal, Semele, who falls in love with Jupiter, god of the sky. One day, after a postcoital nap, Semele can't understand why Jupiter seems distracted; she doesn't yet know that his vengeful wife, Juno, is plotting to send a thunderbolt her way. Oblivious to the dangers of loving a married deity, Semele sings of restoring her "wandering love" through the transformative power of sleep. The Handel aria became my signature song. I sang it at recitals, school assemblies, even after a practice air raid in second grade when some of my high-strung classmates were hyperventilating and Sister Margaret turned to me for something soothing to get our minds off a possible communist takeover. I sang it for my parents' friends, for the neighbors, and for my piano teacher, who, being a narcoleptic, slept through it, as she did through all twelve years of my piano lessons. Yet in all the times I performed the song, I never once thought it was weird that I was singing "O Sleep, Why Dost Thou Leave Me?" when sleep had already left certain members of my family and was, with grinding relentlessness, in the process of leaving me.

"Sleep architecture," along with "sleep hygiene," is one of those mysterious phrases that crop up regularly in sleep books. It refers to the overall pattern of a person's sleep—how fast one falls asleep, how long one stays asleep, how often one wakes up, and how that sleep is distributed across the multiple "stages" of sleep. When I think of sleep architecture, however, I immediately picture my family home in Andover, Massachusetts—the House of Punk Sleep. It was named in honor of my mother, who, invariably upon rising each morning, would dramatically announce that her sleep had been "punk." *Punk* was my mother's favorite synonym for anything weak, dispiriting, or well below par. She was so protective of her fragile sleep that if any of us got up at night, we were forbidden to run the water or flush the toilets or make even the slightest noise lest it wake her. That she was probably wide awake was totally beside the point. The inherent message was that sleep wasn't a natural process but a gift from fickle gods, who at any moment could snatch it away.

The House of Punk Sleep had three incarnations, the first a two-bedroom apartment in a white Victorian near the center of town. For the first two years of my life, I shared a room with my Irish grandfather, who lived with us on weekends. The other part of the week he was in idyllic Manchester-by-the-Sea, where he worked as the majordomo for a socially prominent Boston Brahmin. My grandfather, whom I'd nicknamed Bumpa, was also a concert singer, a voice teacher, an opera aficionado, a superb chef, and a delightful storyteller. Bumpa claimed that he inherited his poor sleep genes from his Irish mother, who, in turn, inherited them from her Irish mother, who inherited them from hers, and on and on. If you listened to my grandfather, Ireland produced light sleepers the way it bred poets and priests, but the Flynn family was particularly vulnerable for reasons he couldn't explain. He referred to it half-jokingly as "the Flynn curse," but what exactly did that mean? Did the Flynns carry a gene for "fatal familial insomnia," an inherited prion disease that kills through lack of sleep? That was highly doubtful, as Bumpa died at eighty-six, and my own sleep-deprived mother, at eighty-nine, is one of the most energetic people around. Maybe the Flynns were "short sleepers"—people who only needed four or five hours a night. Or maybe they were "secret sleepers"—people who got enough sleep but complained that they didn't. Or maybe there *was* a curse.

A few years ago, hoping to get to the root of the problem, I traveled to Ireland to search for my grandfather's relatives in his native County Cork. He had eight brothers and one sister, but all were deceased. I did, however, manage to locate a widowed niece, who was then in her late eighties and was getting ready for a night out dancing with a "gentleman friend." She was pressed for time, although she did mention that her grown children didn't approve of her gallivanting. "They want me to be home in bed," she said, which prompted the obvious question: "Do you get much sleep?" She shook her head vigorously. "Not a wink, dear. I'm too busy dancing."

Before high-stepping out of her small house, she provided directions to the overgrown cemetery where my great-grandparents are buried amid the ruins of a twelfth-century Cistercian abbey. Both had lived to their mid-seventies, which was fifteen years over the norm, proving again that however poorly they slept, it hadn't affected their longevity. From the cemetery it was a short distance to my grandfather's birthplace in Upper Aghada, where the architectural precursor to the House of Punk Sleep bears the name Careystone Cottage. Set against a lush backdrop of green pastures, wildflowers lining the entranceway, the house was so quaintly Celtic that I wanted to move in to it immediately. I was loitering in the driveway when a short, dark-haired woman opened the door. After I explained my connection to the house, she invited me inside, confiding that she could never figure out how the Flynns slept. "The house had only two rooms when we bought it," she explained.

"No wonder they didn't sleep," I said. "My grandfather had nine siblings. Imagine twelve people in two rooms."

"Actually, *one* room," the woman said. "The other had a piano in it."

While Bumpa may have been a poor sleeper, he was a prolific dreamer and it wasn't uncommon for him to start a conversation with "The weirdest thing happened last night." The deceased might appear to him "as real as life," or he might interpret a dream as a warning, such as the one foretelling the end of his career as a merchant marine. As he told it, and he did many times, he dreamt that he was sailing past the Rock of Gibraltar when he saw a mermaid sunning herself on the limestone promontory. With a nod to both Homer and the Starkist Tuna, the mermaid, whose blond hair cascaded down her shoulders, called his name and cried, *"Beware of drowning! Beware!"* He was docked in New York at the time, and heeding the siren's warning, he jumped ship. "And a good thing, too," he always said, long after I knew the punch line. A steward on White Star's *Oceanic,* he was about to be reassigned to the company's newest luxury liner—the RMS *Titanic.*

In New York, without a job or connections, Bumpa was walking down Fifth Avenue when he literally bumped into the woman who'd become his wife. My English grandmother had recently moved to New York from a country estate in Leesburg, Virginia, where she'd worked as a lady's maid for Mrs. William Corcoran Eustis, whose in-laws had started the Corcoran Gallery of Art in Washington, D.C. Mrs. Eustis's father, Levi P. Morton, was Benjamin Harrison's vice president and so rich that Henry Adams, the Washington chronicler, referred to him as "Money Bags." Through Morton, my grandmother secured Bumpa a job at the Metropolitan Club, which had been designed by Stanford White for the railroad tycoon J. P. Morgan. Morgan had helped finance Thomas Edison, who, in 1879, had invented the incandescent lightbulb, which would forever change modern sleep habits. Bumpa, whose Zelig-like ability to insert himself in the popular culture never ceased to amaze, claimed to have met Edison through the Irish tenor John McCormack, who recorded some ballads for Edison's company. The astoundingly prolific Edison—he held more than one thousand patents—was said to get by on only four hours of sleep a night. Bumpa delighted in quoting Edison's dictum that extra sleep made people "unhealthy and inefficient," to which he'd invariably add, "and dull, too."

When, in 1953, we moved to the second House of Punk Sleep, Bumpa lived with us full-time; my grandmother had died a few years earlier and he'd retired from his duties on the North Shore. Our new house, a charming 1930s Cape Cod, had three bedrooms; Bumpa shared one with Buff, my new cocker spaniel puppy. It was Bumpa's job to paper-train him and make sure he didn't bark at night, so my mother was free to toss and turn to the syncopated rhythm of my father's snoring. How my father managed to sleep was one of life's great mysteries, for in addition to probably having sleep apnea, he had bruxism, grinding his teeth so badly that he later needed extensive dental work. My nickname for him was "Mr. Pressure Cooker Head." Yet despite the snoring and gnashing of teeth, he was an extremely deep sleeper. You could scream his name and punch him in the arm, which my mother often did, and he wouldn't flutter an eyelid, whereas Bumpa, even with bad tinnitus, could hear a pin drop.

In theory, Bumpa's nightly routine should have encouraged good sleep. He never drank tea after 4 P.M. and abstained from cigarettes and alcohol. He ate early and lightly and rarely watched television. After cleaning up after the puppy and putting him in his little wicker dog bed, he'd say his prayers and then do eye exercises from the book *Sight Without Glasses*. He usually dropped off right away, awakening around 2 A.M. Instead of going downstairs, which he couldn't do without inciting seismic tremors that would awaken my mother, he stayed in bed, copying bits of Shakespeare onto pieces of Kleenex that he kept for transcription purposes on his night table. His favorite quotes were sleep-related, such as *Hamlet*'s

"To sleep, perchance to dream" or *Romeo and Juliet*'s "Where care lodges, sleep will never lie." Bumpa's "Shakespearean Kleenex" used to drive my mother crazy, and one day she left his bedroom window open and all the tissues flew out. You'd have thought they were part of the original folio edition for all the importance I attached to them. Running outside, I chased them around the neighborhood, salvaging a scrap of *The Tempest* from our birdbath. After plucking off a few stray feathers, I pinned "We are such stuff as dreams are made on" to the clothesline and hung it out to dry. From then on, Bumpa always joked that my mother had "murdered" sleep by tossing Shakespeare out the window, and disheartened, he switched to Webster's dictionary, transcribing vocabulary words onto Kleenex. I could always tell how badly he'd slept by the number of new words foisted on me at breakfast. "You better eat your Cream of Wheat," he'd say, "so you will feel *satiated*." Or "May I offer you some *delectable* donuts? Don't eat too many of them, however, or else it could prove *deleterious* to your *burgeoning* waistline." Pockets bulging with words, he had to be careful not to let my mother get near his plaid bathrobe in case Webster wound up in the wash.

With Bumpa as my role model, it's easy to assume that I'd been groomed for punk sleep from the cradle. Certainly, I knew that sleep wasn't a simple matter of drifting off to Dreamland. It involved Shakespeare and superstitions and vocabulary words. It was about prescient dreams and sight without glasses. It was the complete opposite of everything sleep was supposed to be, and yet my nights were pretty restful until Sister Margaret entered my life in second grade. The nun had linebacker's shoulders, a shiny red face, and thick meaty hands that reminded me of raw hamburger patties. It was rumored that she'd killed a student at another school for failing a math test. She'd punched him so hard he went brain-dead, and then, to elude the police, she stuffed him in a supply closet behind the carbon paper. It was also rumored that she'd started the rumor to keep everybody in line. To be fair, she needed every advantage, since she was clearly outnumbered: eighty to one.

Sister Margaret presided over her multitudinous kingdom from behind an oak desk, a large crucifix suspended over her head. Whenever she moved, it was usually to swat someone with the wooden signal stick she brandished like a police club. You never knew what would set her off. Once I got hit for biting my nails, which, considering how nervous she made me, wasn't an unreasonable habit. When she wasn't focused on our plentiful shortcomings, she directed her wrath at the Soviets. They'd recently launched *Sputnik,* and if we intended to beat them to the moon, we had to buckle down and study hard. In the more important "race to heaven," however, we were the odds-on favorites, for the Soviets lived in such a godless society that they sent a dog on *Sputnik 2,* letting it die in orbit. To make sure that in our rush to the moon we didn't leave God behind, Sister Margaret devised a brilliant plan: Every Wednesday we would change our seats according to our religion-test scores. This would serve two purposes: One, it would strengthen our knowledge and understanding of the Catholic Church; and two, it would sharpen our competitive instincts for the space race.

Due to my excellent memorization skills, I was fluent in the *Baltimore Catechism* and confident that for the rest of second grade I'd be safely ensconced in the first or "Gold" row. But then Sister Margaret dealt the death blow. Since we were too young for astrophysics, she expected us to shine at basic addition and subtraction. First thing Monday morning she'd administer a math test, and we'd change our seats accordingly. Math wasn't my strong suit. In comparison with religion, which relied heavily on the unknowable aspect, it was too black and white, too logical. For three straight Mondays I was banished to the last row for failing my test. Moving seats wouldn't have been so bad if we could have picked up our books and walked to our new locations, but Sister Margaret was too much the sadist for such a simple solution. When she shouted

"Go," we had to "drive" to our new locations in our ancient slant-topped desks, shoving them forward with our feet while we remained in the attached seats. It was like "Dodge 'em," with eighty kids shouting "Beep, beep" and screaming at one another to get out of the way. The last row, nicknamed "the Garbage Row" for reasons that will soon become obvious, attracted the kids who not only failed math but failed everything. Today they would have been diagnosed with ADD or autism or any number of learning disabilities, but in the late 1950s they were viewed simply as "retards."

For years I had nightmares about them, and even today I can still remember their nicknames. "Knuckle Boy" had light brown hair, with a Friar Tuck bald spot. While some kids might have been self-conscious about going bald in second grade, he didn't care because he lived for his knuckles, chewing them until they were raw and bleeding, then chewing the scabs and beginning the cycle anew. I never once heard him speak, but then again, I never saw him without his knuckles in his mouth. "One-Armed Boy" actually had two arms, but whenever he was called upon to go to the blackboard, he'd grab an arm and collapse on the floor. The other boys used to imitate him, and sometimes you'd have five or six kids up at the blackboard grabbing their arms and falling down. "Garbage Boy" lived next to the town dump, where he picked up his hygiene habits, dumping his luncheon leftovers inside his desk. If you sat behind him, which I did on multiple occasions, you'd almost pass out from the stench. Knowing that on Monday I'd have to say goodbye to my friends in Gold to drive cross-classroom to Garbage totally wrecked my Sunday nights. It took me hours to fall asleep, and when I finally did I'd frequently be awakened by my baby sister crying in the next room. After several miscarriages, my mother had recently given birth, so with the noise and the excitement, my struggle with sleep went largely unnoticed. Once, Sister Margaret, remarking on my listless behavior, sent me to the school nurse, who let me rest on a cot while she manicured her nails. But after an older kid suffered a mild seizure and I watched her depress his tongue with what looked suspiciously like a nail file, I returned to the classroom.

If the Garbage Row had been the full extent of my worries, my sleep system might have regained its youthful robustness, but Sister Margaret, in preparing us for our first Holy Communion, managed to take her obsession with the Soviets to even more absurd heights. After the moon, nearby Andover was apparently one of their prime targets, and since they loved nothing better than to prey on little Catholic children about to receive the Holy Eucharist, we had to prepare for martyrdom. If the communists demanded that we spit on a crucifix, even if they ripped out our fingernails and tongue, we couldn't, under any circumstances, even salivate. While battling the communists, we also had to contend with the devil, whose malevolent tricks included throwing little children down the stairs at night. For a poor sleeper, the prospect of a communist-satanic conspiracy was very bad news indeed. Ultimately I conflated these two "monsters" into one entity: the "Commu-Devil." Imagine Khrushchev's fat face peering out of a devil costume and you get the idea.

Even after my *annus horribilis* ended, Sister Margaret's scare tactics had left an indelible mark on my sleep habits. I fell back on one of the few resources available to a child: magical thinking. Sweeping the room for the Commu-Devil became a torturous ritual that involved checking beneath the bed not once but twelve times. In case he'd scurried off into my closet, I'd have to look in there, too. And behind the boudoir chair. And the desk . . . My parents were vaguely aware of my obsessive-compulsive rituals but chalked it up to my being "high-strung." They'd both gone to Catholic schools and wouldn't dream of contradicting a nun. My mother warned me that under no circumstances should I burden my father with depressing stories of Garbage Rows, devils, or martyrdom. "Your father's under a lot of pressure," she'd say. "Do you want his brains to snap?" All along I'd been worried about steam escaping from his pressure cooker head, and now I had a new thing to fear. As usual, I turned to Bumpa, who suggested I invent an ally, a "sleep sprite," who would protect me at night. I named her Felicity after a beautiful blonde I'd seen executing perfect toe loops at the Phillips Academy skating rink. Felicity worked her magic until I lost one of my front teeth; after my mother forgot to put the obligatory quarter beneath my pillow, she suggested the sleep sprite might have stolen it. I had my doubts, but to be on the safe side, I began casting about for another good-luck charm, seizing on Santa's reindeer.

Clement C. Moore obviously didn't have sleep psychology in mind when he wrote "'Twas the Night Before Christmas." His wide-awake narrator actually *sees* Santa, while his sleeping children, for all their good behavior, are rewarded with visions of candied fruit. The inherent message was that sleep didn't pay, so on Christmas Eve I'd keep vigil at my bedroom window, Bumpa's opera glasses in hand, searching for Santa's sleigh. I had it in my head that once I caught a glimpse of his reindeer I'd drift happily off to sleep. In those days, a white Christmas often meant a blizzard, so I was usually too excited to waste time in bed anyway. After my father shoveled the driveway, he would build an igloo, which I'd decorate with castoffs from our basement—a lawn chair, a frayed Oriental runner, a broken Wedgwood candlestick. I'd sit in there and read my Nancy Drew books, pretending I was an Eskimo princess keen on solving mysteries. One of my favorite places was a local theme park called Santa's Lookout, which had a puppet theater, a toy factory, and a reindeer that looked suspiciously like a cow. Then the place hit hard times, and if there's anything that's depressing, it's a run-down North Pole, in August, with Santa sitting in the equivalent of a Native American sweat lodge. While "Jingle Bells" played over the loudspeakers, the "reindeer," which now had lost a leg, limped around the center ring, scaring kids away.

It was then I began having doubts about Santa. Finally, my mother set me straight after I grilled her about the doll I'd requested from him. I'd seen it in the window of a local store, and after putting it down on my list, I noticed it was gone. "You bought the doll, didn't you?" I asked, figuring she'd do the right thing and lie. "Of course I bought the doll!" she said, tired of playing along. By then, I was in sixth grade; some of my friends were already in training bras. Nevertheless, I was heartbroken and remember thinking that if Santa was make-believe, what about his all-important reindeer?

I wrote a short story about it for my eighth-grade English class. It had something to do with a little girl who couldn't sleep and the reindeer that rescued her. Sister Ethelburger, whose name nicely captured her personality, gave me a D, explaining that while the story showed imagination, the overall message was disturbingly pagan. Little girls who couldn't sleep, she said, would be far better off reciting the rosary than worshipping false idols. If I continued on this destructive path, she warned me, I'd wind up like Elizabeth Taylor, who, after playing a pagan in *Cleopatra*, cheated on Eddie Fisher with Richard Burton.

"Do you want that to happen?" she said, as if having an affair with Richard Burton was a real possibility.

I shook my head no.

"Then get some sleep," she said.

In 1964 we moved into the third and final Punk House, a four-bedroom colonial across the street from Jay Leno, who would later go on to keep millions of people up past their bedtimes when he became host of *The Tonight Show*. No one in our house watched TV after eleven o'clock, but even if we'd wanted to, there were only three channels back then, and after Johnny Carson signed off, we were left with the late-night movie. It was truly the Dark Ages, yet Marshall McLuhan, the communications theorist, was already considering the social impact of the electronic media. Three decades before the Internet, he coined the term "global village" to underscore his observation that an electronic nervous system was integrating the planet. With everybody in immediate touch, it was fostering a "retribalization" of human life. During the live coverage of the events following the Kennedy assassination, when everyone watched Jack Ruby shoot Lee Harvey Oswald in real time, I remember overhearing several women in the neighborhood telling my mother they'd been up all night. It was one of the first times TV exhibited the power to actually change social patterns. "A medium is not something neutral—it does something to people," McLuhan said. Even then, it was starting to impact our sleep.

In our new house, Bumpa no longer had to sleep with the dog because the dog was "put to sleep." After developing cataracts, Buff went blind and then turned into the neighborhood scamp, attempting to impregnate all the female dogs within a five-mile sniffing radius. I don't know what was worse for my mother, the dog's blindness or his voracious sexual appetite, but he clearly had to go. From then on, whenever my middle sister, Marise, asked where the dog went, my mother told her that he was "sleeping." This amounted to the longest nap in history, and when Marise finally realized that he wasn't sleeping but was, in fact, dead, she was devastated. But at the same time, Marise had gained a sibling, for my mother, at forty-two, had recently given birth to my youngest sister, Nancy. Ultimately, Marise and Nancy bunked together and I was given my own room and a new bed—a white-canopied four-poster "Provençal" style with a double mattress that the salesman at Furniture Barn decreed the height of elegance. My mother envied my Marie Antoinette model, which she referred to as "the Big Bed," as in "Now that you've got that Big Bed, you'd *better* sleep."

Living up to the Big Bed was a lot of pressure. Sinking into the cushy mattress, I'd stare up at the white eyelet canopy and feel bad for not sleeping when less fortunate children were. When I consulted with a sleep therapist years later, she wondered why my parents had never taken me to see a specialist, obviously forgetting that in the sixties the "specialist" was usually the family physician, whose attitude could generally be summed up as "If you're tired enough, you'll sleep." Our family doctor took that philosophy to the extreme. Bounding out of his black Mercedes, burnished leather bag in hand, he was the picture of rigorous good health and had no tolerance for anybody who fell short of that mark. Since by definition that included his patients, he approached their medical issues with Spartan skepticism. Eyeing my canopy and me beneath it, my grandmother's satin bed jacket around my shoulders, he diagnosed my problem as "Princess and the Pea syndrome." He whipped out a prescription pad and scribbled something down. I tried to decipher his deplorable handwriting. Did it actually say *"Head to the wilderness?"* Before I could object, he began telling my parents that what I needed most was fresh air and extreme physical challenges. Someone he knew from our town had started the American branch of Outward Bound, and he'd be glad to put in a word for me. This "someone," he explained, had been a battery commander under General Patton and a teacher at the physically rigorous Gordonstoun School in Scotland. I knew I had to speak up. "I'm already committed to Girl Scout camp," I said. Camp Merrymeeting was on Pomps Pond, two miles from our house, which wasn't exactly the "wilderness," but it did have fresh air, a pine forest, and a few snapping turtles.

"Well, well," the doctor said, shaking his head in disgust. "For someone so 'exhausted,' you're quite opinionated, aren't you?"

My parents didn't insist on Outward Bound, so I was left with punk sleep, which isn't to say that I never slept at all. Some weeks I'd average eight hours a night, but my insomnia inevitably kicked in right before I confronted a test of any sort. As a result, I scored so poorly on my SATs that my guidance counselor, Sister Rose Carmel, sadly informed me that I wasn't "college material" and that I should apply instead to secretarial school. "I have one word of advice," she said, pausing for dramatic effect. "And that word is . . . *steno!*" Sister Rose Carmel primarily taught gym, and since her idea of exercise was prancing around doing the Pony in a spastic manner, I ignored her suggestion and went to college.

For someone brought up in a house where flushing a toilet at night was a capital offense, living in a dorm was like being inside a pinball machine. How did people sleep with stereos blaring and doors slamming and people showering at 2 A.M.? Recently, my mother gave me a box of letters I'd written home my freshman year. Here's the first one I opened:

Dear Mommy,

A couple of days ago I met this really nice boy and he asked me to a party Saturday night. He's really good looking, has his own car and he's traveled all over the world because his father's a foreign correspondent. Well, Friday night there was so much noise in the dorm that I didn't get to sleep until 5 and then got up at 7. At the party, I was so exhausted I couldn't keep the conversation going. Dancing was even worse. My coordination was off completely. When I went to introduce him to someone, I couldn't even remember his name. He kept asking if I wanted to go home because I seemed bored. He'll probably tell everyone I have the worst personality, although who wouldn't on TWO HOURS OF SLEEP!!!

Of all the places to eventually wind up, I probably should have thought twice about making my home in "the city that never sleeps." Thirty years later, I'm still trying to find a quiet apartment in Manhattan. There was the Lincoln Center two-bedroom that was directly beneath a woman who sleepwalked in stilettos; the studio on West Seventy-fourth Street, where the elderly man next door whispered death threats through the wall; the one-bedroom on West Seventy-fourth Street, where I'd fled the death threats, only to find myself living below a music critic with a taste for punk rock, which, when combined with punk sleep, was a bad mix indeed. The quietest place I ever lived in wasn't even mine—it belonged to a boyfriend, but I slept so well there that I stayed with him even though we fought so much that friends nicknamed us "the Battling Bickersons." Good sleep makes strange bedfellows. He was a writer and film archivist, with an apartment on Riverside Drive filled from floor to ceiling with books, newspapers, and videotapes. It was like a womb—or a tomb. I was in heaven. My boyfriend was sensitive to morning light, so in addition to shrouding the windows in heavy, fog-colored drapes, he wore a cowboy bandana around his eyes. And because he wore one, he strongly suggested that I follow suit. When we got a dog, she had to wear one, too. So there we were, three heads aligned on two pillows, cowboy bandanas masking our eyes. I felt like a hostage, which in fact I was, but not to my boyfriend. I was a hostage to that apartment and to sleep. Eventually I got my own place, but the bandana trick, which had been so successful on Riverside Drive, didn't work on West Seventy-fourth Street. When my boyfriend went to Spain for a month, I agreed to house-sit for him. Here's how well I slept: When a burglar roamed through the apartment, stealing thousands of dollars' worth of my boyfriend's electronic equipment, I only woke up *after* he'd climbed out the window.

When Lee and I got married, we bought a co-op around the corner from my ex-boyfriend's. From a sleep perspective, I figured it wasn't a bad idea to hedge my bets, and besides, my ex had become one of my closest friends. For five years I did pretty well. I didn't sleep like a baby or anything as dramatic as that, but it was no longer a big issue, primarily because I had bigger issues to worry about, such as trying to have a baby and writing dozens of magazine articles and a biography. Then in the midst of fertility treatments that ended with no baby but a serious case of pneumonia, new neighbors moved downstairs.

On the surface they seemed normal enough. The husband was a lawyer; he and his wife had two boys, and they were below, not above us. The first night they arrived, however, Lee and I were awakened by someone chanting *"Whooooo! Whooooo! I'm the devil!"*

We went down the back stairs and listened at their door. It was definitely the lawyer, and it was totally creepy. I tried to cut our neighbor some slack, hoping the stress of moving had brought out his kinky side, but no such luck. The man had such a loud voice that I was privy to the most intimate details of his life. When he wasn't chanting *"Whoooo! Whoooo!"* he was screaming about his in-laws, his wife's spending habits, and his bowel problems. We complained to the co-op board, but while they were extremely picky about whom they let into the building, once you'd passed the board, you could apparently morph into Beelzebub with little consequence.

My sleep disappeared. The devil had stolen it, so we had to move. I looked at eighty-eight apartments, relentlessly quizzing the doormen about the neighbors. Did they play piano? Did they throw frequent late-night parties? Was there anything about their clothing that might lead one to suspect that after midnight they became the devil? Finally, I found the perfect place in Carnegie Hill, a sedate family neighborhood, where little pigtailed girls in starched uniforms marched up Madison Avenue on weekdays and disappeared to their country houses on weekends. Our upstairs neighbors were fairly quiet, our downstairs neighbors even quieter. I still struggled with intermittent insomnia but didn't let it control me. More recently, I'd fallen into a pattern of sleeping from 10:30 to 2:30 A.M., staying up until 4:30, followed by another three hours of sleep. Instead of fearing the middle-of-the-night awakenings, I began to look forward to them as a time to analyze my dreams. It was such a creative and productive period that I labeled it "My Year of Beautiful Sleep."

And then my year of beautiful, recharging, regenerative sleep ended when the upstairs neighbors moved to the country. The wife, whose office had been close to the Twin Towers, had developed insomnia after 9/11 and wanted to escape from the city. The new neighbors embarked on an eight-month renovation, breaking a hole in our bedroom ceiling. The couple had two small children, who, at the crack of dawn, proceeded to run up and down the hallways. The mother referred to them as "Little Elephants," complaining that she couldn't control them. With *Wild Kingdom* overhead, I couldn't relax enough to fall back asleep. Now I was waking up at 2:30 A.M.—and staying up. To block out the noise, I bought a sound machine, trying every setting from "Brook" to "Jungle." Then I went to an audiologist who fitted me with specially designed earplugs that wouldn't stay in because apparently I've got "tricky" ears, and after numerous attempts, the audiologist gave up and quit his job.

It was particularly bad when the Little Elephants returned from one of their foreign safaris. Still on European time, they'd begin the stampede at 3 A.M. and I'd have jet lag without having gone anywhere. After their latest trip, knowing I'd have to endure a week of gradual time-shifting, I decided to get out of town entirely. I flew to Boston to stay with my sister Nancy, who ranks sleeping as one of her favorite activities. Though she has TMJ (temporomandibular joint disorder) and wears a bite plate at night, for the most part it doesn't interfere with her sleep. But even when Nancy doesn't get adequate sleep, she always takes a nap. I've never taken a nap in my life and have always been highly suspicious of people who do, but Nancy has even trained her two miniature poodles to nap with her. When she had a baby, Isabel, who woke up every hour or so, she was totally unprepared for the disruption and was so exhausted that she now wonders if what she presumed was postpartum depression was sleep deprivation. Her pediatrician suggested swaddling Isabel. Babies have a startle reflex that can easily waken them from deep sleep, and swaddling, which has been used for centuries to prevent movement, is supposed to help. Isabel, however, was a Swaddle Houdini, so Nancy turned to the Miracle Blanket—or "the Baby Straightjacket," as I called it. Though it made Isabel look like Hannibal Lecter, it worked and she slept. Then, around the age of two, Isabel turned into a late-night entertainer, performing a soliloquy that encapsulated the day's events. Her monologue could go on for several hours and involved the participation of a band of traveling mimes, including Dirty Little Poodle, a plush toy she wouldn't let Nancy wash; Whitey Bulger, a white horse named after the notorious Irish-American crime boss; and a half-dozen supporting players, all named Duckie. In addition to the toys, Isabel insisted on sleeping with at least a dozen fabric swatches that Nancy was afraid to return to her decorator because they all functioned as one-hundred-dollar-a-yard "blankies."

The night I was there, Isabel fell asleep right away and so did I. Then, around 2 A.M., I heard a little voice singing at the top of her lungs: "Row, row, row your boat, gently down the stream . . ." followed by *"Take it away! Duckies!"* The next morning I immediately went to the House of Punk Sleep—to try to sleep. Lee flew in from New York to join us for dinner, after which we watched TV in Bumpa's former bedroom, now the den. Since my mother sleeps in the Big Bed to escape my father's snoring, we were left with the twin beds in my sisters' former room, which is still stocked with all their old toys. Lee and I climbed into our small beds, where he fell asleep immediately and began to snore like my father. When Lee snores at home, which he does only occasionally, I can usually nudge him and he stops. But in twin beds, with a night table between us, I couldn't reach him, so I listened to my father and husband snoring in unison. Then I listened to my mother groaning in the Big Bed because she heard them snoring. Getting increasingly frustrated, I grabbed the Raggedy Ann perched on my headboard and threw it at Lee. It didn't wake him up, so I tossed Raggedy Andy. Still nothing. I then hurled *Make Way for Ducklings* and *The Adventures of Uncle Wiggily.* Lee kept snoring. Finally, a teddy bear in a HOME SWEET HOME sweater bounced off his head and got his attention.

Lee fumbled for the light on the night table, squinting at the menagerie on his bed. "A person can't sleep in a house like this," he mumbled.

"Precisely!" I said.

2

LADY IN THE DARK

The lunar moth is everywhere—on TV, in magazines, even on the wall clocks in the Manhattan sleep-disorders clinic, where I'm waiting to see the director. Since Lunesta hit the market in 2005, its ubiquitous trademark has become the twenty-first-century Tinker Bell. *Clap if you believe in sleep!* It's taken me a month to get an appointment, and the doctor is running late. I watch the lime-green moth on the minute hand circumnavigate the clock at least fifteen times. Later, when I Google "lunar moth," I learn that it flies only at night, spending its days napping beneath leaves. If it can't sleep at night, how is it going to help me?

I filled out my sleep history prior to my appointment, answering detailed questions about my own medical and psychiatric issues, as well as those of my parents, siblings, and second-degree relatives. My immediate family has been blessed with good health, and no one has had a problem with drugs or alcohol. Most of my parents' siblings moved away from the East Coast, so I'm unaware of their particular issues. I hoped my five-page sleep history would provide the doctor—a slight man who has been involved in sleep research for over three decades—with adequate information, but he insists on doing a sleep study, which involves spending a night in the hospital. I hate overnights, except when I'm on vacation, staying at a quiet hotel. Years ago, when my college boyfriend and I were working for a travel publication, we were trapped on a tall sailing ship with a dozen drunken honeymooners. I was so distressed at the sight of my small leaking cabin and so convinced that for the next five days I'd never sleep that midway between Saint Bart's and Saba I happily climbed into a dinghy and was rowed to shore. I won't have that option in the hospital. There will be no lifeboat, just a sea of wires and electrodes pinning me to the bed.

The American Academy of Sleep Medicine, which sets the clinical standards for the field, recommends overnight studies for all people with sleep complaints. But what's the point of watching someone *not* sleep? Insomnia is a unique disorder in that the patient is also the chief diagnostician. No one knows my sleep better than I do, although there's always the possibility that I've missed something. Could I be a secret snorer? Or sleepwalker? Maybe I have "sleep-state misperception" and think I'm sleeping poorly when I'm actually getting a full night's rest. Quite possibly I'm having a sleep study because it generates the most revenue. In 1975 the United States had only three accredited sleep labs; today there are 1,782, not including an equal number of unaccredited labs. Rates vary around the country, but my overnight will cost $3,200, largely reimbursable through insurance.

When I call the hospital to make an appointment, I learn that the next available opening isn't for another three weeks. That makes it a total of two months from the time I arranged for my initial consultation, and while my situation is hardly an emergency, I'm worried about serious long-term health consequences. You can't read about sleep deprivation without encountering the name of Dr. Allan Rechtschaffen, who conducted a series of experiments on rats at the University of Chicago in the 1980s. Remember *They Shoot Horses, Don't They?*, the 1969 movie about the marathon dancers starring Jane Fonda? Well, this is the rat version. Rechtschaffen and his colleagues placed pairs of rats on a turntable above a pool of cold water.

Whenever the rats got tired and began to nod off, the turntable would tilt toward the water, forcing the rats, who apparently hate cold water, to keep "dancing." Just like in the movie, things got pretty desperate. Despite consuming more food, the animals lost weight; they developed unsightly sores that wouldn't heal, and their fur turned rattier than usual. After a few weeks the rats died, and to this day, nobody can fully explain it. Why couldn't they maintain their body weight and temperature despite increased food intake? Did lack of sleep actually kill them?

I ask the doctor's assistant if they can squeeze me in. They can't. There are thirty people ahead of me, and if I want to sleep, I'll have to wait my turn. The National Sleep Foundation, a nonprofit organization based in Washington, D.C., has just released its annual "Sleep in America" poll to promote National Sleep Awareness Week. According to the NSF, forty million Americans suffer from a chronic sleep disorder and another thirty million from intermittent sleep problems. That's seventy million sleepy Americans—more than the entire population of France.

"I don't suppose there'll be a cancellation?" I ask.

"Doubtful," the assistant says.

On a chilly night in late March I'm packing for the hospital while Lee watches a DVD of his favorite movie—*The Adventures of Robin Hood*, starring Errol Flynn. Robin looks remarkably clean and rested for someone who lives in a forest, and this gets me wondering how the real Robin—or his thirteenth-century equivalent— slept in the woods. Going online, I find an article on "Seasonal Survival in Medieval Sherwood Forest," by the writer and historical consultant Richard Rutherford-Moore, who leads "Robin Hood tours" through Nottingham, England. After I email him, he sends me a picture of himself as his alter ego, "Blacke Dickon—Forester of Royal Sherwood." "The first thing that would strike a modern person if they slept in medieval Sherwood is how totally quiet and dark it is," he writes in an email message. "After 1066, the Normans introduced *couvre-feu*—the modern term is 'curfew.' If it was too dark to do any work, you went to bed. When the sun came up, you got out of bed and started work." To re-create medieval sleeping conditions, Rutherford-Moore has bedded down in sticks and boughs packed over with pine needles and bracken, slumbered inside a tree hollow and up in a bough. ("In Robin's day that would have afforded protection from wolves or thieves," he writes.) Though historians describe tents made of leather or canvas, Rutherford-Moore thinks it's more likely that Robin sought refuge from the cold in a nearby cave, placing his pack on a stone to use as a pillow.

Come to think of it, where's *my* pillow? According to the sleep lab's instructions, I'm allowed to bring my favorite, so I tuck my Bloomingdale's down pillow beneath my arm for the journey uptown. "Good luck," Lee says, happily ensconced in our bed while I head off into the night.

A cab drops me off in front of the hospital's main pavilion, where, according to my instructions, I'm to report to the security desk. The officer on duty is supposed to telephone the sleep technician, who will escort me to the lab, but there's no one at the security desk. "Well, he *was* there," the receptionist says. When I explain that I need to get to Room 34, the receptionist waves me in the general direction of the sleep lab, which is "over there, over some more, and then up." Did I hear that correctly? I turn right, which I guess is the "over there" part, but soon I'm totally lost. I wonder if it's a cognitive test. I return to the lobby, where I wait in line for the receptionist, who is only marginally more helpful. Frustrated and annoyed, I strike out for Room 34 again. The hospital is huge and seemingly empty. Still carrying my pillow, I wander up and down the hallways like a *Peanuts* character stuck in a *Twilight Zone* episode. Does Room 34 even exist? I spot a wall phone and ring reception, only to get a recorded voice telling me that reception is closed for the night. I run toward a cleaning man at the end of the hallway. "I'm trying to find the sleep clinic," I say. "You know, Room 34." He doesn't know but points upward, as if it's in heaven.

Now I'm wandering around the third floor, which is also deserted. I'm about to give up when I bump into the sleep technician. "I've been looking for you," he says. He opens the door to the mysterious Room 34, which looks like my college dorm room, circa 1971. There's a twin bed, with a navy quilt, matching bolsters, a wicker nightstand, harsh fluorescent lighting, and a TV on a file cabinet. The technician tells me to "get comfortable" while he attends my sleep-deprived colleague two rooms away. "Oh, by the way, don't drink the water," he says nonchalantly. I later learn that the hospital had a deadly outbreak of Legionnaires' disease and was being cautious in case bacteria lurked in the water pipes.

After brushing my teeth with bottled water, I slip into sweatpants and a blue T-shirt from the New York City Opera's production of Stephen Sondheim's *A Little Night Music*. The T-shirt is decorated with stars that glow in the dark, which will be helpful if I need to navigate my way home. I test out the bed. The sheets are wrinkled and itchy. I pick up the *DSM-IV—Diagnostic and Statistical Manual of Mental Disorders*—that someone has left on the night table. I never realized that punk sleepers were such a varied lot. There are breathing-related sleep disorders; circadian-rhythm sleep disorders; hypersomnia; insomnia; narcolepsy; nightmare disorder; REM behavior disorder; night terrors disorder; and sleepwalking disorder. And those are just the ones that fall under the umbrella of "mental disorders." According to *The International Classification of Sleep Disorders, Diagnostic and Coding Manual*, there are more than eighty recognized sleep disorders, ranging from period limb movement disorder to sleep-related painful erections.

At 10:45 P.M., the technician summons me to the monitoring room for the polysomnography (PSG), which will provide a continuous recording of the specific physiologic parameters that occur during sleep. For the next hour he wires me up, pasting about twenty-five electrodes and sensors on various parts of my head and torso. These will record brain-wave changes, eye movements, muscle tone, respiration, heart rhythm, leg movements, level of oxygen in the blood, and sound or neck vibration indicating snoring. Though I want to know exactly what's happening, the technician steers the conversation away from sleep to keep the experience as neutral as possible. He tells me he wants to become a better writer and asks if I can recommend a book to help him with grammatical usage. I suggest *The Elements of Style,* and he asks another question about writing. I ask about sleeping. It becomes a subtle contest between writing and sleeping. I casually inquire about the man in the next room, fearing he might be a sexsomniac. Sexsomnia is a "disorder of arousal," in which people engage in sexual activity while asleep but don't remember it later. The technician is the epitome of discretion but alludes to the man's snoring issues.

"What's the name of the book on grammar again?" he asks.

"Isn't it awful working the night shift?"

"Terrible."

An hour later, after I'm all hooked up and ready for bed, the technician finally gives me some advice. "Someone once told me that whenever they can't sleep, they just push all thoughts from their mind and say, *'I'm sleeping now, I'm sleeping now.'*" He puts on a sound machine and turns out the lights.

"By the way," he adds, "if during the night one of the wires comes unattached, I'll quietly come into the room and put it back and hopefully you won't wake up."

"If I were the type of person who didn't wake up when a strange man came into my room to reattach electrodes to my head, I wouldn't be here."

"Have a good night," he says, closing the door.

The video camera's infrared light is bothering my eyes. As part of my sleep study, I'm also being filmed so doctors can compare my physical movements with the polysomnogram. I hope I don't do something unexpectedly weird, like pretend I'm a cat, which is what happened to a nineteen-year-old at the Minnesota Regional Sleep Disorders Center. Not long after falling asleep, the teenager climbed out of bed and began growling and crawling along the floor. Then he started chewing the mattress. He later told technicians that he was having a recurrent dream, in which he was a large cat following a female zookeeper carrying a bucket of raw meat. As I'm trying to fall asleep, I think about how a sleep lab would be the perfect place to set a horror movie about "Cat Boy, the Feline Sexsomniac." *I'm sleeping now.* I think of my husband sleeping comfortably in our bed without electrodes attached to his head. *I'm sleeping now.* I think of all the possible casting choices for Cat Boy. *I'm sleeping now.* I think about my parents and wonder if it's their fault that I'm starring in a sleep video, in which I don't sleep. *I'm sleeping now.* Johnny Depp as Cat Boy? *I'm sleeping now. I'm sleeping now . . .*

I look up at the glowing red camera and then at the glowing stars on my T-shirt. *Why is it so bright in here? I want a glass of water. Is the guy next door snoring? Do I smell food? Is the technician eating pizza? I'm sleeping now. I'm sleeping* not. I am not sleeping. I am, most definitely, WIDE AWAKE!

In 1974 paleontologist Donald Johanson made one of the most exciting discoveries in the study of human evolution when one of his team members unearthed the fossil skeleton they would name Lucy. Even though Lucy was 3.2 million years old and literally a sack of bones, Johanson and his colleagues were able to put together an extremely detailed picture of what she would have looked like. They knew that Lucy was an adult apelike female who lived on a lake near the edge of a forest in Hadar, Ethiopia. They knew that she stood 3.8 feet tall and weighed between sixty and sixty-five pounds. They knew that she walked upright, ate high-bulk foods, and had a big belly. What they didn't know was anything about Lucy's sleep habits—or if in fact she did sleep. The toe bone may be connected to the foot bone and the foot bone may be connected to the ankle bone, but since there's no "sleep" bone, it's impossible to say how sleep evolved. "To the best of our knowledge, there are no sleep organs that we can identify in fossils and observe across species," writes Stanley Coren in *Sleep Thieves*. "There are no special sleep structures and no specific body shape or size seems related to the sleep process."

We know that sleep must have an important adaptive value—otherwise we wouldn't still be doing it. While we're sleeping, we can't eat or drink. We can't socialize or reproduce. Even worse, without an adequate hideout while we're sleeping, we're more vulnerable to predators, which over the centuries have ranged from saber-toothed cats to saber-wielding ninja. "When an animal is disturbed from sleeping it accumulates a sleep need that takes precedence over everything else," Dr. Jerome Siegel told me when I visited him at his lab at UCLA. Siegel is a professor of psychiatry and a leading expert on mammalian sleep. "If an animal is stressed and in danger, from a survival standpoint, the last thing you'd want is *increased* sleep," he said. "To me, that's the mystery. What is going on that is more important than other behaviors that would seem to have greater survival value?" As Rechtschaffen once said, "If sleep does not serve an absolutely vital function, then it is the biggest mistake the evolutionary process has ever made."

Sleep remains the great unsolved puzzle, the big black hole in the scientific universe. If you ask the average person to define sleep, you'll invariably hear about how wonderful it *feels*. Yet that lighter-than-air sensation of sinking into a mattress and drifting off to oblivion is merely the prelude to a remarkable theatrical event that we are both starring in and absent from. Except for "lucid dreaming"—the conscious realization that we are dreaming while we're "inside" the dream—we don't know we're sleeping when we're asleep. While we're doing it, we're pretty much dead to the world, which is why sleep and death have long been intertwined.

The ancient Greeks, in their typically inventive style, created a colorful genealogy to explain it. Nyx, the goddess of the night, gave birth to twin boys: Hypnos (sleep) and Thanatos (death). Hypnos fathered Morpheus, the god of dreams, who lived surrounded by opium poppies, the giver of dreams. While there would be no Morpheus without Hypnos, the Greeks treated sleep like a dull relative, preferring to focus their attention on his magical offspring. From about the fifth century B.C., they made pilgrimages to special "dream temples," which functioned as antiquity's version of Lourdes. After spending the day offering sacrifices and bathing in sacred waters, they'd enter a special part of the temple, where Asclepius, the healing deity, would appear to them in dreams, curing their ailments. Around the same time, the medical writer and philosopher Alcmaeon proposed the first scientific explanation for sleep. He believed it occurred when blood flowed into the head. Blood flowing out of the head caused us to wake up. Hippocrates, the father of Western medicine, thought that sleep was caused by the *warming* of the blood as it flowed to the center of the body, while Aristotle and Plato theorized that vapors from food decomposition rose into the brain.

The nineteenth century witnessed the popularity of behavioral theories based on the concept that the brain shut down at night due to insufficient outside stimulation. Countering the predominant view that sleep was a passive state, the Swiss psychologist Édouard Claparède saw it as an active process that countered the "fatigue toxins" that would otherwise build up in our bodies. In 1907 the French psychologist Henri Piéron took issue with Claparède's "biological" approach, proposing a "chemical" theory that revolved around his canine experiments. Like Rechtschaffen with his rats, Piéron sleep-deprived his dogs, forcing them to either sit or stand or else risk strangulation. After the dogs died, Piéron and a colleague extracted a substance they called "hypnotoxin," which they then injected into normal animals, causing them, they claimed, to sleep longer and more deeply than usual.

Beginning in 1917, the epidemic of encephalitis lethargica, or "sleeping sickness," that spread through Europe and North America piqued the general public's interest in sleep. It played on fairytale notions of spells and somnolent princesses, and it didn't discriminate between rich or poor, young or old. One of its most famous victims, the banker J. P. Morgan's wife, drowsed for eight weeks and then never woke up, prompting Morgan to donate $200,000 to the Neurological Institute of New York to study the disease. By dissecting the brains of its victims, the Viennese neurologist Constantin Von Economo was the first to identify a "sleep center" in the midbrain. As Kenton Kroker describes in his excellent history of sleep research, *The Sleep of Others,* encephalitis lethargica brought the "concept of a 'sleep centre' to the forefront of neurological research, emphasizing that sleep had both a structure and a function."

A major breakthrough came in 1925, when German psychiatrist Hans Berger invented the EEG machine and began to record brain waves, employing a primitive instrument used for recording electrocardiograms. In 1929 he published a seminal paper that offered a description of how brain waves shifted depending on the subject's state of consciousness. In the mid-1930s, Alfred Loomis, the amateur scientist and multimillionaire, recognized the EEG's enormous potential, creating the first sleep laboratory in his own state-of-the-art lab in Tuxedo Park, New York. Elaborating on Berger's findings with a machine called a "kymograph," Loomis and his colleagues were able to identify five distinct sleep "stages" based on different brain-wave patterns. Interestingly, Loomis failed to discover rapid eye movement, the one observation that wasn't dependent on hugely expensive machines. All anyone had to do was stay up all night watching someone sleep.

In the mid-1950s, Eugene Aserinsky, a doctoral student at the University of Chicago, was given the job of observing babies' eye movements as they slept in their cribs. He then began to make all-night sleep recordings of adults, correlating the jerky movements of the eyelids with the EEG. What he discovered came as a revelation. While the subjects appeared to be sound asleep, the brain waves indicated that they were wide awake. Aserinsky and his advisor, Nathaniel Kleitman, who is considered the Father of Modern Sleep Research, went on to correlate rapid eye movement, or REM, with dreaming, publishing their findings in the journal *Science*. "The history of modern sleep science really begins at the discovery of rapid eye movement," Kroker told me. "Yet when Aserinsky and Kleitman's two papers came out, they hardly attracted any attention. I went back to see how many times rapid eye movement was cited in the scientific literature, and it got mentioned only six or seven times. By contrast, Watson and Crick discovered the structure of DNA the same year, and that discovery was all over the place. But they had an advantage: Molecular biology was practically a ready-made field. That wasn't the case with sleep research. It had no popular cachet."

It did, however, hold great promise to psychiatry. Dr. William C. Dement, who'd joined Kleitman's lab not long after the REM discovery, was given the task of waking people up to inquire about their dreams. With his continuous all-night studies, Dement found that REM sleep was a part of a ninety-minute sleep pattern separate from the other four sleep stages. Dement also believed there was a simple reason for why people's eyes moved in REM sleep: They were watching their own dreams. At the time, Dement's patients were exclusively male, as it was considered immodest for women to be involved in sleep studies. "I remember wanting to record a woman for REM sleep," Dement said, "and Kleitman told me, 'Absolutely not!' He wanted to protect his lab's reputation." After moving to New York, Dement set up his own sleep lab in his Upper East Side apartment building, where, in response to a classified ad for study volunteers, one of the Radio City Music Hall Rockettes showed up. After she gave out his name to her colleagues, Dement's apartment became a crash pad for exhausted dancers. They'd arrive after the show in full makeup, asking the doorman to be shown to the sleep doctor's apartment. "It was actually a good deal for them," Dement said, "because they needed money and they needed sleep."

Ultimately there was nothing novel about women's REM cycle. In fact, the whole REM phenomenon, which had originally held so much promise as a means of uncovering the unconscious, wasn't bearing much fruit. More and more "dream labs" were opening up, but to what purpose? "Basically the dreams that patients were relating during REM awakenings weren't any more interesting than the normal ones they talked about during their sessions," Kroker said. "In addition, you had all these built-in difficulties. What patient wants to be woken up at 2 A.M. so he can tell his dreams? And what analyst wants to hear them, particularly if being in the lab has 'corrupted' the dreams and they're about the experimenter and electrodes?"

Sleep and dreams parted ways, with dreams abandoning the lab for the couch and sleep still struggling to find a niche. Dement, who'd set up a sleep lab at Stanford in the early 1960s, realized that if sleep was going to be taken seriously, it needed a disease to call its own. He found it with narcolepsy, a disorder characterized by extreme daytime sleepiness and abnormal REM sleep activity that can only be identified in a sleep lab by someone monitoring a patient's EEG. "Narcolepsy became the first 'sleep disorder,'" Kroker said. "For sleep, it was like, finally we've got our own territory! The only problem is that narcolepsy is fairly rare, but it did show that sleep had the potential to become a distinct medical specialty."

Scientists threw their energies into identifying and treating a growing list of sleep disorders, and then in the nineties advances in neuroimaging revived interest in the old nagging question: What is sleep for? Among the possibilities is that sleep doesn't really serve a purpose at all and that it basically evolved as a means of keeping animals in a protected environment and out of trouble. Other theories are that sleep boosts memory and learning, or that it "restores" whatever has been depleted during the hours spent awake. Siegel has studied the sleep habits of different mammals, noting that dolphins have no REM sleep and yet still manage to learn. If they can do that, why should humans limit sleep to one basic function?

It's been three weeks since my night in the sleep lab, and I'm in the doctor's office awaiting my results. I have a hazy memory of waking up after a night of horrible sleep and being handed two things: the bill and bottled water. After I wrote out a check, I brushed my teeth and washed my face with the water and then, with the remaining few droplets, attempted to get the electrode paste out of my hair. But what's a bad hair day if the end result is good sleep? As it turns out, I really do have something wrong with me. The doctor shows me the printout of my EEG, which is composed of squiggly lines like the Palmer penmanship exercises we did as children. In 1968, Allan Rechtschaffen and another sleep researcher, Anthony Kales, developed a sleep scoring system that divided non-REM (NREM) sleep into four stages, with REM sometimes described as stage five. In 2007, however, the American Association of Sleep Medicine set new standards, with NREM sleep divided into three stages. N1, or "light" sleep, is marked by the transition from alpha to theta waves; we move from feeling relaxed to growing increasingly sleepy, often experiencing flashes of dreamlike imagery and sudden twitches. N2—average sleep—is characterized by two sleep-specific brain waves, the short, choppy "sleep spindles" and huge "K complexes." About forty-five minutes later we enter N3—deep or "slow wave" sleep, during which giant delta waves devour the tiny theta waves, rendering the sleep spindles and K complexes nearly invisible on the EEG. In Stage R (REM sleep), we experience weird dreams and, depending on our sex, penile erections or clitoral engorgement. Our muscles are paralyzed so we can't move. The journey from N1 to Stage R takes approximately ninety minutes and happens four to six times every night, with our deepest sleep occurring mostly during the first part and our dream sleep mostly but not exclusively in the second part.

Normal sleepers spend 5 percent of the night in N1; 50 percent in N2, 20 percent in N3, and 25 percent in Stage R. So how did I do? During my seven-hour study, I slept for all of three hours and forty-one minutes, experiencing three extended awakenings of sixty-seven, ten, and sixty-five minutes. I spent 22 percent of my sleep in N1; 76 percent in N2; and no time at all in N3 or Stage R. But how closely did the study reflect my normal sleep habits? That night it took me forty-three minutes to fall asleep, when I usually drop off in five. I typically go to bed around ten-thirty, but the technician kept me up until midnight. I surely would have slept later in the morning, but he woke me up at 7 A.M. More to the point, I never go to bed wrapped in wires, in a hospital room, with a stranger watching me, and where I can't use the water for fear of contracting a disease. I rarely experience three long extended nighttime awakenings, and I'm a prolific dreamer.

According to my official report, I have "sleep maintenance insomnia—organic, psychological, psychophysiological, and behavioral factors contributing." The doctor explains that among the other waves on my EEG, he spotted "alpha, delta, theta bursts," ranging from three to seven seconds in length, which were "mild to moderately" disruptive of my sleep. "So this is real," he says, going on to explain that he almost never finds these atypical EEG-arousal bursts in normal sleepers. What he's describing, however, is called a "nonspecific finding," which means that it can be seen in a variety of unrelated conditions, including chronic pain, anxiety, subtle respiratory disturbance, and, as one sleep tech described it, "just being bummed by uncomfortable surroundings and the presence of observers while you're trying to sleep."

The doctor wants me to try a low-dose version of doxepin, a tricyclic antidepressant that is compounded especially for him. (I later discover that he'd obtained a patent from the U.S. Patent Office for the use of low-dose doxepin as a treatment for chronic insomnia.

Somaxon Pharmaceuticals later licensed the drug from the doctor, who served as a consultant and a member of the Scientific Advisory Board.) Until I receive the doxepin from a Florida pharmacy, I'm to continue taking my usual dose of one milligram of Ativan, which I've been taking for the past six months. The doctor also wants me to keep a sleep diary so I can better understand my cycles of sleep and wakefulness.

Before he moves on to another patient, he warns me that my biggest problem may be getting another appointment with him. He's booked solid for months, but at least I'm armed with the best that modern sleep science can offer. I've got Ativan. I've got a prescription for doxepin. I've got the diaries. I've got everything I could possibly hope for except for the one thing I really need: sleep.

3

ARE SLEEPING PILLS MORE DANGEROUS THAN AL QAEDA?

My doxepin arrives in the mail today from Winter Park, Florida—America's most famous sinkhole city. In 1981, a four-hundred-square-foot cavity opened up in the ground, swallowing a three-bedroom bungalow, an Olympic-sized swimming pool, and five new Porsches. The site quickly became a tourist attraction, with thousands of people flocking to the city to stare at the gaping hole and get their pictures taken with an enterprising local dressed as "the Sinkhole Monster."

I open the package and find two bottles of pills, at two different strengths—.5 milligrams and 1 milligram. Doxepin has been around for thirty-five years, but at the regular doses of anywhere between 75 and 300 milligrams, most people found it too sedating. As doxepin hydrochloride, it is also the active ingredient in several skin creams used for dermatological itch. People have gotten drowsy using the skin treatments, so I guess that's a good sign. Most sleep medications attach themselves to receptors in the brain's GABA (gamma-aminobutyric acid) neurotransmitter system, which is thought to promote sleep and relaxation. These drugs include the older benzodiazepines, such as Dalmane and Valium, as well as newer sleeping pills—Ambien, Lunesta, and Sonata (they're known as "Z drugs" because the letter Z appears in their generic names). Doxepin is different in that it blocks the wake-promoting neurotransmitter histamine, which in turn decreases the drive for wakefulness.

I once took 25 milligrams, and it gave me weird psychedelic dreams that were the visual equivalent of Jimmy Webb's 1960s hit song "MacArthur Park," about the cake left out in the rain, the sweet green icing flowing down. In my doxepin dream, the frosting was a blinding Technicolor green that didn't merely flow but surged through the park like a biblical mudslide. Just before I woke up, it was heading straight for me, having wiped out most of L.A. In my sleep history, I'd warned the doctor that doxepin had given me "weird, LSD-type dreams," but maybe he forgot or else figured that .5 milligrams wouldn't cause the same reaction. But it does. MacArthur Park melts in the dark, or maybe it's Winter Park. When I call the doctor and tell him what happened, he says, "I've never heard anything like that before," which isn't entirely true—he heard it from me, in my sleep history. I don't correct him, though. I just listen while he says, "Well, well" and "Imagine that." I detect a tone of disappointment in his voice. I've let him down. Maybe I should try it again. Since I've already taken the smallest dose available, the doctor suggests I open one of the capsules and lick a few granules.

The following night I spread a Kleenex out on the sink, and after twisting apart one of the capsules, I tap out three neat lines of white powder and quickly do some calculations. If three lines equal the destruction of Los Angeles, what does one line equal? The end of Burbank? If I lick a few grains, will it only rain terror on the Bel-Air Hotel? Between brushing and flossing my teeth, remov-ing makeup, and applying moisturizer, my bedtime routine is busy enough without having to compound my own sleeping pills. "This is ridiculous," I say, tossing the Kleenex away, all the sweet white powder flowing down the toilet.

Curious to discover what other sleep drugs are in development,

I head to 500 Patriot Way, in Lexington, Massachusetts, not far from where the first shots of the American Revolution rang out. Here, in state-of-the-art bunkers, America's best-trained rats are helping us fight the global war on insomnia so that every man, woman, and child in the United States can have the right to Life, Liberty, and the Pursuit of a Good Night's Sleep. These are my kind of rats. I can't wait to meet them, but first I have to talk to Dale Edgar, their Pied Piper and one of the co-founders of Hypnion, the biotechnology company at which they are employed. Prior to my visit, Hypnion, which develops drugs for sleep disorders, was purchased for $315 million by the pharmaceutical giant Eli Lilly. Most of the employees have already packed up their belongings and left the company. *Hypnion* means "new sleep," and if you wanted to nod off, I could imagine no better place than the company's reception area. The room is decorated in pale blues and greens, with the circular Hypnion logo representing the sun or the moon or perhaps a sleeping pill. I take a seat inside, where it is so quiet I can hear the receptionist breathing. I'd love to open the package of Mentos in my pocketbook, but I'm afraid I'll scare her.

"It sure is quiet here," I say when Edgar enters through a glass door.

"Well, it *is* a sleep lab," he jokes.

Edgar is in his early fifties and has a round face, red hair, and the friendly, open manner of a grown-up Opie from *The Andy Griffith Show.* Walking down a pristine corridor, we pass a male employee dressed in baggy jeans and sneakers, carting away the last of his boxes. He and Edgar say goodbye, and I take a seat in Edgar's office, which was once the hub of the Hypnion universe but is now the center of 33,000 square feet of empty office space. It feels lonely, but Edgar is in a buoyant mood, the result, no doubt, of the recent Hypnion sale. (Six weeks after our interview, he took a job with Lilly, heading up the company's discovery sleep-research program in England.)

"I consider myself a translational neuroscientist working to translate scientific discoveries into practical applications," he tells me. "A lot of people are driven to do science for the sake of asking a scientific question. I'm driven to do it for the sake of helping people, and if I can't connect the two, I'm not happy." Edgar's mother suffered from dystonia, a painful movement disorder that causes the muscles to contract and spasm involuntarily. "It's a horrible way to go," he says, "and of course the sleeping problems are just tremendous. So I chose to dedicate my life to finding solutions for the tough nuts to crack in medicine." One of the toughest may be insomnia, which Edgar knows from personal experience. He routinely wakes up in the middle of the night and can't get back to sleep—a pattern, he says, that is common to 70 percent of people with chronic insomnia. And it only gets worse with age. With 76 million baby boomers in the United States, one hitting fifty every seven seconds, it's not surprising that Hypnion's contribution— an insomnia molecule currently known as HY10275—was formulated with them in mind. Americans spend $4.5 billion on sleeping pills a year, but some analysts estimate that since only a fraction of insomniacs now use them, the market could be worth $7–10 billion.

Edgar first came to prominence for his pioneering work not in the sleep area but in what is known as the "wake" space. I'm not used to thinking of the time we spend not sleeping as "wake." You never hear people say, "I'm going to catch some wake now," or "How was your wake?" but in scientific circles that's what it's called. For the longest time, the general dogma was that something in our brains—a master switch—made us sleep. While getting his Ph.D. in biology at the University of California, Davis, in the mid-eighties, Edgar revealed it to be a far more complicated process involving our biological clock. I'd only heard of the biological clock as it applied to reproduction, as in "You better have a baby before your biological clock runs out," but Edgar tells me that it is connected to everything and that it's located in the suprachiasmatic nucleus. *Supra-chi-as-ma-tic.* It sounds like something Mary

Poppins might have coined, although SCN, discovered in 1972, actually refers to a group of neurons in the brain's hypothalamus. Light and darkness "set" this master clock, determining when we go to bed and wake up. Most sleep scientists believed that our biological clocks controlled both wake and sleep, but Edgar discovered, while studying the sleep patterns of squirrel monkeys, that if the SCN no longer functions, it's not possible to stay alert during the day. This discovery meant that the brain's Big Ben wasn't essential for sleep after all but served as an alarm clock promoting wakefulness.

But if the biological clock controls wake, what controls sleep? And how do we explain the intricate balancing act between the two? Teaming up with William Dement, who founded Stanford's Center for Human Sleep Research, Edgar came up with what is now called the "opponent-process model." Basically, our sleep drive—the "sleep homeostat"—runs counter to the clock's waking mechanisms. The longer we're awake, the greater the drive to sleep. Opposing this process is the alerting action of the biological clock, which, depending on the time, can be stronger or weaker. Interestingly, the clock's alarm softens after lunch, which accounts for the midafternoon coffee break or siesta. "Initially I was reluctant to publish a paper on this for fear that it would be discounted out of hand," Edgar says. "And so I basically started doing the lecture circuit, talking to different groups and making presentations. Then over time and thinking it through with Bill Dement, we published our findings in *The Journal of Neuroscience,* and it's now in textbooks."

While at Stanford, Edgar developed SCORE, a sophisticated computer system that evaluates drug effects on sleep-wakefulness in rodents. Tired of hand-scoring miles of polygraph records whenever he collected animal data, Edgar, collaborating with a computer programmer, devised a way to monitor the animals' behavior in real time. SCORE became the platform technology for establishing Hypnion and one of the reasons Lilly purchased the company. Appearances to the contrary, we've got a lot in common with rats. While their sleep is polyphasic, meaning they sleep only a few hours at a time, their sleep architecture is fundamentally like ours. Rats dream (of navigating through mazelike structures), and as they get older, they sleep poorly, too. What's more, the drug compounds that make us sleepy have the same effect on them, so whatever works for rats should, in theory, work for us.

I figure now would be the perfect time to see them, but Edgar has bad news. The rats can't be disturbed. He says he's very sorry, but they're in the middle of an experiment. If I *were* to see them, though, he is sure I'd be impressed. "One of the things we take great pride in is the fact that the only way to get good sleep quality is from a healthy animal," he says. "Our facility has extraordinary temperature, humidity, and lighting control. They get nothing but the best bedding, which is all cuddly and cozy, and the best food. If you were to go over to the facility, you'd go, 'Wow! They look really happy.'"

I'm not so sure that's what I'd say because weighing in on the collective happiness of rodents is totally beyond me. It is not, however, beyond SCORE, which makes discovering new drugs easier by allowing different compounds to be fed to the rats with instant results. The rats are wired with miniature radio transmitters that send signals through the SCORE system, which then tracks reactions remotely over a network. "This is what's really cool!" Edgar says. "You can bring up all the data over the Internet. The system monitors body temperature, locomotor activity, heart rate, feeding and drinking habits, and sleep patterns. I can do this anywhere in the world, so when I travel, I can take my notebook computer and see all my animals live."

As a wake expert, Edgar already helped Cephalon to develop Provigil, currently the only wake-promoting drug on the market, and he hoped to create a line of anti-drowsing pharmaceuticals at Hypnion. "Helping people with impaired alertness is important— ask anyone who works the night shift—but the need to help people with insomnia is more broadly recognized by physicians," he says. Consequently, Edgar and the Hypnion team decided to first develop a better sleeping pill, or hypnotic. "We didn't want to do the same thing somebody else was doing," he says. "We didn't want a 'me, too' sleeping pill." Instead, working backward, Edgar and his colleagues initially targeted their audience—older people with sleep-maintenance insomnia—and then attempted to develop a drug that would address their specific needs. Having created the world's largest integrated nonclinical database on sleep pharmacology, they were quickly able to compare novel compounds with currently approved medicines, identifying those molecules with the best chance of offering new benefits for insomnia patients when tested in clinical trials.

While current drugs help people fall asleep faster, they don't help two-thirds of the people with sleep-maintenance insomnia. Edgar's challenge was to figure out what part of the brain was preventing people from falling back to sleep. "I'd been looking at the opponent process all my life, and I suspected that the histamine neurons in the brain were the bad boys behind sleep-maintenance insomnia," he says. "You get those histamine cells going and it's like a screaming baby, and it starts a snowballing process. That's how we normally start to wake up in the morning and then stay up throughout the day. But this can happen at night, too. The circuits are still there. Normally, the histamine levels would be relatively low at night, but as we get older, those histamine cells are kind of itchy. And it's easy to get them riled up. So it became pretty obvious to us that an important target was histamine. So I said, 'Okay, let's work with this hypothesis and let's try to make some molecules that would be selective.' But SCORE took us down a slightly different path. It taught us that there was a second receptor target that, when controlled together with histamine, produced a better effect on sleep maintenance in laboratory rats than the antihistamine target alone."

Here's what I'm wondering, though: If the histamines are the bad boys of insomnia, then why can't I just take an over-the-counter antihistamine?

"Well, there's more to the story," he says. "The currently available antihistamines labeled as sleep aids are not very selective for the histamine receptor. They have various off-target activities that constrain their efficacy and cause a number of unwanted side effects, some that carry over to the next day and make you feel groggy and lousy."

Over the years I've tried Tylenol PM and all the other PMs that contain antihistamines, and while they eventually put me to sleep, I did indeed feel groggy and lousy upon awakening. But who's to say I wouldn't feel groggy and lousy on his drug? And didn't doxepin target the histamines, too?

"When we tested our new compound preclinically," Edgar says, "it looked far superior to any traditional antihistamine we've ever seen." To help expedite development, Hypnion conducted its initial clinical trials in Europe, where they were completed in almost half the time than it takes in the States, where, on average, it takes eight and a half years for a new drug to get to market, at a cost of anywhere between $800 million to $2 billion. "You know the old adage 'Time is money'?" Edgar says. "It's really, really true in biotech." In one study, test subjects were confined to a large and noisy drug-safety clinic while *Terminator 2: Judgment Day* played full-blast on a wide-screen TV. Every six minutes they were given the drug, with another fifteen minutes allowed for absorption, and according to Edgar, they fell asleep like clockwork, in six-minute intervals. "That's when we started to become really excited about this compound," he says. "I'm not calling this a magic bullet because there's no such thing and we're still a long way from having an approved drug. But we're excited about the potential benefits a new compound like this could bring to sleep medicine."

But isn't the field already overcrowded, with Ambien CR, Lunesta, Sonata, Rozerem, and at least a half dozen others in development, including Intermezzo, a sublingual reformulation of generic Ambien and a new medication that targets the hypocre-tin/orexin system, which helps people stay awake? "A lot of people are doing research in this space because there's a need," he says. "And yes, there's money in it. . . . But if you ask a fifty-five-year-old individual with sleep-maintenance insomnia whether this is just something they have to put up with because they've gotten older, or whether it's something that justifies intervention because other-wise they might die behind the wheel of a car . . . I mean, that's the way I think about this. There are real consequences to sleep dis-orders. People say, 'Oh those wusses! They should be able to deal with not sleeping.' But I've known too many people who have got-ten hurt—*physically maimed*—because of sleep disorders. Insomnia affects a lot of people's lives. Finding a good treatment for it really matters!"

Daniel Kripke is scaring me. He's the author of an ebook, *The Dark Side of Sleeping Pills,* which is illustrated with pictures of the Grim Reaper and scorpions. The warning reads: "Sleeping pills could be hazardous to your health or cause death from cancer, heart disease, or other illnesses." At first I think he's probably one of those cra-zies you frequently run into when doing medical research on the Internet—until I learn that he is a psychiatry professor at the Uni-versity of California, San Diego, and has been involved in sleep research for more than thirty years.

When reached by phone at his office, he tells me that "sleeping pills kill more than Al Qaeda!" I immediately picture thousands of Lunesta moths flying into high-rise buildings. How did he arrive at this alarming statistic? For several decades Kripke has been collab-orating with the American Cancer Society, analyzing its prevention studies for insights on sleep habits and mortality. In 1998, after matching for age, sex, race, and education, and controlling for thirty-two health risk factors, he found that people who took sleep-ing pills every night had a 25 percent higher mortality over a six-year period than those who didn't take them. Even occasional usage was associated with high mortality. His cancer study, however, ended in 1988, before the newer drugs like Ambien and Lunesta came on the market. Is it fair to associate all sleeping pills with a higher death rate?

Kripke believes there is a good chance that the newer pills are dangerous, too, pointing to the number of rats and mice that developed cancer after being given high dosages of Lunesta, Sonata, and Rozerem. But since we're not rodents taking megadoses, I wondered if that data applies to us? In 2008 Kripke did a study that was published in the *Journal of Sleep Research* that found evidence that the newer pills, such as Ambien, Rozerem, Lunesta, and Sonata, possibly increase the risk of skin cancer. While it's not clear why this would happen, Kripke says that since millions of Americans are currently taking sleeping pills, wouldn't it be wise to look into this connection, especially in view of our culture's obsession with getting a full eight hours a night? As part of Kripke's analysis of the cancer studies, he found that individuals who slept eight hours a night were 12 percent more likely to die within six years than those who slept seven hours. Interestingly, those who reported having insomnia lived longer. While he's not suggesting people cut back on their sleep, he doesn't think people should be reaching for sleeping pills in order to get eight hours.

"Look, I've gotten enough NIH grants so that I'm not beholden to the drug companies," he tells me. "Leaders in the field of sleep medicine take millions of dollars a year in research money. They're on the boards of drug companies and have a financial interest in diagnosing insomnia. I don't."

Kripke has a reputation for being somewhat extreme on the issue, but UCLA neuroscientist Jerome Siegel believes he may be onto something. "Today we've got millions of people taking sleeping pills not for a few weeks but for years," Siegel explains when I visit him in L.A. "When they say that the pills have been tested for 'long-term use,' it means they've been shown to increase sleep even when used for a month or two or six months. What's going to happen to people over the long term? Hormone replacement therapy was something that seemed perfectly sensible at the time. Now we know it causes cancer, dementia, and all sorts of other things, and it took twenty years for us to find out. So I think there's a very good possibility we'll find out the same thing about chronic usage of hypnotics. Look, if you're taking a drug for a life-threatening illness and the drug has side effects, at least there's a trade-off. But the trade-off with sleeping pills is rather subtle, and much of it depends on a person's perception of what 'normal' sleep is. Sleep time isn't correlated with IQ or level of achievement. I don't know of any evidence that increasing sleep time produces health benefits. Obviously people need sleep, but to tell them they have to put it ahead of everything else and if they're not getting adequate amounts of it, they should take hypnotic medications . . . well, it's just crazy."

People have been searching for ways to induce what Shakespeare called the "honey-heavy dew of slumber" for as long as they've been able to harvest medicinal plants. A reference to opium poppy was found on Sumerian clay tablets dating back to 3000 B.C. The Sumerians named it "Gil" for happiness. The word *opium* is a Greek derivative, and Homer referred to the plant's sleep-inducing properties in both *The Iliad* and *The Odyssey*. According to Paul L. Schiff, Jr., a professor of pharmaceutical sciences at the University of Pittsburgh School of Pharmacy, the Greeks viewed opium "as a symbol of consolation and oblivion," crowning all their nocturnal gods, including Hypnos and Morpheus, with a wreath of poppy blossoms. For them, "sleep was the greatest of all physicians and the most powerful consoler of humanity." In addition to opium, both the Greeks and Romans relied on lettuce, which produces a milky soporific sap, and the herb henbane, a powerful hallucinogen, to induce sleep. During the Middle Ages, mandrake root was popular, although its resemblance to the human form gave rise to the bizarre myth that if you uprooted the plant it let out a horrible Munch-like scream that caused death or insanity to anyone who heard it.

At the beginning of the nineteenth century, opium was synthesized, followed, in 1832, by chloral hydrate, a rapid-acting central nervous system depressant that was the key ingredient in the knockout cocktail Mickey Finn. Hailed as a major advance over existing drugs, chloral hydrate could put you to sleep, but over time you needed more of it to achieve the same results, leading to fatal overdoses. When Edith Wharton decided to kill off Lily Bart, the heroine of her 1905 novel *The House of Mirth,* she chose chloral hydrate to do the job, igniting a debate that lasted for decades as to whether Bart's death was an accident or suicide. A century later, tabloid readers were wondering the same thing about former *Playboy* model Anna Nicole Smith. She, too, had died of a chloral hydrate overdose, though, modern pharmaceuticals being what they are, she'd mixed the drug with nine other prescription medications.

Chloral hydrate and its chemical relatives, all classified as "bromide salts," dominated the market until barbiturates emerged in 1903. As David Healy points out in *The Creation of Psychopharmacology,* barbiturates were such effective sedatives that doctors used them for "sleep therapy," putting psychiatric patients in a continuous sleep for as long as several weeks in the hope of calming their nervous systems. By the 1940s, doctors began liberally prescribing them for insomnia, and manufacturers started to churn out pills. (In 1948 the output was 672,000 pounds, or twenty-four pills for every U.S. citizen.) Breezy nicknames such as "pink ladies" and "blue angels" obscured their deadly potential. In 1951 barbiturates killed one thousand people, either through accidental overdose or, when combined with alcohol, by suicide. That same year, *The New York Times* ran a front-page story headlined GRAVE PERIL SEEN IN SLEEPING PILLS, quoting a Bellevue Hospital psychiatrist as saying that "addiction to sleeping pills is far more dangerous to the patient and to society than is heroin addiction." Similar stories were published in newspapers and magazines across the country, as sleeping pills, in the words of the popular magazine *Coronet,* were widely perceived as a "Doorway to Doom."

In 1962, President Kennedy signed the Kefauver-Harris Drug Amendments requiring drug manufacturers to prove to the FDA that their products were both safe and effective. Thalidomide, a drug that had been given to pregnant women to prevent insomnia and morning sickness, had resulted in ten thousand babies born with severe defects in Europe, and Kennedy wanted to make sure nothing like that happened in the United States. The changing drug legislation brought pharmaceutical companies into the sleep lab, where they've been ever since. "As sleep research expanded, more and more sleep labs began to appear within psychiatric clinics," Kroker told me. "But as the emphasis shifted away from the study of dreaming, they were looking for ways to use their labs, so they began evaluating drugs in the context of these new FDA requirements."

The 1970s saw a shift away from barbiturates in favor of benzodiazepines, or BZDs, which Leo Sternbach, a Polish chemist, invented in the late 1950s, after fleeing the Nazis to work for Hoffmann–La Roche. The BZDs, such as Librium and the 1960s blockbuster Valium, were developed for anxiety, but their sedating properties made them popular for treating insomnia, although the FDA hadn't approved them for that purpose. When Dalmane came on the market in 1970, it became the first BZD to win FDA approval as a sleep drug, quickly becoming the most popular hypnotic in the country. The BZDs were considered safer than barbiturates because they were far less likely to cause death in overdose, but a 1979 study by the National Academy of Sciences concluded that BZDs were equally if not more risky than barbiturates. Dalmane drew the most fire, with Hoffmann–La Roche criticized for its misleading advertising stating that sleep-laboratory studies had objectively determined that the drug was effective for at least twenty-eight consecutive nights; its findings were based on only two studies comprising a total of ten people. ("Perhaps this is not satisfactory," a company spokesman admitted.) The expert panel also found that Dalmane and the other BZDs leave active substances in the body for long periods, creating a cumulative effect. Though patients were warned not to drive or operate a machine "shortly after ingesting the drug," there was no mention of how the drug and its breakdown chemicals could adversely affect coordination the following day. Ultimately, the biggest safety advantage the BZDs had over barbiturates—that they're rarely lethal by themselves—wasn't critical, because both drugs are deadly when combined with alcohol.

In 1979, twenty-eight years after *The New York Times* published its front-page story on the perils of sleeping pills, it ran another page-one story that reached a similar conclusion. Doctors began writing fewer prescriptions, and the general public grew more skeptical, especially when the drug Halcion appeared to confirm everyone's worst fears. Since its debut in 1982, it had become the most widely prescribed sleep aid in the world, despite several hundred adverse-reaction reports and complaints of memory loss and violent behavior. (The FDA's medical-review officer in charge of Halcion's drug application had recommended against approval for this very reason but was overruled.) In 1989 a Utah woman who had been taking the drug for a year shot and killed her eighty-three-year-old mother. Charges were ultimately dismissed, and the woman sued the drug's manufacturer, Upjohn, which settled out of court. At the same time, William Styron, in his bestselling book *Darkness Visible: A Memoir of Madness,* blamed Halcion for contributing to his amnesia and suicidal thoughts. While it's difficult with any drug to link cause and effect—Styron, for example, had been a heavy drinker—Dr. Anthony Kales, a leading expert on sleep pharmacology, warned *Newsweek* that Halcion was a "very dangerous drug." Ultimately, Britain banned Halcion, although it is still sold in the United States.

With confidence in sleeping pills at an all-time low, the pharmaceutical company G. D. Searle had the task of introducing Ambien to a highly skeptical American public. (The drug, whose generic name is zolpidem, was already available in Europe.) No stranger to controversy, Searle had managed to win FDA approval for aspartame, even after the agency concluded that one of the company's studies on rats showed an increase in brain tumors from the artificial sweetener. Searle's president during much of the aspartame approval process was Donald Rumsfeld, who had made the company profitable (he'd left Searle prior to the Ambien launch). If people thought of sleeping pills as dangerous, then Searle's challenge was to position insomnia as even more dangerous. Searle hired the Edelman public relations firm, which had previously helped establish Butterball Turkey as *the* holiday bird by setting up a hotline at "Butterball University" to give consumers tips on how to overcome "turkey trauma." Needing a legitimate way to address sleeping-pill trauma, Edelman teamed Searle with the recently formed National Sleep Foundation, turning it into the Butterball University of Sleep. To coincide with the NSF's official launch in 1991, Searle paid for a Gallup survey that revealed that 35 million Americans suffered varying degrees of insomnia, recognizing it as America's most common sleep problem. The survey also highlighted the dangers of drowsy driving, a legitimate issue that hadn't even been considered before. The public, however, didn't know that Searle footed the bill for that survey, or that it funded the NSF's "insomnia workshops" that were timed to Ambien's debut, or that the NSF's first president, Dr. Thomas Roth, had extensive ties with drug companies and would ultimately serve on the speaker's bureau of Sanofi-aventis, which now markets Ambien. They just knew that as far as their sleeping patterns went, they were as clueless as Butterball turkeys heading for the slaughterhouse.

While the Ambien campaign was a pivotal moment in creating "sleep awareness," the whole field of sleep medicine, which had previously existed in the margins of science, was finally making some headway. In June 1993, Congress established the National Center on Sleep Disorders Research, which released a report, "Wake Up, America," that further dramatized what was now being labeled a "public health crisis." This in turn generated more articles that stressed the dire consequences of sleep loss. At the time, Medicare and insurance companies rarely reimbursed sleep-medicine services, and the National Institutes of Health practically ignored sleep-disorders research. In order to compete with such known killers as heart disease and cancer, sleep disorders had to be seen as life-threatening. William Dement, taking a cue from AIDS activists, went on the offensive, describing sleep disorders as a "national emergency" that was costing America $70 billion a year in inefficiency, errors, accidents, and health problems.

This was good news for the makers of Ambien and the other new Z drugs, which received a further boost in 1997, when the FDA relaxed the rules governing mass-media advertising for pre-scription drugs. "Direct-to-consumer" ads emboldened patients to ask their doctors for the expensive, brand-name drugs they were seeing on TV. According to IMS Health, a pharmaceutical research firm, between the years 2001 and 2005, sleeping-pill prescriptions grew 55 percent, to 45.5 million. During the first eleven months of 2005, sleeping-pill makers spent $298 million luring consumers to their products, with Sepracor's Lunesta battling with Sanofi-aventis's Ambien CR in an unprecedented marketing and ad blitz. By the time Rozerem was introduced a year later, Takeda, realizing it couldn't outspend its rivals, decided to outdo them on the cre-ative front. Instead of featuring a sleepless person tossing and turn-ing in bed, the ads starred Abe Lincoln and a talking beaver and carried the tagline "Your dreams miss you."

The new Z drugs are generally considered safer and more effec-tive than the older ones because they are more selective in the way they target the sleep-inducing GABA receptors. Unlike the BZDs, which reduce REM and delta sleep, the new drugs don't substan-tially alter sleep architecture. But do they really work? That depends on whom you ask. Dr. Gary Zammit, who runs New York's Sleep Disorders Institute, which treats patients and trains physicians in sleep medicine, is a firm believer. He is also president and CEO of Clinilabs, a company that provides clinical development services to pharmaceutical companies that make sleeping pills. The Sleep Disorders Institute and Clinilabs operate out of the same facility on West Fifty-fifth Street, where patients going in for a sleep evaluation are sometimes asked if they'd like to participate in a clinical drug trial. At one time Zammit was on the faculty of the Sleep Journal Club, an interactive website, where doctors received CME (continuing medical education) credits for listening to authors present recently published articles on sleep. The website was funded by Takeda, which makes Rozerem and also paid Zammit a consulting fee. Zammit has received research support from at least two dozen sleep-related companies, has been a consultant for fourteen of them, and has participated in speaking engagements for Neurocrine Biosciences, King Pharmaceuticals, McNeil, Sanofi-aventis, Sanofi-Synthélabo, Sepracor, Takeda, Vela, and Wyeth-Ayerst Laboratories.

When I visited Zammit in his office at the Clinilabs/Sleep Disorders Institute, he echoed what Dale Edgar had told me. "The risk of having untreated insomnia is far greater than any risk associated with today's appropriate treatment for insomnia," he said. "The person with untreated insomnia is experiencing nighttime distress, possible next-day impairment, as well as impairment in cognitive functions, impairment in occupational settings, in social settings, and impairment in terms of ability to perform in a career. The great tragedy regarding the common portrayal of sleeping pills is that they're portrayed as dangerous, when in fact they've been shown to be safe and effective. Let's say you had high blood pressure and you went to the doctor and the doctor said, 'I want you to take antihypertensive medicine every day.' If you went back a year later and told the doctor what you were doing, the doctor wouldn't say, 'Oh my God, you're addicted!' The doctor would say,

'Good! This is what you're supposed to do, because if you stop the medicine, your blood pressure will go up.' For many people with insomnia, they may need the medicine every day."

Directly across town, Dr. Charles Pollak, who heads the Center for Sleep Medicine at New York-Presbyterian Weill Cornell Medical Center and has been involved with sleep research for more than forty years, is not a fan of sleeping pills. "I remember when Dalmane was supposed to be the answer to everyone's problems," he said. "The newer ones are more effective than they used to be, no doubt about that, but I never thought the real answer rested in a pill. Drug companies have always been mixed up with sleep because it's a very lucrative market. Hypnotics are among the most profitable drugs out there."

They remain profitable even though they don't provide substantially more sleep than placebo pills. In a 2007 study financed by the National Institutes of Health, they reduced "sleep onset"—the average time to fall asleep—by 12.8 minutes, increasing total sleep time by only 11.4 minutes. That doesn't sound like very much considering the pills' side effects, such as daytime sedation and motor impairment. When I asked Dr. Daniel Buysse, an insomnia expert at the University of Pittsburgh School of Medicine, about the relatively small difference between the benefits of sleeping pills and placebos, he explained that even if someone is only getting an extra fifteen minutes of sleep, the *perception* that sleep has improved will often make the person feel better. Dr. Steven Ellman, a psychoanalyst and former sleep researcher, told me about a ten-year-old experiment in which a group of insomniacs were given a drug, while others received a placebo. "The drug group slept markedly better than the other group," Ellman explained. "What was the drug? *Amphetamine!* It worked better than the placebo because the amphetamine group knew they had an active drug inside them. They could feel it and so they ascribed their transference to the drug and the whole research protocol as helping them. Consequently, they slept."

After taking a sleeping pill, people have difficulty forming memories, so when they wake up, they might think they had a good night's sleep even if they didn't. As a group, insomnia patients differ from normal sleepers in several ways that involve sleep-related beliefs and perceptions. While normal sleepers don't pay much attention to their awakenings, insomniacs worry that they won't fall back asleep, thereby keeping themselves awake longer. The sleeping-pill advocates will say that if a medication gets someone over that hurdle, what's wrong with that? No one has yet to make a compelling case that sleeping pills are more effective than placebos for improving the quality of life and daytime functioning. People who take sleeping pills, however, think they do, but since these are the same people who think they're sleeping when they're not, I'm not sure how much credence to give them. Just because people believe they're functioning well doesn't mean they actually are. Or does it? In the end, what's important? Actual sleep? Or the illusion that one has slept well?

I'm getting off Ativan. The doctor thinks it might be contributing to my punk sleep, although I began taking it because my sleep *was* punk, not the other way around. Despite being supersensitive to drugs, I never experienced a drug hangover from Ativan, and in nearly twenty years of intermittent use, I've never upped the dosage from one milligram. But with my current bout of acute insomnia, it hasn't been as effective as it once was, so I'm happy to give it up. My reward for slowly tapering off Ativan is that I can go on Sonata. Of all the Z drugs, Sonata has the shortest half-life, so I can take it when I wake up in the middle of the night without worrying about it lingering in my bloodstream. The only problem, though, is that the drug doesn't work for long enough to make it truly effective. While Sonata has been shown to help you fall asleep, it doesn't keep you asleep or decrease the number of times you wake up. Its benefits, to be generous, are minimal.

Still, I try it because I need to keep faith in my sleep doctor. If I truly believe in him the way some people believe they're sleeping when they're not, perhaps I'll sleep, too. Besides, I'm running out of options. I've tried Ambien, which, of all the Z drugs, has been around the longest, with few reported problems, except for the sleep eaters and sleep drivers. Eating a bag of Doritos while under the influence of Ambien is, to me, a problem. Taking your car for a spin while you're asleep is an even bigger problem, but the number of those cases is relatively small in comparison with the millions of people who've taken Ambien. I've never eaten Doritos or driven my car while taking Ambien. I've also never slept particularly well while taking it. With the five-milligram pill, I woke up after four hours, which I do perfectly well without drugs, so I upped the dose to ten milligrams, only to begin losing my memory. I began forgetting where I put things and once left my reading glasses in the refrigerator. If lack of sleep impairs one's cognitive abilities, it didn't strike me as a huge advantage to be taking sleeping pills to achieve the same effect.

Ambien CR is basically Ambien, at an increased dosage, with a time-released coating. "For some people, Ambien is a pretty good drug," says Dr. Matthew Ebben, a sleep psychologist who works with Dr. Pollak at Weill Cornell's Center for Sleep Medicine. "Many of the people who began sleepwalking while using it were already predisposed to the problem, so you can't blame it all on the drug. Ambien CR, however, is another story. The drug company was losing its patent on Ambien, so they needed to come up with something else." According to advertisements, the first layer dissolves quickly, to help you fall asleep fast; then the second layer dissolves slowly, to help you stay asleep. Since I can fall asleep on my own, I don't need the first layer, and as for staying asleep, according to an FDA statistical review of several clinical studies, that effect is harder to justify. In this warped *Alice in Wonderland* universe, who knows what "staying" asleep actually means? Maybe I'm asleep now.

Trying Rozerem isn't really an option for me, because it doesn't help people with sleep-maintenance insomnia. The drug mimics melatonin, a hormone secreted in the brain that helps our bodies regulate the sleep-wake cycle. It is thought to work best for jet lag or for those with delayed-sleep-phase syndrome, a condition that makes it difficult to fall asleep. However, an article in *The New England Journal of Medicine* cited evidence from one clinical trial that found the drug no more effective than a placebo in helping sleep onset. I did try Lunesta and my sleep was exactly what you'd expect it to be like coming from a lunar moth. It felt strange and hallucinogenic, the kind of sleep that when you wake up from it, you expect to see Bottom from *A Midsummer Night's Dream* staring back at you. Plus, my mouth tasted of metal, which is one of the side effects. To alleviate the metallic taste, a sales rep for the company suggested I take it with a spoonful of maple syrup, but I don't even like maple syrup on my pancakes, so I'm hardly going to use it with my sleeping pills.

So for the time being I'm stuck with Sonata. Waking up around 3 A.M., I take five milligrams and try to fall back asleep. It's not what I'd call a knockout success. It takes me two hours to nod off again, and at 6 A.M. I'm wide awake. This remains the pattern during five months of intermittent use. But for me, the strangest thing about the drug is what happens during the transition from wakefulness to sleep, the borderline or "hypnagogic" state, when people often see weird things—faces, flashes of color, kaleidoscope patterns. That usually only lasts a few seconds, but with Sonata, it's as though I'm trapped in that state and I'm seeing gargoyles. So having weaned myself off Ativan, I'm now taking a pill that doesn't put me to sleep for at least ninety minutes, keeps me asleep for only sixty minutes, and gives me visions of gargoyles. This doesn't sound like real progress. I could drink a bottle of absinthe and probably get the same effect.

After a particularly bad night with Sonata, I get a phone call the next morning from a man I'll call Paul. It puts everything in perspective. For the past decade, Paul has been pestering me to get together with his wife, "the number one personal shopper in New York." I've never met Paul, who has a thick Long Island accent, and I don't know how he got my number. "Pat, Pat, Pat," he'll say, using my least favorite nickname. "Do you like Armani? Do you like Fendi? Well, my wife is representing a new designer who is *better* than Armani, *better* than Fendi, and he makes couture. Pat, Pat, Pat . . . couture! AT WHOLESALE!"

On this particular morning, with visions of gargoyles dancing in my head, Paul is offering to get me into Bob Mackie's showroom. I tell him I wouldn't wear Bob Mackie and that I don't need custom clothes, and he tells me that I do need them, desperately. "Pat, Pat, Pat, as we age our body changes," he says. "We're bigger on top, bigger on the bottom. Lots of things go wrong. A few months ago, I was hit by a van. Pat . . . A VAN! I had to have fifty stitches across my nose. I was in a coma, Pat. A COMA! Do you have your health, Pat?"

"I don't sleep very well."

"Listen to me, Pat. I've been taking Halcion for twenty years. My doctors have told me to get off it, but I've begged them for it. I have no memory. I'm not kidding. I keep changing doctors so they'll give it to me. I'm going to die on it. DIE ON IT! Pat, Pat, Pat, I've lost my mind, but at least I've got my sleep."

4

EXTERMINATING ANGELS

Bedbugs are back. I didn't even know they were gone. Actually, I never gave them a second thought until I read in *The New York Times* that they were "spreading like a swarm of locusts on a lush field of wheat." Now I can't stop thinking about them. No one is safe, not even Bill Clinton, whose New York office was overrun with them. And it's no better overseas. England's *Daily Mail* reports that bedbug infestations have increased as much as 500 percent in a recent two-year period, turning Great Britain into "Great Bitten." Entomologists and exterminators have blamed the current epidemic on an increase in international travel, immigration, and the ban on powerful pesticides, but I have another theory. I think bedbugs are trying to remind us that in comparison with the problems we used to encounter, we've got it pretty good.

Back in the old days, sleep hygiene wasn't simply a matter of eliminating caffeine; it was a time-consuming search-and-destroy mission designed to get the bugs before they got you. In his book *At Day's Close: Night in Times Past,* A. Roger Ekirch describes how in preparation for bed, families used to engage in "hunts" of furniture and bedding for fleas and bedbugs, after which they combed the lice from one another's hair. "To keep gnats at bay," he writes, "families in the fen country of East Anglia hung lumps of cow dung at the foot of their beds." Sleep wasn't pretty back then, but if you didn't sleep, at least you knew why. Today, with vastly improved sanitary conditions, we have the luxury of exploring the deeper reasons behind our sleepless nights. Instead of fearing blood-sucking parasites, we're plagued by "restless thoughts."

To help eradicate them and anything else that might be crawling around inside my head, my sleep doctor wants me to see the cognitive behavior therapist who works with him. Cognitive behavioral therapy (CBT) has two components. The cognitive part, which was pioneered by psychiatrist Aaron Beck, is based on the idea that our thoughts cause our feelings and behaviors. So in treating insomnia, if we identify and replace our dysfunctional beliefs and fears about sleep, we can, in theory, greatly improve it. The behavioral part, in relation to insomnia, deals with a basic set of sleep-promoting rules that Dr. Peter Hauri, the former director of the Mayo Clinic's insomnia program, established in the late 1970s. These guidelines, such as avoiding stimulants and alcohol and regularizing bedtime and wake-up time, form the basis of today's sleep-hygiene techniques. A 2009 study, published in the *Journal of the American Medical Association,* showed that for people with persistent insomnia, a combination of cognitive behavior therapy plus Ambien produced better results than either treatment used on its own. However, over the long term, CBT proved to be the most effective strategy in keeping insomnia at bay.

The therapist I meet with, who is in her thirties, is warm and empathetic. I like her immediately. As a twenty-year veteran of psychotherapy, I'm an old hand at talking about myself, and I launch into my sleep history; but since CBT, unlike psychoanalysis, isn't an open-ended process—the average number of sessions is anywhere from four to eight—she gently pushes her agenda. Taking out a piece of paper, she draws three concentric circles to illustrate the "3P Model," which was devised by two New York psychologists, Dr. Arthur Spielman and Dr. Paul Glovinsky, to help explain insomnia's common characteristics. The first *P* stands for "predisposing characteristics," such as anxiety and hyperarousal, which make a person more vulnerable to insomnia. Physiological hyperarousal is associated with rapid heart rate, heightened muscle tension, faster brain waves, elevated hormones, and a higher metabolic rate, while cognitive hyperarousal translates into obsessive worrying and racing thoughts. Eric Nofzinger of the University of Pittsburgh School of Medicine, who has been using PET (positron-emission tomography) scans to look at brain glucose metabolism—an indicator of the brain's metabolic activity—has found that people with insomnia have more active brains than normal sleepers. A 2008 study published in the journal *SLEEP* demonstrated that adults with primary insomnia have reduced levels of GABA, which helps the brain "turn off." From his experience treating insomniacs, Dr. Ross Levin, a psychologist and sleep specialist in private practice in New York, puts writers in the hyperaroused category. "Being more cerebral, writers tend to think too much," he told me, "and at night, they're thinking too much at the wrong time."

The second *P* is the "precipitating event," such as a job loss, divorce, banishment to the Garbage Row—anything that might spark a sudden bout of insomnia. Some people snap back easily, although in my experience they rarely have "predisposing characteristics." My friend who lives upstairs is the perfect example. Not only are we the same age, height, and weight, we live in the identical apartment three floors apart. When it comes to sleep, however, we might as well be on different planets. Several years ago, after recovering from breast cancer, she learned that her husband of twenty-four years was having an affair with a married woman in the B line of our building. They were both on the co-op board and fell in love during our lobby renovation. After the husband admitted the affair, he refused to leave the apartment, preferring to sleep in the tiny maid's room off the kitchen, and for the next year, he commuted back and forth between the B and D lines. Meanwhile, his new girlfriend, now wife, was placed in charge of the flowers in our lobby, turning them into erotically charged tributes to their backstairs romance. My friend couldn't walk into the lobby without confronting a hideous collection of thrusting stamens and orgasmic blooms. Her sleep fell apart, which under the circumstances was perfectly understandable, yet she recovered within a week. She even gave me her extra Ambien, explaining that I probably needed it more than she did, which, sad to say, was true. If my friend had continued to lose sleep, she might have compensated by drinking too much coffee, napping in the afternoon, or becoming heavily reliant on sleep aids. For Spielman and Glovinsky, such a situation would be an example of the third P—"perpetuating attitudes and practices." Any of these coping methods can transform a case of transient insomnia into something chronic; one bad night builds upon another, and suddenly it's no longer about the divorce that precipitated the initial bout of insomnia but about the person's lack of confidence in her own ability to generate sleep.

The therapist begins running through the rules of sleep hygiene, which I'm pretty much following on my own. I don't drink caffeine after 2 P.M. or exercise too late in the day, nor do I overindulge in alcohol and heavy food. I keep the room cool and clocks out of sight. More challenging are the stimulus-control "tools" that were first proposed, in 1972, by Dr. Richard Bootzin, a professor of psychiatry and psychology at the University of Arizona. Since good sleepers associate their bedrooms with sleeping and poor sleepers with lying awake, Bootzin believes that the bedroom triggers an arousal response that needs to be "unlearned." Following Bootzin's guidelines, the therapist tells me that I should use the bedroom only for sleep and sex, which means no TV watching. If I awaken during the night and don't fall back to sleep within twenty minutes, I should go into another room until I'm sleepy enough to return to bed. While I understand why this method might help people with sleep-onset issues, I'm not sure what purpose it serves for people who fall asleep right away but wake up later. If I associate my bed with lying awake, then why do I routinely fall asleep the minute my head hits the pillow?

The therapist tells me that when I get up at night I should do something "relaxing," such as reading a book, but the last thing I want to do in the middle of the night is read. Books remind me of all the books I haven't written and the ones I'll never write if I can't get some sleep. Books, at four o'clock in the morning, are composed no longer of words but of millions of bedbugs playing bingo on the page. The therapist tries to be flexible and understanding without throwing out the central tenets of CBT. She tells me that surely I can figure out something to do that doesn't involve lying in bed, reading, watching TV, or going on the computer, but I honestly can't. As a parting gift, she gives me more sleep diaries to fill out. They're now called sleep logs, but it's essentially the same thing. Since I already have two months' worth, I'd really hoped my days as a sleep diarist were over, but unlike Weight Watchers protocol, measuring the quality of a person's sleep isn't simply a matter of stepping on a scale. It is equal parts perception and reality. Leaving the office, I bump into the sleep doctor, who says, "I see you've got your homework," and I say, "Yes, I love homework," which isn't entirely true. I don't love it, but after having thrown doxepin—his last suggestion—down the toilet, I want him to think that I'm still highly motivated. Now all I have to do is find something to do in the middle of the night that doesn't involve anything I normally like doing.

I'm hunting for bugs. After waking up at 3 A.M. and waiting twenty minutes or so to fall back asleep, I walk into the kitchen, and there, in the middle of the white-tiled floor, is a cockroach nearly the size of a mouse. By chasing a cockroach around the apartment, I'm undoubtedly breaking an unwritten sleep-hygiene rule about cavorting with nocturnal vermin, but if not for these rules, I wouldn't even be in my kitchen, I'd be in my bed, snug as a . . . well, you know. So armed with a wad of paper towels and the closest blunt instrument, which happens to be a cheese grater, I track the cockroach into the small room off the kitchen. It is filled with cleaning supplies, exotic cookbooks all the more exotic because I don't cook, and dozens of gifts people have given us over the years that we don't necessarily like but can't bear to part with. It's a nightmare, this room, so it feels fitting to be down on my hands and knees, on a Moroccan rug that should have stayed in Marrakech, in search of a gigantic cockroach. It's straight out of Kafka's *The Metamorphosis*. "One morning, as Gregor Samsa was waking up from anxious dreams, he discovered that he had been changed into a monstrous vermin." Kafka, too, was an insomniac. I read his novella in college as part of a discussion on existentialism, the nineteenth-century philosophy that emphasizes an individual's uniqueness; while I don't remember much, I do recall the professor explaining how the existentialists weren't concerned with the question of "What is mankind?" but rather with the question "Who am I?" Poised to kill a cockroach with a cheese grater, I ask myself that very same question, and here's what I discover: Contrary to the opinion of Dr. Bootzin, I am not cut out for stimulus-control therapy. I put the cheese grater away and return to bed.

Over the next few weeks, as my sleep fails to improve, I wonder if I should give stimulus control a second chance. I go on Sleepnet's insomnia forum and learn that some people really swear by it. Getting out of bed at night doesn't work for me, but perhaps I should ban the TV from the bedroom. I make this decision at a particularly bad time, as we've just purchased a new TV, which is located where it shouldn't be. "We can't watch TV anymore," I inform Lee as he searches for the remote. "It's disturbing my sleep." Lee reminds me that I've had sleep problems for a lot longer than we've had a TV in the bedroom. "Yeah," I say, "but television could be making my insomnia worse, but I really can't talk about it." According to Bootzin's rules, one shouldn't discuss upsetting events in the bedroom.

I decide to keep myself very busy at night, making dates with people I don't even like in order to avoid what I do like, which is watching TV in the bedroom. I'm forcing myself to be a night owl when by nature I'm a lark. My new life is making me so miserable that I begin staying home more, which inevitably leads to TV watching. One evening, after seeing Diane Keaton and Jack Nicholson in *Something's Gotta Give,* I sleep a full eight hours and wonder if it has anything to do with the movie. It's about a middle-aged playwright who doesn't sleep much—probably because she's writing a play in her bedroom—and how she loses her heart to an inveterate womanizer, played by Jack Nicholson. The plot is beside the point. What's important is Diane Keaton's beach house. It's totally stunning and I want it, and judging from the number of articles written about it, I'm not alone. Thousands of women also covet this house, even though the interiors were all built on a Hollywood soundstage—it is literally a "dream house."

In my follow-up therapy session, I reluctantly admit that stimulus control isn't working for me. The therapist takes it all in stride, proceeding to the next item on her CBT checklist: progressive muscle relaxation. The method was developed by Dr. Edmund Jacobson, a Chicago psychiatrist who first created the technique more than fifty years ago to help people suffering from "tension disorders," including stomach ailments, hypertension, and insomnia. In his 1938 book, *You Must Relax,* Jacobson describes an overstimulated society that sounds very similar to ours, with children "addicted" to radio and television and parents suffering from "nervous strain" due to the unrelenting demands of modern technology. Jacobson believed that an "over-tense national life" was partly the cause of society's sleep problems but that it was possible to calm "over-active nerves" and achieve a state of deep relaxation by relaxing the muscles. The current method, an abbreviated variation of Jacobson's original technique, involves tensing and relaxing sixteen different muscle groups, paying attention to how the muscle feels tense versus relaxed.

I've done progressive muscle relaxation before as part of a college acting class, where a sadistic Israeli mime made us draw names out of a hat and then instructed us to mimic the physical mannerisms of the student we'd selected. I drew the name of a boy who walked with a bad limp, the result of a childhood accident. I thought it was too cruel to do the limp, so I left it out, and the teacher told me I would never make it as a mime. And then to demonstrate what depths we'd have to sink to in order to succeed in this coldhearted profession, he proceeded to drag his leg across the stage, as if playing Tiny Tim in *A Christmas Carol*. Everybody was so horrified they couldn't speak, which in a mime class was exactly the point, but the teacher, detecting a hostile vibe in our rigid body language, decided to ease the tension with progressive muscle relaxation. While I shouldn't dismiss the whole technique based on one bad experience with a mean-spirited mime, it's hard for me to associate it with a sense of well-being.

The therapist demonstrates how to do the exercises, and then we practice them together, clenching our fists and working our way down to our toes. The exercises take about twenty minutes, and the therapist wants me to do them every day, keeping track on a chart of how "relaxed" I feel after each session. My first instinct is that I probably should be learning how to calm my overactive brain rather than my muscles, but then I remember that Jacobson said, "It is physically impossible to be nervous in any part of your body, if in that part you are completely relaxed."

I practice the exercises, trying to ignore the Little Elephants' determination to undermine my progress by going on a stampede as soon as I start to relax. The therapist has warned me that CBT isn't a quick fix and that I shouldn't expect improved sleep right away. That's fair. But why is my sleep getting worse instead of better? I recently read that chronic insomniacs have a high likelihood of developing depression in the future. I've been starting to wonder if the future is now.

Insomniacs have frequently been portrayed in popular culture as hollow-eyed zombies marching toward the loony bin. The word *lunatic* stems from Luna, the Roman goddess of the moon, and insomniacs, by virtue of their nocturnal patterns, are reluctant moon worshippers. At the turn of the nineteenth century, insomnia was depicted in the American press as a horrible torture that frequently led to suicide. An 1888 article in the *Washington Post* described the suicide of a prominent New Yorker as a "terrible illustration of the desperate straits to which a person can be driven by sleeplessness." The article goes on to explain that "it is a well known fact that loss of sleep, carried to [sic] far, will produce insanity." It was believed that something called the "nerve fluid" was produced at night, and if you didn't get enough of it, the nerves would become "abnormally sensitive and irritable—almost as if they were bare"—and the victim would ultimately go crazy. One way for insomnia sufferers to replenish the mysterious nerve fluid was to drink a "nerve tonic," such as Dr. Greene's Nervura, whose eye-catching ads showed a woman leaping from a window, with the headline SAVED FROM INSANITY. Insomnia was one of the symptoms of "neurasthenia," which in the late nineteenth century had become a catch-all diagnosis for such vague but debilitating complaints as fatigue, weakness, loss of appetite, and generalized aches and pains. Described by the neurologist George M. Beard as "American nervousness," it was thought to be primarily a home-grown disorder brought on by increased industrialization and the vices and virtues of modern society. The majority of sufferers were well-educated middle-class women who sought relief with a variety of treatments, including the popular "rest cure." A mix of pampering and repression, the "cure" itself rested on the notion that neurasthenic women had somehow sinned against nature by engaging in intellectual activities, for which they were constitutionally ill-suited. They could regain their equilibrium through massages, low-voltage electricity treatments, a high-fat diet, sometimes force-feeding, and total seclusion. Women were forbidden to write, read, or otherwise "tax" their fatigued brains.

Even today, insomnia's place in the mix is still somewhat vague. In 1983, when the National Institutes of Health convened a consensus conference on "Drugs and Insomnia," insomnia was defined as a secondary disorder. Physicians were advised to treat the underlying disorder first, believing that the insomnia would then resolve itself. By the time the NIH held its second insomnia conference, in 2005, experts were willing to concede that insomnia wasn't just a symptom, recognizing that even if it was initially caused by a medical or psychiatric condition, once the perpetuating factors set in, it was no longer "secondary" but had a life of its own. If sleep problems were a patient's only symptoms, then insomnia could be categorized as a "primary" disorder. Semantics aside, what's important is not what came first but how sleep and psychiatric disorders coexist and collide. People who are depressed often experience early-morning wakening, which makes them more tired and therefore more depressed. Those with bipolar disorder may sleep too much during a depressed phase and forgo sleep entirely during a manic episode. People with anxiety disorders frequently suffer from poor sleep, which can lead to anxiety *about* the poor sleep, resulting in decreased sleep—and increased anxiety.

From about the mid-sixties, psychiatry held a franchise on sleep, primarily because the field was founded on dream research and Freudian psychology was enjoying renewed popularity. But while Freud was famously eloquent on the subject of dreams, he had much less to say about sleep, treating insomnia as he did many other illnesses, as symptomatic of an underlying neurosis. If you got at the "root" of your sleep issues, he believed, the insomnia would go away. Even with our more sophisticated understanding of the brain's biochemistry, many psychoanalysts still hold to that belief. "I've treated four patients with long-term insomnia and all got better in ten psychotherapy sessions," Steven Ellman told me. "It's like males with impotence. You keep them focused on what's really going on in their life and not just, oh my penis isn't working. What does impotence mean to them? It's the same with insomnia. The patient needs to get at the issues directly related to sleep."

Ellman believes that depressed people often have interrupted sleep because they're avoiding dreams. He and several colleagues conducted a series of experiments in which they deprived animals of REM sleep, with the result that the animals experienced "REM rebound," in which they had more frequent and longer periods of REM. They also sought positive-reward stimulation. In another experiment, in addition to REM-depriving the animals, they gave them an hour of positive reward, and the animals had half their REM rebound. "The positive reward system completely substituted for REM sleep," he explained. "We concluded that what REM does is fire positive-reward mechanisms in the brain—that's one of the reasons Freud thought dreams were wishes. Our hypothesis about depressives is that they're waking up in order to avoid dreams. They're REM-depriving themselves so they will seek more positive reward during the day. REM deprivation is a powerful antidepressant. It's interesting that many antidepressants are in fact REM suppressants. If I had a hypothesis about why you're waking up in the middle of the night, I'd bet you're avoiding dreams."

"I love dreams," I told him.

"You may love certain kinds of dreams, but you may not love others, and when people are more depressed they wake up and follow what is a depressive cycle, which is sleep-interruption insomnia."

"According to my sleep doctor, I'm waking up because I've got these brain irregularities—alpha, delta, theta bursts."

"I don't believe there are brain irregularities that result in sleep issues. There are brain characteristics that are genetic, but once we start calling them irregularities, you are on the wrong track in trying to help a person. My guess is that you have a somewhat screwed-up sleep cycle. You might have some mood-regulation difficulties. I don't think you're doomed to being a poor sleeper. Your issues may be heavily engrained, and you might have to unpack those things with a good therapist."

I was in my early thirties when I first went into therapy. I was prompted by my recent breakup with the Good Sleep Boyfriend, who, as a parting gift, threw me a surprise birthday party. I'd spent the day moving into my new apartment and hadn't taken a shower and was wearing sweat clothes when I showed up. It was quite the surprise. The apartment I'd moved into was a fifth-floor walk-up off Columbus Avenue that had once been a single-family home. An elderly Irishman, who reminded me of Bumpa, lived next door. Returning home from my birthday party, where somebody's date turned out to be an agile pickpocket, I heard the Irishman reciting his prayers through our flimsy common wall. He prayed for a lot of people, including the pope and President Reagan, and then he clipped his toenails. With the poor acoustics, I heard every snip, the nails clattering over the hardwood floor like reindeer hooves. I placed a fan against the wall to block out the noise, not realizing that my neighbor was even more sensitive than I. Several nights later he knocked on my door. He wasn't wearing his dentures, and his wispy white hair was standing on end. Bumpa he was not. "Are you purposely trying to destroy my sleep?" he wanted to know. I explained that I was trying to block out his noise so I could sleep, but he wasn't buying it, and in the end I wound up apologizing. The following night I moved the fan to the opposite wall. I was afraid he'd complain, but all seemed fine until he said his prayers. After asking God to bless President Reagan and all the other Reagans, including Patti Davis and Ron junior, he said, "Dear Lord, forgive me for what I'm about to do," and then, pressing his lips to the wall, he whispered, *"I'm going to get you, miss. I'm going to get you for what you did to me!"*

I moved over to the wall. "Are you talking to me?" I asked.

He didn't answer. I turned off the fan and climbed back into bed, hoping I'd appeased him enough so he'd keep quiet for the rest of the night. *"I know you're in there, miss,"* he said a few minutes later. *"You'll be sorry for what you did to me."* He kept this up for the next hour, and I was so scared I completely froze. For the rest of the night he serenaded me with threats, comparing me to Patti Davis—the "tramp." The next morning, I began looking for another apartment and a therapist. I wasn't making enough money as a magazine journalist to afford the going rate, which was then one hundred dollars an hour, so I found a training analyst through a local psychoanalytic institute that operated a low-fee clinic. The man's office happened to be several floors above the Good Sleep Boyfriend's apartment on Riverside Drive, so I was now back in the building Monday, Wednesday, and Friday mornings. I took an instant dislike to the therapist, who was in his mid-forties, with a moon-shaped face, a monk's bald pate, and the bad taste to mix gray polyester pants with a yellow checked shirt, black socks, and mushroom-colored Hush Puppies. As I lay down on his couch, which he'd covered in itchy camel bags, I thought, "This is a major mistake."

He proceeded to burp and belch during our sessions, the air smelling of salami and pungent cheese. In five years of seeing him, the only change in my behavior was that I swore off cold cuts and Roquefort dressing. I can't even remember discussing my sleep problems with him because *his* problems always seemed to take precedence. When I first started dating Lee, we took a vacation to Barbados, and after my therapist found out we'd stayed at an expensive hotel, he said, *"What?* When my wife and I were in Barbados, we couldn't afford that. We had to stay at some little place that wasn't half as nice. I guess that's because I'm only charging *you* fifteen dollars a session." He told me repeatedly that I was spoiled and expected too much out of life. Whenever I expressed any frustration about anything, he'd turn into Mick Jagger and begin singing "You Can't Always Get What You Want." Years earlier, he'd come to New York to become an actor, but, as he put it, he'd "matured" and gone to graduate school in psychology instead. He was less than supportive of my journalism career, and once, after I'd written a magazine piece that received a lot of favorable attention, his only comment was that he'd counted the number of times I'd used the word *but*. He said he thought it "spoke" to some of my main issues, without giving me any idea what they were. When the magazine made me a contributing editor a year later, he said, "That magazine is a total piece of shit." It wasn't, although I was beginning to realize that he was. Over the years he'd gained a lot of weight, and that, along with the recurrent cheese smell, was starting to make me queasy. One night I had a dream in which he turned into a Macy's Thanksgiving Day Parade balloon, and cutting the wires, I watched him float into the air. "That's it!" he said when I gave him the details. "Life is too short to put up with a patient like you." I got off the itchy camel-bag couch and never returned. He charged me for the session.

Ultimately, I found an excellent psychiatrist who was the exact opposite of the cheese therapist; she was warm and nurturing, and I didn't have to lie down on camel bags but could sit opposite her on a leather wing chair. She was supportive of my writing, even of my vacations, recognizing that I wasn't a spoiled brat but someone who was riddled with guilt. Growing up Catholic at a time when the nuns ruled with iron fists, I experienced religion as something so repressive that instead of allowing one's spirit to soar, it constantly tamped it down. Except for the smell of lilies on Easter Sunday, I rarely felt anything close to joy. I did, however, come away from religion with a strong sense of the excruciating tortures of hell and of how, if I didn't follow the "correct" path, I'd suffer eternal damnation. Since both my parents attended Catholic schools at a time when priests and nuns were even more punitive, they, too, had the fear of God instilled in them. My father, who is the most conscientious man I've ever met, has never once been late to an appointment and insisted on walking my sister Nancy down the aisle at her wedding, even though he wasn't feeling well and was later found to have suffered a stroke. During his forty-year career as a banker, he regularly got up at 5 A.M. so he could attend daily Mass. My mother is equally devout, fearing that she'll be held accountable because her three daughters no longer go to church. As the oldest daughter, I was the self-appointed vigil keeper, who took everyone's problems personally and felt as if it was my responsibility to make things right. *Vigil* is a Latin word meaning "watchful and awake" and is usually associated with the darkest hours of the night. From a psychoanalytic perspective, it's not a stretch to see why I'd be a poor sleeper.

My psychiatrist sent me to a psychopharmacologist, a grim-looking man with an unearthly pallor that didn't telegraph good health. He wrote me a prescription for the antidepressant tra-zodone, the drug most often prescribed for insomnia. (Since the FDA hasn't approved it for that purpose, doctors write it off-label, which is why Ambien is technically the "number one" sleep aid.) I nibbled at a fifty-milligram tablet, but even with such a tiny amount, my sleep felt weird. The next morning, I wrote, "Groggy, Ugh!" in my "drug diary." The doctor next suggested Wellbutrin, which, as "Zyban," is given to people who want to quit smoking. It was quite stimulating, like drinking a cappuccino, and while I liked the way it made me feel during the day, it didn't help my sleep and left me with a headache. From there, I tried Serzone, which was taken off the market after it was linked to dozens of cases of liver failure. (Bristol-Meyers Squibb blamed a decline in sales for the drug's removal.) The doctor then gave me Remeron, with the caveat that I might gain weight. "How much weight?" I wanted to know. He said it was hard to tell, so I went on the Internet and found lots of people who'd gained thirty pounds or more on it. I tried it anyhow. ("Groggy *again*. Ugh!") Admittedly, I'm a tough patient, and finding the right antidepressant is a matter of trial and error, but I was getting the distinct impression that the doctor was throwing anything at me. We moved on to Celexa, which made my insomnia worse, and then in what may have been either a brilliant or crazy idea he told me to try Ritalin. The doctor explained that for some individuals the drug's stimulant action can slow racing thoughts, but since Ritalin's most prominent side effects are nervousness and trouble sleeping, I was highly skeptical and never filled the prescription.

Next up was a psychopharmacologist who preferred older drugs, probably because he was older himself and these were the drugs he'd grown up with. The doctor was best known for administering electroshock therapy to a world-renowned musician, short-circuiting his depression and allowing him to continue his career. He told me that he'd treated many creative individuals, including a famous playwright, and that at my age—I was then in my late forties—I shouldn't worry about getting hooked on drugs. He went on to explain that Eugene O'Neill in *Long Day's Journey into Night* had been quite wrong in making the elderly Mary Tyrone a morphine addict, because in real life that probably wouldn't have happened. I'd never pictured myself as a character in *Long Day's Journey,* but after the doctor prescribed phenobarbitol, and then Dalmane, Elavil, and doxepin, I could definitely see myself in *Valley of the Dolls.* I didn't like any of them—"heart palpitations," I wrote in my journal—and I threw them away.

My psychiatrist, giving up on the idea of psychotropic drugs, suggested I consult with a colleague who also happened to be a Jesuit priest as well as a gynecologist. "Don't you think it's odd," I asked, "that a psychiatrist would be a priest *and* a gynecologist?" "Hmmm," she said, "I never thought about it, but then again, I'm not Catholic." When I finally met the priest/shrink/gynecologist, he was dressed in a white doctor's coat. Sitting down in his beautifully appointed office, in front of a large fireplace, I complained about my experience with the nuns, raking Sister Margaret over the coals one more time. He wondered if perhaps I wasn't sleeping not because she'd exiled me to the Garbage Row but because I'd lost my faith. "Would you ever consider returning to church?" he asked. Viewing insomnia as a crisis of faith was something I'd never considered before, and after I left his office, I thought of Paul on the road to Damascus, blinded by the light.

Light is our most important zeitgeber or "time cue," keeping our biological clock in sync. All living things—human, flowers, even fruit flies—operate on a twenty-four-hour cycle linked to the earth's rotation. Since our biological clocks aren't perfect machines—they can run too fast or too slow—they are "reset" each day when morning light hits our retina, sending a signal to the SCN to synchronize our circadian rhythms with the earth's cycle. To help set my own clock, my cognitive behavioral therapist wants me to go outside first thing in the morning. I'm not supposed to wear sunglasses, even though my ophthalmologist told me never to go outside in bright light without them. I recently made an appointment to see her because with all the talk about bedbugs I was suddenly having visions of them, but it turned out I have "floaters." She explained that the eye is encased in vitriol fluid, and as we age, the vitreous humor often thickens and breaks off to form little clumps. While I may think I'm seeing tiny pinprick-sized bugs, it's actually clumped vitreous gel. The condition is very common, and while it doesn't go away, you apparently get so used to it that you hardly notice. After the ophthalmologist told me that I'd be basically seeing bugs for the rest of my life, she warned me that long-term exposure to UV rays can lead to cataracts and macular degeneration. "So you really should wear sunglasses," she advised.

I'd hate to think that in order to sleep I'll wind up blind, but since I'm not going out at high noon, I figure I'll be okay. I have no idea what I'm supposed to be doing outside. I could take a brisk walk, but I prefer to get my exercise at the end of the day. Exercise raises body temperature, and if done four to six hours before bedtime, it can lead to deeper sleep, the result of a "compensatory cooling effect." I head into Central Park and sit on a bench with a metal plaque that reads, MARRY ME, ANI. For the next several weeks I sit there, and when the weather gets colder, I trade the bench for a light box that is nearly as big as my TV. Light boxes have proven very helpful in treating seasonal affective disorder, which affects an estimated fourteen million Americans, who grow sluggish and depressed during the dark days of winter. Many scientists believe that SAD is associated with shifted circadian rhythms. Dr. Alfred Lewy, who has been studying the disorder since the 1970s, describes it as a form of jet lag, in which people's body rhythms are out of sync with the sun. I bought my light box years ago when I thought I might have SAD, but I only used it a few times. Now I drag it out of my closet, where it's been hiding behind my unused massage table, and plug it into the living room wall. It's supposed to be two feet away, at eye level, so I balance it atop a tower of books on my coffee table and try to read the newspaper. At ten thousand lux—lux being the measurement for the brightness of light—it's the equivalent of sitting outside on a sunny day.

For the next several weeks I increase my time in front of the box so that I'm now spending a full thirty minutes basking in the artificial sunlight. I'm quite happy with the effect. Maybe a little too happy. One morning, after an hour "outside," I'm so energized that I speed-read fifty pages of a novel and two articles in *The New Yorker,* then pay my bills. Because I can't sit still—something of a requirement for a writer—I walk down Madison Avenue, where in record time I buy two pairs of shoes, three sweaters, and a skirt. I feel so totally exhilarated that I drop off the packages with my doorman and take another brisk walk, passing the older woman I always see near Central Park's Boat Basin. No matter the season, she's getting a suntan and looks like a lizard. Today she is dressed head-to-toe in shades of camel and bronze, and when I look down at her feet I notice that she's wearing lizard flats—the same shoes I just bought. I don't need a more dramatic sign. I cut way back on light therapy.

Sleep restriction is the toughest part of CBT, but with the easy stuff out of the way, my therapist thinks I'm finally ready for it. Invented by Spielman in the mid-eighties, the method is designed to limit the hours spent in bed to the time actually spent sleeping. If, for example, you're in bed for ten hours but only sleeping four, you're restricted to four hours of bed time. Essentially, you are being sleep-deprived, which makes you sleepier and more likely to fall into a pattern of sleeping more "efficiently." As sleep amount increases, so does the amount of time you're allowed in bed. My therapist tries to be gentle with me, suggesting I stay up until 11:30 P.M. and then set an alarm for 6:30 A.M. I don't even have an alarm because I've never overslept in my entire life, so I have to go out and buy one. The therapist has given me a full seven hours in bed, which is hardly boot camp, but the mere suggestion of an alarm is so alarming I'm up for six hours. It doesn't get much better during the rest of the week. For an anxious person, sleep restriction strikes me as possibly the worst thing you can do, but Matthew Ebben, a colleague of Spielman's, tells me he's used it effectively for his patients and that it works—provided you stick with it. Seeing my haggard face, the therapist lets me off the hook for a while, advising me to increase my dosage of Sonata to ten milligrams.

A few months later we try sleep restriction again. This time the therapist wants me to set the alarm for 5:45 A.M. Knowing it's going to go off gets me so crazy that in the middle of the night I begin rooting through an old makeup bag for the Valium a friend had once given me. I'd never taken Valium before, and this one proves to be totally useless, possibly because it's about a decade old and covered in pink lip gloss. I decide to visit Spielman in Brooklyn to see what kind of person would invent such a seemingly cruel technique. I find him in a small, cramped office at New York Methodist Hospital, where, as associate director of the Sleep Disorders Center, he works several days a week. (He also teaches psychology at the City College of the City University of New York, in addition to co-directing Weill Cornell's Center for Sleep Medicine.)

Spielman has the booming voice and the powerful presence of an army commander. Calling two female Ph.D. candidates into his office, he tells them to sit in on the interview "to see how it's done" and then goes on to explain the roots of sleep restriction in a very fluid, well-rehearsed way. "Occasionally I'd see a patient and not know what to do," he says, "so I'd tell them, 'If you have trouble falling asleep, just go to bed an hour later.' I started noticing that the patients were getting better. Sleep restriction is a little more sophisticated, but it's the same essence. It becomes easier to fall asleep the later it gets, because your biological rhythm starts kicking in. After the first night, you're accumulating a little sleep loss. Sleep is a self-correcting process. It's just like eating. When you're hungry you tend to eat more, because the body doesn't want you to get in a vulnerable state. It's the same thing with sleep. You'll make people sleep better if you just cut down their time in bed and make them a little sleep-deprived."

"Aren't they sleep-deprived to begin with?" I ask.

"It's not exactly clear that they *are* sleep-deprived. Many of the cognitive behavior techniques don't increase total sleep time."

What? So why am I bothering with them?

"Sleep time is an abstract concept," he goes on. "There's quality of sleep and number of awakenings. If you're just focused on sleep time, you're missing the picture. They still may be sleeping five and a half hours, but they fall asleep faster and sleep deeper and more solidly. Consequently, they feel better."

"But what if they don't?"

"Helping someone may take substantial efforts," he says. "I do all sorts of Draconian things. I take away caffeine, alcohol, and sleep time. When people are better they can have them back. I leave no stone unturned because I want to be the last sleep doctor they'll ever see. I tend to see people who have seen other sleep doctors, because sometimes I feel I'm the court of last resort. I have lots of dramatic stories of helping people in only one or two sessions. I call them my 'heroic treatment patients.' They're so filled with suggestions they could write a book themselves." He raises his voice. "I tell them to CUT IT OUT. ALL OF IT! You're seeing an expert and I've seen everything and know everything you're doing. STOP IT ALL! JUST GET BACK TO YOUR LIFE! They get better in two sessions. You want to sleep well? Don't think about it! Don't do anything! Sleep is automatic! It's repetitive! It happens every twenty-four hours! JUST GET OUT OF ITS WAY!"

It's been six months since I've seen my original sleep doctor, so I make a follow-up appointment to discuss my progress and to let him know that I've become so interested in sleep that I've decided to write a book about it. I thought he might be pleased, but he's not. "It's a terrible, terrible idea," he says, urging me to reconsider. Unfortunately, it's a little late because I already have a book contract. He wonders if the only reason I went to his sleep clinic was to gather information for my book. I explain that I went to his sleep clinic because I wanted to sleep, not because I wanted to write about sleep. The book came later. Things get tense. I don't blame the doctor for being upset. He has a reputation to protect and doesn't want me to dissuade people from going to a sleep clinic. I explain that I'm only writing about my experience, and each person is different, but the doctor suggests that I might be *really* different. "You couldn't even handle setting an alarm," he says, "and have you ever wondered why you're so sensitive to medication?" He reiterates my issue with the "alpha, delta, theta bursts," which none of the other sleep doctors I've spoken to think is a problem, and then explains that I'll never be a "champion sleeper" just like some people will never be champion runners. I'm prone to stumbling. Okay, so now I'm a sleep stumbler. "I wanted to help you get well," he says, shaking his head. "How do you expect me to do that now?"

Three weeks later I'm back in his office suite for my appointment with the therapist. Recently, they've moved to a luxury high-rise, where they share space with a slick-looking man who appears to be renting rooms to non-English-speaking tourists. It's Halloween and the receptionist is wearing a sparkly cat mask. I wish I had a mask. Knowing your sleep doctor is mad at you isn't the best dynamic if you're looking for sleep. When the therapist asks how I've been doing, I tell her that I've been getting light in the morning and practicing muscle relaxation, but that I'm experiencing memory loss from the Sonata. She suggests I cut back to three nights a week, and I immediately start bargaining with her. "What about four nights a week?" I say. "Can I alternate with Ambien?" Then I realize I'm practically begging for a drug that doesn't help me sleep and is impairing my memory. She suggests I try sleep restriction again and hands me more sleep logs, but I've already done that. On the way out, I bump into a woman dressed as an angel in a miniskirt. "Trick or treat," she says.

Lately I've been seeing more gigantic cockroaches, so I make an appointment with a real exterminator. "When other tenants renovate their apartments," he says, "the bugs move around and come in through the water pipes." He begins squirting insecticide everywhere, telling me it's safe for humans but not, apparently, for bugs. After washing up that night, I spot a huge cockroach outside my bedroom closet. I grab one of my lizard flats and, channeling Dr. Spielman, bring it down on the insect, shouting "CUT IT OUT! ALL OF IT! STOP IT!"

Spielman was right. It slept.

5

ASTEROID LAS VEGAS

At the MGM Grand in Las Vegas, "Sleep Disorders: All You Ever Wanted to Know About Sleep" is running simultaneously with Cirque du Soleil's *Kà*. That a continuing medical-education course for three hundred doctors and medical technicians and a $165 million martial-arts extravaganza are being held under the same roof tells me everything I need to know about Las Vegas and to some extent about sleep. A sign in the hotel's lobby says it best. With haiku simplicity, it reads:

SLEEP

DISORDERS

LAS VEGAS

I've enrolled in the sleep course, booking a room at the Signature, MGM's "smaller, non-gaming, non-smoking hotel." Hopefully, it will translate into "quieter, pro-sleeping hotel." I haven't been to Las Vegas in thirty years, so I'm not sure what to expect. Taking the elevator up to the twenty-third floor, I steel myself for something totally tacky, only to find a sleek, semi-tasteful room. While I wouldn't have necessarily chosen acid-green leather for my own headboard, I love the room's pillow-top mattress and Egyptian-cotton sheets. And how often do you get an unobstructed view of the Eiffel Tower? If I ignore the casinos, the construction cranes, and everything I know about geography, I could almost be in Paris. Both cities are famous for their lights: Paris is the official City of Light, Las Vegas the City of Neon. Las Vegas glows so brightly that its lights are visible from eight national parks. The city is so invested in its identity as a megawatt town that for its one-hundred-year anniversary the Centennial Committee requested that an asteroid be named in its honor. Due to its reputation as a major light polluter, scientists on the committee of the International Astronomical Union—the group in charge of naming asteroids—weren't too keen on calling one after a place that practically invented the term "sky glow." But since they'd already named one Elko, after a Nevada town famous for its legal brothels, it seemed unfair to penalize Las Vegas when all it had done was potentially damage the ecosystem and not, like Elko, help further the state's reputation as an epicenter for prostitution and sex trafficking.

Asteroid Las Vegas isn't the only trace of Vegas in the firmament. The tip of the Luxor's pyramid contains a forty-billion-candlepower spotlight so bright that astronauts reported seeing it as they hurtled through outer space. In his book *Neon Metropolis,* the late Nevada historian Hal K. Rothman describes the city as a symbol of the "new America," and states that "what people see in Las Vegas today . . . is what they can expect everywhere in the near future." And what is that? Gazing at "Paris," which isn't far from an equally incandescent "New York," "Venice," "Lake Como," and "Mandalay Bay," I see the whole electrified world before me—and it's not sleeping.

Doctors drink lots of coffee. Outside of Starbucks, I can't remember the last time I saw so many people consume so much caffeine.

The physician sitting next to me has four large cups lined up in front of him. Doesn't he know that caffeine is the sworn enemy of sleep? Surprisingly, the average M.D. doesn't know all that much about sleep. The American Medical Association didn't even recognize sleep medicine as a self-designated practice specialty until 1995, and most primary-care physicians have only had two hours or less of formal sleep education. Dr. Richard Strobel, who heads the Sleep Disorders Clinic at Lehigh Valley Hospital in Allentown, Pennsylvania, told me: "I graduated from med school in 1985, and I didn't get a single hour on sleep. We spend a third of our lives sleeping, and physicians had no clue about it at all."

The coffee smells delicious, and even though I've sworn it off, I immediately go looking for some. Outside the conference room, there's a smaller room, where an elaborate buffet breakfast is laid out within salivating distance of the drug reps from Rozerem and Lunesta. After watching doctors pile fattening food onto their plates, I pile some on mine and then belly up to one of the massive coffee urns and pour myself a really big cup. It's only 7:45 A.M. and I've already consumed more calories and caffeine than I normally do in an entire day. The whole setup feels unhealthy—and I'm not just referring to the food. Since most doctors have to earn a certain number of CME credits each year to maintain their medical license, these conferences are a way of life for them. In the past, universities and medical associations produced and paid for continuing medical education, but today, drug companies finance half the cost of CME courses in the United States. As a result, physicians have grown accustomed to running a gauntlet of drug reps to get to the scrambled eggs. While the CME course promises to be "evidence-based" and "free of commercial bias," Takeda and Sanofi-aventis are two of the commercial sponsors, and both give money to the National Sleep Foundation, one of the co-presenters. They also provide financial support, either through consulting or speaker's fees, to five out of the fifteen lecturers. Dr. James K. Walsh, who is giving the talk on the pharmacologic treatment of insomnia, lists on his disclosure form financial ties to no fewer than twenty-two drug companies.

At exactly 8 A.M., I'm back inside the massive beige conference room staring at an empty stage. Lined up in front of us on the long tables are number 2 pencils and bowls of hard candies. The lights dim and William Dement, who has inherited the title "Father of Modern Sleep Medicine" from his mentor, Nathaniel Kleitman, begins speaking in a low, husky voice. Though Dement has accomplished much in his sixty-year career, from helping discover REM to establishing the world's first sleep-disorders clinic, he derives the greatest satisfaction from his role as an old-fashioned, fire-and-brimstone evangelist. At eighty-two, with a full head of white hair and indomitable energy, he's still running around the country preaching the Gospel of Sleep. In the bleary-eyed universe over which he presides, people aren't merely tired but "sleep-sick." They carry around a "sleep debt," which accumulates over time and can only be reduced by obtaining extra sleep. The larger the sleep debt, the more tired and impaired they become, leading to drowsiness, leading to falling asleep faster, leading to . . . death.

Dement reminds us that we're sleeping one and a half hours less than we did a century or even fifty years ago, and as a result, the average American is walking around with a sleep debt of between 25 and 30 hours. This sounds serious. But is he right? According to a National Sleep Foundation poll, the average American gets 6.9 hours of sleep during the week, rising to 7.5 hours on the weekend. Since doctors recommend between 7 and 8 hours, I'm not sure how a differential of a few percentage points constitutes a national crisis. And did our ancestors really sleep 9 hours a night? Jim Horne, the director of the Sleep Research Centre at Loughborough University, United Kingdom, claims the evidence is based on a 1913 Stanford University study that tracked schoolchildren, not adults. Since children are longer sleepers, the study set the bar artificially high, at 9 hours. After comparing data from the Bureau of Labor Statistics' American Time Use Survey from 1965–1985 and 1998–2001, Horne found that the average amount of sleep during that particular period changed by less than 0.7 percent.

Dement sprinkles his lecture with words like *disaster* and *catastrophe,* reeling off a well-rehearsed litany of tragedies, starting with the *Exxon Valdez.* When the tanker ran aground off Alaska in 1989, spilling eleven million gallons of crude oil and damaging thirteen hundred miles of shoreline, Dement says it wasn't because the captain had been drinking but because the third mate, who was left in charge, had slept only six hours in the previous forty-eight. (According to some reports, the captain had consumed at least five double vodkas in the hours before the disaster, which surely didn't help.) Dement attributes the 1986 explosion of the space shuttle *Challenger* to the severe sleep deprivation of NASA managers who had been working twenty hours straight after only two or three hours of sleep the previous night. He blames the 1995 grounding of the Liberian passenger ship *Star Princess,* which ruptured oil tanks and caused $27 million in damages, to the pilot's obstructive sleep apnea. He tells us that the nuclear accidents at Chernobyl and Three Mile Island and the industrial disaster at Bhopal were the result of judgment errors made in the middle of the night when operators were dangerously fatigued. More recently, security guards at Peach Bottom nuclear power plant in Pennsylvania, Indian Point in New York, and Turkey Point in Florida were all caught napping on the job.

Death could come just as easily on a highway, he reminds us, where, according to the National Highway Traffic Safety Administration, at least 100,000 police-reported crashes are the direct result of driver fatigue each year. That translates to an estimated 1,500 deaths, 71,000 injuries, and $12.5 billion in monetary losses. Being awake for more than twenty-four hours degrades performance as much as having a blood-alcohol level of 0.1 percent—the equivalent of being legally drunk. "If you're in a car with someone who is sleep-deprived," Dement says, "you should ask the driver to pull over and *get out*. A severely sleep-deprived person can go from feeling wide awake to falling fast asleep *in as little as ten to fifteen seconds*." Long-haul truckers are the most vulnerable to drowsy driving, sometimes dozing with their eyes wide open. These "microsleeps" can last from a few seconds to several minutes, and while the brain is technically asleep, the trucker may still be driving, oblivious to stop signs and sudden curves in the road.

While highways are dangerous, Dement tells us to be equally wary of hospitals. With their eighty-hour workweeks, medical interns are among the sleepiest people in the world. In 2004, researchers at Brigham and Women's Hospital in Boston conducted the first study to measure the impact of sleep deprivation on interns' medical judgment. The results, which were reported in the *New England Journal of Medicine*, showed that the interns on the traditional long schedule, working at least twenty-four hours on every other shift, made one-third more serious mistakes than they did during "short" sixteen-hour shifts. He holds up a newspaper article with the headline: SURGEONS ASLEEP AT THE SCALPEL.

Dement's time is nearly up, and I can't say I'm sorry. Does the man have any good news? Before he finishes, he attempts to lift our spirits with his favorite bedtime story. It goes something like this: In 1989, Dement started a program in his hometown of Walla Walla, Washington—"the place they liked so much they named it twice." In this town, there were thousands of sleepy people who couldn't understand why they were tired all the time, so Dement began to train and educate local doctors in the basics of sleep medicine. As a result, the sleepy people found "clinical salvation" and the National Sleep Foundation named Walla Walla the Healthy Sleep Capital of America.

Oh, to be in Walla Walla instead of in a cab with a crazy driver who is barreling down the highway at eighty miles per hour. I'm heading to Summerlin Hospital to interview Dr. Robert Troell, one of

Dement's former students and the first surgeon to be certified in sleep medicine, but my driver isn't inspiring much confidence.

"Do you know where you're going?" I ask.

"No problem," he says. But it is a problem, because he can't find the hospital and because he's driving so erratically we nearly get hit. With Dement's words still fresh in my mind, I think about asking him to pull over so I can get out. But then what? Hitch a ride with a sleep-deprived trucker who might fall asleep at the wheel, sending me into the arms of a sleep-deprived, scalpel-wielding surgeon?

"Are you visiting a patient in the hospital?" the driver asks.

"I'm interviewing someone," I mumble. "For this book I'm writing on sleep."

"*Sleep?*" he says, swiveling around so we can talk face-to-face.

"Don't do that!" I say. "Watch the road!"

The driver, who is originally from Kenya, tells me that he's on the eleventh hour of a twelve-hour night shift and is totally exhausted because he has never adapted to night-shift work. "I spend the night going from hotel to hotel," he explains. "People, they gamble all night long, so they need someone to drive them around. When I go home, I collapse on the sofa and fall asleep in a minute, but then the people in my family are noisy, and since it's daytime, they wake me up." I feel bad for him, I really do, but it's now apparent that we're totally lost and that I'm going to be late. The driver calls for directions and speaks to the doctor's receptionist. "Yeah, yeah," he says, nodding his head. "Okay, right and then left. Okay, got it."

"So, now do you know where you're going?" I ask.

"No."

He calls again. "Okay, *now* I know. We were heading the wrong way."

He makes a U-turn on the highway with cars speeding toward us, and by the time we reach the hospital I'm ready to check in to it. "I hate Las Vegas," he yells out the cab window as I walk away. "The people, they're all crazy!"

Troell's receptionist tells me the doctor is running a little late, but I'm to make myself comfortable in the waiting room, which is decorated with dreamy paintings of nude women flying through woodland groves. Aligned on a coffee table are two brochures, one for restless leg syndrome, the other for the dermal filler Restylane. A third brochure, on a side table, features a picture of one of the woodland nymphs with the words "Beauty by Design." I hadn't realized that Dr. Troell is both a sleep doctor and a plastic surgeon. As weird as it seems, it does make a certain sense. If people aren't getting their beauty sleep at night, at least they can acquire beauty "by design" during the day.

"Oh, so the doctor isn't just involved in sleep," I say to the receptionist.

She smiles. "No, he's involved in making America beautiful."

"Sorry, sorry," Dr. Troell says, rushing into the waiting room dressed in his surgical scrubs. "Just came from a full-body lipo." Troell looks a little like Mel Gibson in his *Lethal Weapon* period and exudes some of the actor's manic energy. He speaks rapidly and appears to be jumping out of his skin, but since I'm trying to picture full-body liposuction, I could be projecting a bit. Troell has an intense stare, and sitting across from him, I can't help wondering if he's thinking, "This woman has sleepy eyes. She needs them fixed." Maybe I do. If sleeping pills and CBT don't necessarily improve sleep time but make you feel better about the sleep you've had, then shouldn't plastic surgery do the same thing? If I looked less tired, would I *be* less tired?

I ask Troell if he thinks it's a little unusual that someone board-certified in sleep medicine is now doing facial-fat grafting, liposuction, and lip augmentation. Troell explains that since his original expertise was in the surgical aspects of sleep, treating people with obstructive sleep apnea, he was already board-certified in otolaryngology-head and neck surgery, facial plastic and reconstructive surgery, and sleep medicine. When he moved here in 2001, he was able to take full advantage of his various specialties, for if Las Vegans are preoccupied with anything, it's looks and lack of sleep. The city has more than a dozen sleep labs, with names like Desert Moon and Nocturna, all competing to sound like deluxe hotel/casinos. Christina Molfetta, the former owner of Nocturna (in 2008 she sold it to Graymark Healthcare), even posed for the journal *Sleep Review* wearing a halter top and rolling a pair of dice. But even with all the supposed luxuries, such as cherry-wood sleigh beds and matching armoires, many sleep clinics can't make a profit because the competition has resulted in aggressive underbidding. "You really can't do a sleep study for less than about $650," Troell tells me, "so if you're trying to go below that, you're going to lose money. Some people will say, 'Oh, I can make a buck,' so they open a sleep clinic, but some of them are so bad that when I look at their test results, I can't even interpret them. One place was even closed down by the FBI." In 2005, SDI Future Health was indicted for Medicare fraud, after a federal grand jury found that five Las Vegas doctors were prescribing sleep-apnea tests to patients who didn't need them. "If you look at Vegas," Troell says, "I wouldn't exactly call it the Mecca of ethics."

It's not the Mecca of good health, either. According to a recent Burt Sperling/Centrum study that issued a "health report card" on the fifty largest metro areas in the United States, Las Vegas received especially poor marks for physical activity, stress, alcohol consumption, and smoking. A Sperling/Ambien poll ranked it the seventh-worst city for sleeping. (Detroit came in last.) "People who come to me often have multiple sleep problems," Troell says. "Many people in Nevada are over their ideal body weight, so a lot of them have sleep apnea. Seventy percent of people with apnea are overweight. Then they often have what we call 'insufficient sleep syndrome,' which basically means they're not sleeping enough. Vegas is a 24/7 type of town. At four in the morning the casinos are still open, so we have more sleep problems related to all that stimulation. Then, of course, you have the shift workers."

If tourists come to Vegas to forget temporarily who they are, people move to the land of reinvention to forget who they were. Yet second chances often come at a price, and finding a job in an unconventional town frequently means keeping unconventional hours. Of the approximately 860,000 employed in Las Vegas, 155,000 work in the casino/hotel industry, with a third on the night or "graveyard" shift. While a person working from 11 P.M. to 7 A.M. should in theory be able to sleep when he gets home, it isn't as simple as putting on an eye mask and pulling down the blackout shades. Daytime is synonymous with being awake. Phones ring, dogs bark, babies cry. The outside world is noisy and intrusive. Many parents prefer the night shift so they can take care of their children during the day, but even if workers don't have family responsibilities, their own bodies frequently rebel, the result of disrupted circadian rhythms. In addition to the "master clock" located in the SCN (suprachiasmatic nucleus), scientists have discovered clocklike genes in all our major organs, which may explain why sleep deprivation, in addition to affecting brain function, also raises the likelihood of gastrointestinal disorders, obesity, heart disease, and cancer. In 2007 the International Agency for Research on Cancer, part of the World Health Organization, after following eight epidemiological studies, found the evidence so persuasive that it listed the graveyard shift as "probably carcinogenic to humans." Six out of the eight studies found a modest increased risk of breast cancer in women who worked nights. It is thought that exposure to light at night interrupts the production of melatonin, a hormone produced by the brain's pineal gland. Melatonin peaks at night during sleep and is believed to act as a protective agent against cancer. Interestingly, studies have shown that blind women with no light perception have a decreased risk of breast cancer.

The graveyard shift, as bad as it sounds, is actually easier on the body than a rotating shift. "That's the absolute worst," says Troell. "While I try to regulate their sleep-wake cycle as best I can, by the time they've adjusted to one shift, they're switching again. It's like permanent jet lag. I had several patients where things got so bad I had to tell them to switch their jobs, and they did, and they got better."

Approximately 8.6 million Americans work the night shift, opening up a market for drugs to counteract the effects. In Las Vegas, however, people tend to stick to the tried-and-true remedies, such as caffeine, energy drinks, and stimulants. "In my experience, shift workers rarely show up at sleep clinics, unless they have apnea," says Molfetta. "They tend to figure, 'Well, this is my life and I just have to deal with the insomnia,' so they self-medicate with stuff like Red Bull, caffeine, and Tylenol PM."

Dr. Mel Pohl, the medical director of the Las Vegas Recovery Center, tells me that Las Vegas's twenty-four-hour lifestyle creates major challenges in treating addicts. "Seventy-five percent of our patients have sleep-related issues," he says. "They often turn to opioids, such as Vicodin and Lortab, and stimulants, such as Ritalin, cocaine, and amphetamines, to get an energy surge when they need to be awake. Then they take sedatives or alcohol to even themselves out so they can eventually fall asleep. This upper/downer syndrome is very common. And when they try to stop, the sleep problems are terrible, so it's tough. We try to counsel people to get jobs that are more compatible with life, but in economic downturns, they often don't have a choice."

A bartender I'll call Joe was on the night shift for seven years, taking speed, cocaine, anything he could get his hands on to stay awake. "I don't think I ever had a good night's sleep the whole time," he said. "Sometimes I'd stay up for one, two days, and then I'd sleep for a whole day. Sometimes I'd play golf after work before going to sleep. It all just depended on how I felt." Joe ultimately ended up in rehab, and after he got out, he quit the night shift. In the forty years he's been working in Las Vegas, he doesn't think the city has become any more accommodating to shift workers. "The only thing the hotels care about is making money," he said. "For the worker the whole place has changed for the worse. This is a city where you're forced to face your demons. If I were twenty-one and came to Las Vegas now, I'd leave and never come back. Las Vegas is terrible for your family life. It kills your kids." While one in every twenty weddings takes place in Las Vegas, for the people who live here, marriage is often an impossible balancing act between two partners working different shifts. Adolescents are often left unsupervised, with the result that Las Vegas has one of the worst high school dropout rates in the country, along with soaring rates of teen suicide and drug abuse. "If you look at the statistics," Troell says, "American workers put in more hours than anyone else in the world—even the Japanese. If you're working sixteen hours a day, you don't have much time for a lot else, so people have to sacrifice one thing, and usually that's sleep."

After the interview, Troell drives me to a nearby casino, telling me I'll have an easier time getting a cab there than at the hospital. I spot a cab but there's no driver inside, so I stand around in the sun for the next fifteen minutes staring into the desert. In the fifties and sixties, 120 atomic bombs were detonated in the Mohave Desert, right outside the city. Casinos packed "atomic bomb lunches" so guests could picnic near "Ground Zero." I'm contemplating the insanity of it all when an obese man eating an ice cream cone emerges from the casino. "Hello," I say. "Are you the cabdriver?" He nods and gets into the cab, while I climb into the backseat. He starts up the motor while still eating his melting cone.

"I don't mind waiting if you want to finish that," I say.

"No, not a problem," he says, continuing to lick it. "This is my lunch."

"You wouldn't be at the end of your shift, would you?"

"No, I just started."

"That's good," I say, telling him about my last cabdriver.

"You won't find me working a crazy schedule. I'm kind of a health nut."

"Oh?"

When asked for his definition of a non-crazy schedule, he tells me that he drives a cab for twelve hours a day, four days a week.

"So that's not too bad," I say.

"Yeah, that way I've got more time . . ."

"To rest?"

"No, to hang drapes. I do upholstery the other three days."

Back at the conference, Dr. Fred Turek is showing the roomful of doctors the face of sleep deprivation, and it belongs to Ann Curry, a co-host of the *Today* show. "Just look at this," he says, pointing to an old 1998 newspaper headline that reads, AWARD-WINNING MOTHER CHOOSES KIDS OVER SLEEP. "What kind of message does that send?" Turek asks. "I mean, *this* is the 'Outstanding Mother of the Year,' and she does it by skimping on sleep!" Turek is so worked up he reminds me of Tom Cruise talking to Matt Lauer about anti-depressants. Would Turek have been happier if Ann Curry had chosen sleep over her kids?

Turek, a circadian biologist at Northwestern University, is on safer territory when he's talking about what he knows best, which is the effect of sleep deprivation on mice. He shows us a picture of a mouse. It's so fat it doesn't even look like a mouse but like a cir-cular bath mat with eyes and a tail. Turek led an important study in which mice were genetically engineered to lack a working version of a gene called Clock, which controls daily rhythms in the brain and throughout the body. Without Clock, the mutant mice lost their bearings, snacking when they should have been sleeping. Within weeks, the ravenous mice not only got fat but developed symptoms similar to those seen in overweight people, such as dia-betes and high cholesterol. Since the mid-seventies, the prevalence of obesity has increased sharply in this country, with nearly two-thirds of the adult population now overweight. According to the Centers for Disease Control, 24 million Americans now have type 2 diabetes, which is associated with poor diet, excess body weight, and infrequent exercise. That number is up 3 million from the pre-vious two years, with another 27 million Americans at high risk of developing the disease. Our super-sized, all-you-can-eat culture is perhaps the biggest factor contributing to the problem, but biologists like Turek are suggesting that lack of sleep is another culprit.

Dr. Eve Van Cauter, a professor of medicine at the University of Chicago, has been studying the effects of circadian rhythms on metabolism and hormones for the past twenty-five years. Her laboratory produced a series of studies showing the effects of short-term sleep deprivation in healthy young men. After two nights of four hours of sleep, the men had lower levels of leptin, a hormone that suppresses appetite, and higher levels of ghrelin, a peptide secreted by the stomach that acts as an appetite stimulant. What's more, the ravenous men began craving carbohydrates, opting for breads and pasta over proteins, vegetables, and fruits. Taken together, Turek's and Van Cauter's experiments suggest that short sleep can wreak havoc with the body's ability to regulate appetite, placing people at an increased risk for obesity and diabetes. However, a 2008 review of the epidemiological evidence found that it wasn't yet strong enough to warrant telling the general population that sleep duration was definitely related to obesity. Van Cauter told *Nature* that she'd been approached by one pharmaceutical company to discuss the possibility of a sleeping pill that could double as a diet pill. One can only imagine the commercial: *"Can't sleep at night? Afraid to step on the scale in the morning? We can help you lose weight while you sleep . . ."*

Turek believes that one of our big problems is that we're increasingly out of sync with nature in many aspects of our lives. As a growing number of women married later and entered the workforce, they were forced to confront the reality of their diminished fertility. Advances in reproductive medicine helped push back the clock, and what had once been the stuff of science fiction became the highly profitable fertility industry. In recent years, scientists have used stem cells to grow healthy human eggs, a development that might enable women to delay menopause by a decade. Since the majority of women aren't likely to return to the days when they had children during their peak fertile years—the clock begins to slow down at twenty-seven—they will undoubtedly rely more and more on technology to pick up the slack. Will it be the same with sleep? In our 24/7 world, we may become increasingly dependent on drugs to help us override our natural timekeeper. "We're the only species that doesn't listen to our biological clock," Turek says, "and we ignore it at our peril."

Today is Valentine's Day, and I'm at an insomnia workshop inside the MGM Grand. It's just me, twenty doctors, and the workshop's leader, Dr. Anne Germain, an assistant professor of psychiatry at the University of Pittsburg School of Medicine. Dr. Germain is a tall, striking brunette, who in her black clothes and stylish glasses could easily play a brainy scientist in a Bond film. Her specialty is sleep and post-traumatic stress disorder, but she also trains therapists in behavioral techniques to treat insomnia. Germain takes a practical approach to the problem, believing there is as much variation for sleep as there is for height, weight, and other factors. "It's unrealistic to think that everyone should sleep basically the same number of hours," she explains. "Eight hours is actually a lot for an adult. There's only so much sleep your brain can produce. What's important is that you sleep as much as you need. If it's four hours, it's four hours. Insomnia is a problem when it starts to interfere with daytime functioning."

A doctor raises his hand. "From my experience," he says, "insomnia can become a lifestyle, like with chronic pain. Patients don't want to give it up. They hold on to it because they're getting some benefit out of it."

"How insulting," I think. True, I parlayed my insomnia into a book, but my life isn't all about sleep. It's only about sleep when I'm trying to sleep and when I'm writing about sleep. That leaves eight hours to pursue all my non-sleep interests, which I've had to curtail because of my sleep book, but I'd hardly call insomnia my "lifestyle." Several other doctors express irritation about their insomniac patients, categorizing them as unpleasant whiners who probably sleep more than they think they do. "A doctor I trained under likes to tell the story of a patient who claimed she hadn't slept in twenty years," says a sleep tech from Las Vegas. "She came for a sleep study and fell asleep in five minutes and remained asleep the whole night. The next morning, she said, '*See?* I told you I didn't sleep.'"

Earlier in the day, we'd all listened to James Walsh deliver an enthusiastic lecture on the pharmacologic treatment of insomnia. In fact, during the formal presentations, I didn't hear one negative comment about sleeping pills, but the doctors at the workshop, citing their own experience with patients, are considerably more skeptical. "I have patients who want pills to wake up and pills to go to sleep," says a neurologist. "What are we supposed to do?"

A worried internist adds, "We still don't really know the effects of these drugs. You have doctors telling patients to go on higher and higher dosages, but on higher levels of Ambien, bizarre behavior has been seen."

Another internist says, "Personally, I think these drugs are very habit-forming. At the very least, patients develop a psychological dependence, and I find it very hard to get them off the medications."

Dr. Germain outlines the benefits of cognitive behavior therapy, giving a passionate defense of sleep restriction and stimulus control. "If your patients can't sleep," she says, "tell them to get out of bed, keep the lights low, and do something boring, like sorting buttons." *Sorting buttons?* Where would I get buttons? Her other suggestion is knitting, which I haven't done since sixth grade, when I created an impossibly long multicolored scarf that I never wore. I think that if we were living in a nineteenth-century world where people sorted buttons and knitted, we might all be sleeping better.

At the far end of the room, a pulmonary specialist raises his hand, expressing his concern that insomniac patients are getting all the attention when everybody knows that doctors have the worst sleep problems. "What about us?" he says. "Aren't the consequences of what we're doing just as important? We're terrible at following our own advice. We don't get enough sleep, so we drink six cups of coffee and think that's perfectly fine." Another doctor brings up Libby Zion, an eighteen-year-old college freshman whose death at New York Hospital, in 1984, spawned the rule limiting residents to an eighty-hour workweek, with no single stretch of duty of more than twenty-four hours. (The two residents taking care of Zion had been on duty for eighteen and nineteen hours.) While an eighty-hour week still sounds brutal, residents used to routinely work a hundred hours a week, often for thirty-six hours at a time.

"Sleep deprivation among doctors is still rampant," the pulmonologist says. "If we don't sleep, how can we expect our patients to?"

Everybody nods in agreement. For the stowaway insomniac, it's a very sobering moment.

The NBA All-Stars are in town for the big game, and I spend my last evening dodging hordes of basketball fans as I attempt to stroll down the MGM Grand's promenade to the casino. I'm not a gambler, and except for my previous trip to Las Vegas, I've only been in a casino one other time, when I was writing a story about Atlantic City's emergence as a gaming resort in the late seventies and my personal tour guide turned out to be a member of the Gambino crime family. We got a lot of free drinks and I won eighty dollars in the nickel slot machines. This time I quickly lose a hundred at the slots. Despite the incessant ringing, which indicates (falsely) that people are winning, I grow bored and move on to the Lion Habitat, where, oblivious to the constant barrage of noise, two lions are fast asleep on a glass walkway. Looking up at them, a woman cries, "Oh my God! I think they're dead!" In this environment, death seems far likelier than sleep. While it "feels" like night-time or some hellish approximation—there are no windows and few visible time cues—casinos are purposely designed to keep people awake through sheer sensory overload. Then, to make sure they're not *too* alert, cocktail servers in skimpy red outfits, sporting voluminous cleavage, solicit drink orders. As a result, gamblers often exist in a quasi dream state where their money doesn't feel any more real than their artificial environment. If Asteroid Las Vegas actually fell from the sky and hit Las Vegas, I doubt anyone at the casino would even notice.

Jim Horne believes that one reason casinos stay open all night is to take advantage of a sleepy gambler's penchant for risk taking. He and a colleague conducted an experiment in which a group of play-ers, after a night of no sleep, became increasingly less inhibited, placing larger and larger bets. This pattern of risky behavior was borne out in a 2007 study published in the journal *SLEEP* that found that sleep deprivation had a negative effect on a gambler's judg-ment. Duke University researchers studied the brains of healthy subjects using functional magnetic resonance imaging (fMRIs), an advance in magnetic technology that allows researchers to map changes in blood flow that correspond to brain function. They dis-covered that the part of the brain involved with anticipating rewards became more active when the sleep-deprived "gamblers" were presented with risky payoff choices. According to the study, not only does sleep deprivation adversely affect a person's decision-making ability by elevating expectations of gains, but it also mutes the emotional impact of losing.

Interestingly, drugs for restless leg syndrome have been linked to compulsive gambling. In 2007 the Mayo Clinic reported that some patients being treated with medications known as dopamine agonists had developed an unusual urge to gamble, even if they'd never been inside a casino before. (The neurotransmitter dopa-mine not only helps control movement and balance but is active in the brain's reward system.) One woman, who had previously viewed gamblers as "unfortunate individuals," lost more than $140,000. While the Mayo Clinic study was based on the experience of only three people, it's considered significant because two years earlier the clinic had reported pathological gambling as a side effect for people taking dopamine agonists for Parkinson's disease, and in 2009 it reported that one in six such patients developed compulsive gambling or hypersexuality. The Mayo Clinic now advises doctors to monitor their RLS patients for any signs of compulsive behaviors.

After spending an hour or so watching people lose money, I'm ready to leave but can't find my way out of the casino, which is basically a huge maze with no visible exits. Everywhere I go I keep running into the robotic gorilla at the Rainforest Café, where Gorillas in the Mist Cheesecake is on the menu. Who'd name a dessert after a movie in which the lead character, the primatologist Dian Fossey, is brutally murdered in her sleep? The real-life Fossey may have been taking pills and drinking alcohol to alleviate her insomnia, and according to one theory, she might have survived the attack if she'd been more alert.

I've never wanted to get out of a place so badly in my life, and now the concierge is telling me that due to a snowstorm my flight has been canceled and I'm stuck in Vegas another night. "Just take a day off, enjoy yourself," Lee says when I tell him. But how am I supposed to enjoy myself *here*? Except for my outing to Summerlin Hospital, I've now been inside for four straight days and have totally lost my sense of time and place. I decide to go for a walk, but the air quality is awful, so I take a cab to the Venetian, where I can be indoors and outdoors simultaneously. I feel like buying something, but there's nothing that appeals to me. I ride the elevator up to the fifth floor, where I stroll around Saint Mark's Square and watch gondoliers in straw hats take tourists down the Grand Canal. Overhead, the artificial sky changes color. It feels like rain.

Maybe I should buy an umbrella in case the ceiling rips and the heavens open.

The next day, finally leaving Las Vegas, I share a cab to the airport with a New Jersey couple who have spent the past four days at an apparel trade show. "Is this your first time in Vegas?" the man asks.

"Second," I say.

"So, what did you think?"

I think that as far as sleep goes, Las Vegas is the Village of the Damned. Inside the airport, a female voice announces over the loudspeaker, *"Will Lebron James please come to the information counter . . . Laker Girls, Laker Girls, Laker Girls, your transportation is ready . . . Will the person who left five thousand dollars in cash wrapped in a yellow elastic band please reclaim their money at the information counter."*

I look down at my watch, a 1938 Rolex that I bought twenty years ago at a store called Time Will Tell. It has stopped running. The watch has always given me trouble, but I keep having it repaired because I like it so much. The back is engraved TO DOUGLAS, FROM DEREK AND CYRIL, and while I have no idea who these men are, I've always imagined them as fellow actors in a Noël Coward play. Now my watch is broken and poor Douglas, Derek, and Cyril are probably all dead. If there's a lesson to be learned, I'm reasonably sure it's not to be found in Vegas.

6

BREATHLESS

My psychotherapist has a new idea for my insomnia: hypnotism. I immediately picture an evil Svengali with a flowing black cape, Brylcreemed hair, and a buxom assistant named Lola. "No thanks," I say. "Too scary." My therapist explains that the hypnotist she has in mind—he's actually a *hypnotherapist*—is not only a brilliant psychiatrist but also a specialist in psychopharmacology, neuropsychiatry, stress management, family counseling, cognitive/behavioral therapy, and psychosomatic and sleep disorders.

"Yeah, but he still could be a diabolical huckster," I say.

"Except he isn't. He's very nice."

So I make an appointment to see him, receiving in return a thick questionnaire inquiring about my religious beliefs, menstrual and sexual history, spouses, friends, lovers, addictions—everything you could possibly think of, if you were a CIA profiler or, apparently, this doctor. Several weeks later I take the subway to his office, which is located in a large hospital complex across from the Eye Institute. Maybe it's because I've got eyes on the brain that when I meet the doctor I can't help noticing that his own eyes are gigantic. Or perhaps it's an optical illusion, the result of his very large aviator-style glasses. Whatever the reason, I feel as if I'm staring into the yard-high retinas of Dr. T. J. Eckleburg, the all-seeing, all-knowing oculist from *The Great Gatsby.*

"Dr. Eckleburg" sits at a desk, while I sit next to him, and we talk about my need to "keep vigil." He wonders if I ever experienced a childhood sexual trauma, one that I failed to mention in the tell-all questionnaire or at any time during twenty years of therapy. I tell him that as far as I can recall—and I'm pretty sure I'd remember— I was never sexually abused. Instead, I tell him about my recently formulated hypothesis, which I've dubbed the Cocoon of Sleep. As long as I can remain enveloped in a cozy, silky cocoon, even if I have to get up and go to the bathroom, I can usually fall back asleep. But if I fall out of the cocoon (and it's not as if I'm doing it on purpose; it just happens), then I'm totally wide awake. The doctor listens very intently, while I try to remember what Dr. Eckleburg in *The Great Gatsby* symbolized. I think he was a metaphor for either the American Dream or God. Eckleburg, as if reading my mind, begins talking about religion and the power of ritual. It's undoubtedly fascinating, but his voice is so monotonous I'm already getting sleepy, and we haven't even started yet. He tells me to look up at the ceiling while slowly closing my eyes and then to float my arm in the air "just like a bah-*looon.*" Next he tells me that I can't move my arm, and suddenly I can't. He tells me to lower it, and luckily it descends on cue, but he wants me to try it a second time.

"Now, float your arm into the air just like a bah-*looon,*" he says, but this time my arm won't budge. Clearly, this isn't the desired result, but he tells me that since I exhibited hypnotic potential the first time around, he believes I'm still a viable candidate. He begins speaking into an audiocassette recorder, preparing the tape he wants me to listen to every night. Meanwhile, I follow along, floating my arm, which, as he explains, is my "signal to enter a deeper state of consciousness known as self-hypnosis." He tells me to imagine that I'm flying on a magic carpet, "away from home, away from work, away from worries and hassles and problems and cares." I picture myself on a deserted island, where I'm cultivating the Cocoon of Sleep—something larvae of butterfly and other species generate on their own. He offers the suggestion that "cooped-up feelings and worries generate tension, and tension interferes with the sleep process, and over time this exercise will get easier and easier." After I count to three and take a deep breath, I slowly lower my arm. Opening my eyes, I feel totally relaxed, something I haven't felt in ages, or maybe ever. It's amazing. He gives me the tape, and I float out the door and down Amsterdam Avenue. I have no idea where I'm going, but who cares? I'm light. I'm buoyant. I'm just like a bah-*looon*.

Nobody fully understands how hypnosis works. The word comes from Hypnos, the Greek god of sleep, but the hypnotic state isn't a state of sleep; rather, it's an artificially induced state of consciousness characterized by heightened suggestibility and receptivity to direction. A growing body of research suggests that it is an effective tool in treating a variety of problems, from calming migraines and irritable bowels to reducing anxiety and nicotine dependence. Several studies published in the *American Journal of Clinical Hypnosis* showed that it could even augment a woman's breast size, the study participants experiencing an average increase of two cup sizes.

In ancient healing rituals, people chanted magic words while lapsing into a trance, believing they'd be more receptive to messages from the gods if they achieved an altered state of consciousness. Indian fakirs induced self-hypnotic trances, walking on hot coals or eating fire without experiencing pain. In A.D. 167, the Roman emperor Marcus Aurelius wrote in his *Meditations* that "our life is what our mind makes it," and both the Greeks and the Romans made various allusions to the mind-body connection. The modern age of hypnotism began in the late eighteenth century, when Austrian physician Franz Anton Mesmer, whose name is the root of the word *mesmerize*, began using magnets to treat disease.

He believed that humans were filled with magnetic fluid and that illness resulted from an interruption of that flow. With his method of "animal magnetism," he achieved such an impressive cure rate that King Louis XVI invited him to France, later convening a panel of scientists, including Benjamin Franklin, to investigate the practice. They concluded that magnetism had no scientific basis, relying as it did on "imagination, imitation, and touch"—elements that would later be seen as a critical part of the healing process.

The Scottish neurosurgeon James Braid is widely credited with developing the procedure we think of as "hypnotism" when, in 1842, he produced a "mesmeric trance" by holding a shiny object in front of a patient's eyes for a prolonged period. Another Scottish surgeon, James Esdaile, who was appointed surgeon to the government of India, performed hundreds of painless operations using hypnotism, including one in which he removed a 103-pound testicular tumor. (To make sure patients were suitably "anesthetized," Esdaile would drop a hot coal on their inner leg or deliver a strong electric shock.) Before he could win support from his colleagues in the West, ether and chloroform were invented and anesthetic hypnosis went the way of the medical leech. French neurologist Jean-Martin Charcot treated hysteria with hypnosis, although he believed mistakenly that hypnosis was an indication of pathology and thought that only hysterics were hypnotizable. Freud studied with Charcot, and after returning to Vienna, he and the psychiatrist Josef Breuer used hypnosis to target the root cause of hysterical symptoms. He ultimately abandoned the method in favor of "free association," a technique similar to hypnosis in that patients were required to lie on a couch, in a relaxed state, with their eyes shut.

The role of hypnosis in modern medicine was influenced by psychiatrist Milton Erickson, who established the American Society of Clinical Hypnosis and whose approach combined psychoanalysis and hypnotic suggestion. In 1958 the American Medical Association acknowledged its value in healing, and in 1966 the

National Institutes of Health issued a statement indicating that there was "strong evidence for the use of hypnosis in alleviating pain associated with cancer." Still, the medical community has been slow to embrace it, partly because of the difficulty in studying the technique in a classic clinical-trial setting. Techniques for hypnotic inductions can vary widely, and the method's success is largely dependent on the rapport between the individual patient and hypnotherapist. Several studies using PET scans have demonstrated what happens to the brain during hypnosis. In one study, hypnotized volunteers were shown a black-and-white pattern and told they were looking at color. The color-perception areas of the brain were subsequently activated, implying that if a person thinks he is seeing color instead of black and white, he actually does see color. What's more, the brain acts as if he is seeing it, which suggests that hypnosis isn't merely following instructions but involves a shift in the brain's perception.

On my first "date" with Dr. Eckleburg, I send Lee out of the bedroom so we can be alone, and then I place the self-hypnosis tape in an old cassette player. After floating my arm in the air, I take off on my magic carpet, landing on a deserted beach, where I snuggle in a comfortable lounge chair and weave my cocoon. Halfway through, though, I realize that I've forgotten to use sunblock and begin obsessing about skin cancer. I stop the tape and begin again. This time I picture myself beneath a large umbrella, with my tube of sunblock and a tropical drink. Though I'm skeptical it's going to work—isn't the magic-carpet device a little hokey?—I have one of the best nights of sleep in my life. After ten days of glorious, uninterrupted sleep, I've become so attached to Eckleburg that I can't live without him. It's almost like being in love. Who cares if he speaks in a monotone with a slight Queens accent? He taught me how to weave a cocoon and saved me from being a Sleep Stumbler. There's one little problem, though. I've signed up for the first National Patient Sleep Conference in Minneapolis, and I'm supposed to leave tomorrow. What if he doesn't travel well?

"I don't feel like going to the conference," I tell Lee.

"But you've already paid for it."

"Yeah, but I'm sleeping, so why ruin a good thing?"

"I'm sure you'll sleep in Minneapolis," he says.

If Las Vegas is among the worst places to sleep in America, Minneapolis is supposedly the best, so I tuck Eckleburg in my pocketbook and get on a plane. We arrive in Minneapolis just as the sun is setting over Fort Snelling National Cemetery, which I can see from my room at the airport Hilton. While some people might find sleeping next to a cemetery off-putting, I am not one of them. Years ago, we almost bought a summerhouse that had nothing going for it except that it abutted a cemetery, which meant no noisy neighbors.

After unpacking my clothes, I venture downstairs for the meet-and-greet. Immediately, a short woman with a round face and white hair approaches me. "Hi, my name is Ann," she says. "I have narcolepsy, sleep apnea, and rheumatoid arthritis. I lost my husband, lost my job, and spent two years in a psychiatric hospital because I was misdiagnosed. So, what's your sleep issue?"

"I've got insomnia," I say.

She nods encouragingly. "*And . . . ,*" she says. But there is no "and." That's it. I've just got insomnia—or, rather, *had* insomnia. Ann's eyes begin to dart around the room. Obviously, my sleep issue isn't interesting enough. I wonder if insomnia has become too commonplace. "Excuse me," she says, "but I think I'll get something to drink." A few minutes later, I hear, "Hi, my name is Ann. I have narcolepsy, sleep apnea, and rheumatoid arthritis. . . . So, what's your sleep issue?"

I look around for someone else to talk to. Since it's a sleep conference for patients and I'm a patient, I should be able to find plenty of available candidates among the 160 people here. The conference has been organized by Talk About Sleep, an online service company that was founded, in 1999, by Dr. James O'Brien, a Boston area pulmonologist, and Tracy Nasca, a former florist.

Realizing that people were increasingly turning to the Internet for medical information, O'Brien, who goes by the name Dr. Jim, and Nasca decided to create an advertising-supported website as a way for patients with sleep disorders to share experiences. With my name tag dangling from my lanyard, I head to the cash bar, order a glass of white wine, and listen to Dr. David Rapoport, the medical director of New York University's Sleep Disorders Center, discuss sleep apnea with a young man. "I'm totally passionate about it," Rapoport is saying. "I think it's the most fascinating aspect of sleep."

"I have insomnia," I say, inserting myself into their conversation. "That can be pretty fascinating, too."

"You don't have apnea?" Rapoport asks.

"No, sorry."

Rapoport and the man return to their conversation, while I listen to the Blue Daddies, a rhythm-and-blues band stuck with the unenviable task of playing for people with sleep disorders. Three women are sitting inches away from the band, and during a brief lull between numbers, I tell them about my book. One woman nods off, which is hard not to take personally. Before heading to my room for the night, I take a look at the Dream Quilts, which are prominently displayed near the conference area. Like the AIDS Memorial Quilt, which helped focus attention on the AIDS pandemic, the Dream Quilts were designed to spread public awareness of sleep disorders. The first was created in 2003 to celebrate the fiftieth anniversary of the discovery of REM sleep, and every year a new one is unveiled to coincide with National Sleep Awareness Week. All conference participants are encouraged to contribute to the next quilt. According to the instructions, the artwork or message must be "sleep-related" and fit on a seven-inch square of off-white muslin. We're free to use appliqué, embroidery, stenciling, and fabric paint. "Puffy paint" is frowned upon, as it gets "sticky." I don't know how to appliqué, embroider, or stencil. I've never even heard of puffy paint, although it sounds like fun. Looking for inspiration, I study all four quilts but don't relate to any of them. Inside one seven-inch square, a woman is lying next to a mouse. DARN MOUSE, it reads, IF I COULD ONLY TELL YOU THAT I'VE FALLEN AND CAN'T GET UP. BUT DON'T WORRY. MY MUSCLE TONE WILL RETURN IN A FEW SECONDS AND I'LL BE FINE. Another square is dedicated to someone's dog—SWEET DREAMS TO THE DOBERMAN WHO HELPED US UNDERSTAND OUR NARCOLEPSY AND CATAPLEXY.

If I were to make a square for a Dream Quilt, what would I possibly design? Nothing, I think, because I'd never make a square for a quilt. I don't even like quilts. But then I get a stroke of inspiration. I'll paint a bah-*looon* adorned with Eckleburg's gigantic eyes. Then, in puffy paint, I'll write, I LOVE YOU, DR. T. J. ECKLEBURG.

The first event on today's schedule is the Rise and Shine Breakfast in the Wildlife Meeting Room. At the buffet, we've got donuts, muffins, assorted pastries, pancakes, blintzes, French toast, fried eggs, fried potatoes, hickory-smoked bacon, big sausages, little sausages, meats that aren't sausages but are probably related, and vats of whipped butter. If this is what's being served at a health seminar, it makes you wonder what you get at a fast-food expo. Walking around the corner to the exhibit area, I'm confronted with a smorgasbord of breathing devices and masks. There's the Mojo, the "marital aid that saves relationships"; the Mini-Me, for people with small noses; the Phantom, with "flexible outer shell and pliable nose clip"; and the Rudolph 7600 Vmask, whose motto is "Just try one on."

"Would you like to see anything?" a sales rep asks.

"Oh no," I say. "I've got insomnia. Just insomnia."

"Are you sure?"

"Positive."

Another sales rep hands me a T-shirt. "Take it," he says. "It's free." It's also an extra, extra large. I buy several Relax Wraps, including a pair of herbal-infused booties that can be placed in the microwave. I'm not sure when I'll wear them, but I'd like to think it will be sooner than when I'll wear a Mojo or a huge T-shirt that reads SLEEP APNEA KILLS—REAL MEN GET TESTED.

Does sleep apnea really kill? Before it became a major sleep disorder—arguably *the* sleep disorder—people thought of it as "snoring." My father snores—and still does, and while it once drove my mother crazy (before she inherited the Big Bed) it never crossed her mind that snoring was a harbinger of death. It was just one of my father's irksome habits, like his tendency to eat his meals too quickly. But in the 1980s, snoring became akin to a death rattle, signaling respiratory distress. With obstructive sleep apnea (OSA), the most common form, throat muscles fail to keep the airway open, resulting in pauses in breathing that last at least ten seconds. (*Apnea* is a Greek word for "absence of breath.") In severe cases people can stop breathing as often as one hundred times an hour—anything above thirty is considered severe—with no memory of waking up short of breath. Because the airway obstruction causes the level of oxygen in the blood to fall, it can increase stress on the heart and raise the risk of hypertension, as well as memory and mood problems. More typically, people who have OSA are often very tired and don't know why. Before apnea came into vogue, it was Pickwickian syndrome, hardly a flattering designation. Named after Charles Dickens's *The Pickwick Papers,* it referred to the fat, lazy servant boy Joe, who was so tired he'd fall asleep standing up. Why this comic character would later inspire a medical definition says as much for Dickens's enduring talent as it does for how Pickwickians were viewed. Robert Macnish, the author of *The Philosophy of Sleep* and a contemporary of Dickens, believed that chronically sleepy people were also fat, sluggish, and mentally slow due to their character and temperament.

While no one would draw that conclusion today, obesity does significantly raise the risk of sleep apnea, and dieting was once viewed as the main remedy. In extreme cases, patients were urged to have a tracheotomy, a surgical procedure in which a breathing hole is placed in the throat. It wasn't until the early 1980s that people with OSA had a third and significantly less painful option: CPAP, or continuous positive airway pressure, which was invented by Colin Sullivan, an Australian medical and clinical researcher. Essentially, it's a facial mask hooked up to a small respirator that blows air into the nose to keep the throat open. It looks like a small vacuum cleaner—in fact, Sullivan's first model *was* his vacuum— and as a result, CPAP wearers often refer to themselves as "hose heads."

It's hard not to walk around the exhibit area without thinking that the hose heads have taken over the sleep world. "By the late 1980s, insomnia had become almost irrelevant to sleep medicine," Kenton Kroker tells me a few weeks later. "While it created the need for sleep labs, it didn't really benefit from them. Besides, it was too idiosyncratic a disorder for sleep medicine to rally around. With sleep apnea, you had this thoroughly organic disorder that could be diagnosed through polysomnography, and with CPAP, you had a ready-made solution. So that made apnea *huge*." While insomnia affects more women and is still a bit of a mystery, sleep apnea is a meat-and-potatoes kind of problem. More men than women suffer from it, and for the most part, they look more like Tony Soprano than Michael Phelps. (In fact, both Tony Soprano and Uncle Junior had sleep apnea.) There are, of course, exceptions. It can afflict thin people with small, receding jaws, as well as menopausal women—it may be related to lowered levels of estrogen and progesterone. "We see young women who are three hundred pounds with no apnea at all," says Matthew Ebben of Weill Cornell Medical College. "And then you have older women who have it because they no longer have the hormonal protection." Sleep apnea plays such a dominant role in sleep medicine that the National Center on Sleep Disorders Research is part of the National Heart, Lung, and Blood Institute of the NIH. Today a "sleep doctor" is more likely to be a pulmonologist or cardiologist by training than a neuropsychiatrist. Sleep research, once focused on the mind and dreaming, is now all about the very tangible and highly profitable world of CPAP. "There's even a question of whether or not sleep apnea is a real disease, as opposed to a symptom of obesity or aging," Kroker says. "With sleep labs cropping up everywhere, people needed to justify their use, and it could be an example of 'technology creep.' In 1972, it was considered a 'rare syndrome.' Now eighteen million Americans have it. Prescribing CPAP is extremely lucrative. Are too many people being diagnosed with something they don't really have?"

Tracy Nasca, Talk About Sleep's co-founder, certainly doesn't think so. A heavyset woman with short brown hair and large eyes, she suffered from OSA for decades without a diagnosis. Depressed, suicidal, and morbidly obese—Nasca once weighed close to three hundred pounds—she was so tired that customers at her flower shop would often find her napping in the back room. "People thought I was fat and lazy," she told me. "It was hurtful and made me even more depressed." When her gynecologist informed her that she had polycystic ovarian syndrome, which is marked by high levels of androgens, or "male hormones," she was relieved. (At the time, she had no idea that POS can predispose a woman to sleep apnea.) POS can result in weight gain, and at the age of thirty-two, Nasca readily submitted to a hysterectomy, believing that once she slimmed down she'd no longer be so tired. The hysterectomy, however, sent her into premature menopause and she began gaining more weight. Ultimately Nasca quit her job, and even though she had two children in grade school, she spent much of her day in bed suffering from a variety of symptoms, including migraine-like headaches. Waking up one morning with blurred vision and excruciating head pain, she feared she was having a stroke and went to see a neurologist, who diagnosed her problem as severe sleep deprivation. The neurologist then referred her to a pulmonologist, who, at last, got it right. "At thirty-five, I was diagnosed with profoundly severe obstructive sleep apnea," she says. Nasca was advised to have an uvulopalatopharyngoplasty (UPPP), which removes the uvula—the little piece of flesh that hangs down from the back of the soft palate—along with excess tissue. She had the surgery, but it didn't work, so under a doctor's supervision, she went on OptiFast, a liquid diet program. Nasca lost one hundred pounds, but her sleep apnea improved only slightly. At the time, she was using CPAP but having trouble with it. (The masks can cause nasal congestion and claustrophobia, and as a result "CPAP compliance" is low.) Nasca's doctor told her that if she couldn't keep the mask on for more than a few hours, she'd have to undergo a tracheotomy. Without it, she'd probably be dead in five years. Nasca consulted with another sleep specialist, who suggested she try a BiPAP machine, which for some patients is easier to tolerate. Unlike CPAP which delivers air at a constant pressure, BiPAP delivers it at one pressure upon inhalation and another upon exhalation. Today she credits it with saving her life.

"Apnea is the real fire in my belly," she tells me. "It's so important for people to get tested. Have you been tested?"

"I don't snore," I say.

"Well, you should really look into it. Maybe you're not sleeping because you have it."

"I'm pretty sure I don't."

"Listen, there are twenty million people walking around with undiagnosed apnea. People die each day from cardiovascular deaths related to it. Apnea can *kill!*"

For the rest of the day, I sit through a half dozen lectures, including one by Dr. Jim, who advises us to think of sleep as a multi-course meal, describing the various stages as the "cheese and crackers," the "hearty soup and salad," and the "big main course." Speaking of food, there's a dinner symposium tonight hosted by ResMed, a medical-supply company that designs and markets breathing devices. The subject is "Making CPAP Work for You," although based on the accompanying photograph in the workbook, you'd be forgiven for thinking the topic was "Dinner Rolls." There's a close-up of a bread basket, along with what I presume is either chicken in cream sauce or vegetable lasagna in cream sauce. Since I didn't sign up for the dinner, I decide to spend Saturday night at the nearby Mall of America, which is the nation's largest retail and entertainment complex, covering 4.2 million square feet. According to the Mall of America's website, the space can hold 32 Boeing 747s, 7 Yankee Stadiums, and 258 Statues of Liberty lying end to end. The website even tells us that one hundred pounds of food are fed daily to the animals at the mall's Underwater Adventures Aquarium, plus an extra ninety pounds when the sharks are fed. Even without the sharks, there's a ton of food being flung around here—Hooters, Bubba Gump Shrimp, and all the other junk-food restaurants that make up the heart and stomach of the Mall of America—and it's not hard to understand why so many Americans are suffering from sleep apnea. While I realize there may be a reciprocal relationship between OSA and obesity—obesity can cause apnea, while apnea can also cause obesity—wouldn't it be helpful for doctors to stress nutrition a little more? A steady diet of junk food can also *kill*, but I've never seen a T-shirt sporting that logo. After wandering around for an hour, I go back to the hotel and order a glass of wine from room service. *The Devil Wears Prada* is on cable. It's always on cable, which is why I can practically recite the whole movie verbatim. I watch it again and then cap off the night with Dr. Eckleburg, drifting off to sleep on my deserted island.

I'm being attacked by a rhino. I turn on the light and hear someone snoring through the wall. While I realize I shouldn't assume it's a man, I'm highly confident it's not a child or a woman. This is Tony Soprano, *guy*-type snoring, and it's awful. I try to stay calm, reminding myself that this person has a legitimate sleep disorder, one that could kill him, but you know what? *I* want to kill *him*. I grab my cassette recorder, hoping Eckleburg's voice will drown him out. I float my arm in the air, I fly away on my magic carpet, I land on my deserted island—only it's been invaded by Conan the Barbarian. And he snores. This isn't good. I can't elbow him in the ribs or go to another room because I am in another room. I'm tempted to run down the hallway, grab a Mojo, and stick it on his face. I look in my gift bag for some earplugs but only manage to come up with playing cards from Puritan Bennett—"the maker of the Good Night 420 series." On the back of each card is a true or false question, such as "The risks for obstructive sleep apnea include a large neck, obesity, and snoring." I pound the wall with one of my boots. Since I'm not about to move rooms in the middle of the night, I take an Ativan. An hour later, I'm still captive to the snoring man, so I take another. I've already had wine. What if I overdose? What if sleep apnea really does *kill*?

I've lost my faith in Eckleburg. I'm back in New York, and in my darkest hour, he fails to perform. Who could have predicted that he would have turned out to be the unreliable type? True, he failed to protect me from the snoring succubus, but that was under the noisiest of circumstances, far away from home. Not long after I return from Minnesota, my mother calls to ask me to help fix an ongoing family issue. There are certain problems you don't want to think about before going to bed. This is one of them. So I turn to Eckleburg, hoping he'll help me. But Eckleburg is powerless against her, so I take an Ambien, and then, at 2 A.M., the New York City Department of Transportation decides it's the perfect time to rip up the street. Getting up to investigate and still in a drug haze, I walk into the bed's wrought-iron footboard and break my little toe. Now it's official: I really am a Sleep Stumbler.

The incident marks a turning point for Eckleburg and me. I don't lose faith immediately. I keep listening to the tape the way I once listened for reindeer long after I knew there wasn't a Santa, but after a while, I have to confront the hard truth: I've hit a dead end. Just as I'm reconciling myself to the fact that I'll always have insomnia, I get a call from my former dentist, Michael Gelb, who's heard through Lee that I'm writing a book on sleep. Gelb thinks I might benefit from an oral appliance. "I fitted Raquel Welch with one," he says, "and she's never slept better, and now she uses it for rejuvenation." Since Welch is nearing seventy and looks great, I make an appointment to see Gelb at his Madison Avenue office.

Gelb and I first met twenty-five years ago, when I interviewed him for an article totally unrelated to dentistry. After studying my face, he placed his fingers in my ears and told me to bite down. It really hurt, so Gelb suggested that I might have TMJ, which is when the temporomandibular joint that lies in front of the ear becomes misaligned. TMJ can cause headaches, jaw pain, and sleep problems resulting from nighttime clenching of teeth. Gelb is one of the leading authorities on the disorder, having gone into business with his father, Harold, a TMJ pioneer. Since my sister Nancy has TMJ and my father grinds his teeth, it didn't seem out of the question that I could have jaw issues, too. I wasn't suffering from any of the usual symptoms, however, so I didn't think anything more about it. Gelb is now treating patients with sleep-related breathing disorders, which he believes is a logical extension of his work studying facial anatomy. He co-invented the NORAD, or Nocturnal Oral Airway Dilator appliance, which reduces snoring by positioning the patient's tongue and jaw to allow the airways to stay open. "Today, the future of sleep is with the dentists," Gelb tells me as he checks out my jaw. "Pulmonologists aren't going to like it, but it's true. They buy CPAPs for six hundred dollars and sell them to patients for eighteen hundred. There's tremendous profit in it, but a lot of patients can't tolerate wearing the mask, and if you travel a lot, it's totally inconvenient. In many cases, CPAP is overkill. An oral appliance can work just as well." (The American Academy of Sleep Medicine recommends dental devices only for mild to moderate OSA.)

Before I can say, "No, not *that!*" Gelb sticks his fingers in my ears and tells me to bite down. *Ouch!* He then informs me that I have the kind of face that's typical of someone with a sleep-related breathing disorder. This isn't a compliment. With her large mouth and strong jaw, Angelina Jolie does *not* look like she has a sleep-related breathing disorder. I, on the other hand, have a small mouth and receding jaw, which marks me as a potential snorer. I don't snore, but apparently I look as if I do.

"We know that you had braces that pushed back the top half of the front of your mouth," Gelb says. It's true. I did have braces for three long years. I finally got them in ninth grade (after a brain-damaged kid on the school bus pointed at me and kept screaming "Bucky!"), and Jay Leno rescued me from further humiliation when he let me sit up front with him. I had eight teeth extracted and was still wearing braces at my junior prom when my date, who was my drama teacher's nephew and doing her a favor, said, "I'm not crazy about the metal." Consequently, when Gelb tells me that my braces might be part of the reason I'm not a good sleeper, I want to cry. "The braces created less room in your mouth and constriction of the palate," he says. "As a result, you breathe more through your nose. When kids get braces today, they usually move the jaw forward. Back in the 1960s, they pushed the upper teeth back, and it's spawned a whole new generation of snorers and sleep apneacs. Primitive man had much stronger jaws. With the softer food we're eating, our jaws have become smaller. Babies who breast-feed have stronger jaws, because all that sucking brings the jaw forward."

"My mother didn't breast-feed me," I manage to get out while he's fitting the appliance.

"Bottle-fed babies often develop unnatural swallowing patterns and tongue-thrusting motions that can result in narrow faces, weak-looking chins, and crowded teeth. Breast-fed babies don't snore."

He asks if I sleep on my back, and when I tell him I do, he says there's a good chance that my recessive jaw is falling back even farther. As a result, I'm experiencing breathing-related "arousals" during the night. "Or you could also be waking up because you're clenching your jaw at night," he explains. "Once you're up, anxiety takes over."

Several days later, I pick up my new appliance, which I'm supposed to wear at night to prevent my jaw from slipping back. Gelb hopes it will keep me in a deeper sleep longer and that I won't experience as many arousals. I wear the appliance for a week but don't notice much of a difference. Then again, I'm so aware of having something in my mouth that I may be thinking about it too much. I store it away in my medicine cabinet with the intention of trying it several weeks later. At my regular checkup, I happen to mention to my dentist that my top teeth feel as if they're starting to move forward. He says it may have something to do with my bottom teeth, which used to be straight (thanks to the braces that ruined my jaw) but have grown progressively crooked. He refers me to an orthodontist, who also happens to be a NASCAR driver and who gives me the impression that he'd rather be looking into the hood of his Porsche than in my mouth. The orthodontist advises me to try Invisalign, a series of clear, removable braces. I only need to wear them for five months, which in comparison to three years is nothing. So now I have a new dental appliance. It probably won't help my insomnia, but if I'd been breast-fed or born during the Stone Age, or as Angelina Jolie, I'd have the perfect jaw and wouldn't need a thing.

I decide to give Eckleburg one last chance. The deserted-island scenario had gotten stale, so I tell him that the best sleep I ever had was at a former hunting lodge in India, midway between Jodhpur and Jaipur. Lee and I spent the evening sitting around a campfire with several other guests, including an Indian family who were avid hunters and whose son pleaded, "Oh, Daddy, please tell them about the time you were horribly mauled by a tiger." We then had to sleep in a tent, on the former site of royal hunting grounds, which should have been reason enough for me to stay up all night, but for some reason I slept soundly. "So in order to sleep I think I need adventure," I explain, failing to mention the other fifteen nights in India when I hardly slept at all. Eckleburg listens very intently, nodding every so often and saying "I see" in the voice I've come to know so well. He tells me that we're going to make another tape, and we go through the induction—the bah-*looon*, the arm float, et cetera. "Now imagine that you're flying to India or to an extraterrestrial planet," he says.

"*What?*" I think. I meant "exotic," not outer space. Hasn't he seen *Aliens,* where Ripley wakes up after fifty-seven years in "cryo-sleep," only to discover human bodies wrapped in *cocoons?* Even with my eyes closed and my arm floating in the air, I must seem agitated, because Eckleburg quickly steers the flying carpet in another direction. "Or you could be having adventures, like Alice in Wonderland," he says. Now I see the Mad Hatter, the Cheshire Cat, and the Queen of Hearts, who's screaming, "Off with her head!"

"How was that?" he asks when he finishes the tape.

"*Awful!*" I say. "Alien planets? Alice in Wonderland? Falling through a rabbit hole? These aren't exactly soothing images."

"Perhaps they weren't the best suggestions. Well, you can't always get it right. . . . I'm afraid our time is up."

7

ALERT! AWARE! AWAKE!

David Blaine can't think of anything worse—and he's got quite the imagination. Over the past decade, the magician and self-described endurance artist has spent a week buried in a coffin; sixty-three hours encased in ice; forty-four days fasting in a box; seven days submerged in water; thirty-five hours balanced atop a one-hundred-foot pole; forty-eight hours shackled to a gyroscope; and sixty hours dangling upside down from a thin wire above Central Park. So when Blaine says that "sleep deprivation is one of the most horrific things a human being can experience," I'm taking him at his word.

Following Blaine's written instructions, I've just spent twenty minutes roaming around a maze of alleys searching for his office in downtown Manhattan. It's somewhere near Chinatown, but I couldn't tell you exactly where because Blaine's street address doesn't seem to exist. When I finally call his assistant, she comes running out of an alley and motions me inside. There's an easy-to-find front door, she explains, but Blaine prefers that his guests enter through the dark, subterranean alley. She gets a call on her cell. It's Blaine. He's running late. Ten minutes later the phone rings again. Blaine is still running late. A few minutes later, Blaine suddenly appears, as if he's been waiting in the back alley for the right moment to materialize.

Blaine looks stronger and considerably healthier than the last time I saw him, which was on TV, at the end of his "Drowned Alive" event, when divers were pulling his emaciated and shriveled body out of the water. He'd just spent a week floating inside a two-thousand-gallon sphere at Lincoln Center, where, for the grand finale, he'd been trying to break the record for breath holding while also breaking out of chains. When I ask him what it was like sleeping in the equivalent of a gigantic fishbowl, Blaine looks at my digital recorder, opens his mouth, and struggles to speak. This goes on for several uncomfortable minutes, when Blaine suddenly starts to giggle. "Wasn't that funny?" he says, looking at his assistant and then at me. When neither of us answers, he repeats the question until we both agree: It's funny.

With that weird bit out of the way, Blaine gets down to business. "Living underwater makes sleeping very difficult," he explains. "The first night I couldn't sleep, the second night I was able to sleep for about twenty minutes, the third night maybe an hour, but that was enough for my brain. During 'Vertigo,' when I stood on the pole in Bryant Park, I didn't sleep at all, and by the second night the buildings began to look like animals' heads." When he did "Frozen in Time," however, he went without sleep for five straight days and feared he was losing his mind. Being encased in a block of ice might have had something to do with it, but that was merely a minor inconvenience in comparison with the mental pain of sleep deprivation. Though Blaine trained for the stunt by learning to sleep standing up, he couldn't put his skills into practice because if he nodded off, he might get frostbite. "By the third night with no sleep," Blaine says, "I began to have really vivid hallucinations. Even though it was really scary, it was beautiful, too, like having dreams and nightmares with my eyes open. At one point, I thought I'd died and I was in purgatory waiting to see if I was going to heaven or hell. When they started cutting me out of the ice, I turned to an EMT and asked him if my mind would ever feel right again."

Blaine would still like to break the world's record for sleep loss. He once conceived of a stunt that involved standing on a platform above a pit of hungry lions. If he fell asleep, he'd activate a lever that would open a trapdoor and tumble into the pit. He's read widely on the subject of sleep deprivation and has consulted with medical experts, such as William Dement, but the challenge remains a daunting one. "There's no way to know how to offset brain damage from staying awake so long," he says. "There just isn't enough research on the subject."

Guinness World Records no longer supports a sleep-deprivation category, citing it as a potential health hazard. As a result, it's difficult to know who holds the record and for how many hours of wakefulness. In 2007, Tony Wright, an English horticulturist, went without sleep for over 11 days, or 266 hours, with thousands of Internet viewers watching him on webcam. But since nobody was monitoring his brain activity and his stunt came after the Guinness ban, the official record holder remains Randy Gardner, a seventeen-year-old American high school student, who in 1965 remained awake for 264 hours. Dement was eager to prove the connection between sleep deprivation and mental illness, and when he learned that Gardner wanted to break the world's record for the longest time awake, he volunteered to supervise the experiment.

Six years earlier, Dement had participated in one of the first scientific studies of prolonged sleep deprivation, when he observed New York disc jockey Peter Tripp's two-hundred-hour "wake-a-thon" to raise money for the March of Dimes. Tripp's symptoms were similar to Blaine's; as the days progressed, he began to hallucinate, at one point imagining that the neurologist sent to examine him was actually an undertaker preparing to bury him alive. After his ordeal, he was indicted in a payola scandal and then left his wife, lost his job, and, according to various accounts, became a "drifter."

Dement had initially interpreted Tripp's sad demise as further evidence for Freud's theory that if people are deprived of dreams, taboo impulses and desires can bubble up, leading to mental instability. After observing Gardner, however, he changed his mind, for the teenager was still beating Dement at pinball and basketball during the final days of his stunt. (Grainy footage shows Gardner, in a dress shirt and narrow tie, shooting hoops.) Looking back on the Tripp episode, Dement attributed the DJ's paranoia and hallucinations to the amphetamines he was using to keep him awake. Yet Gardner wasn't taking any stimulants, and while his reactions weren't as extreme as Tripp's, he, too, began to hallucinate and experienced fleeting bouts of paranoia. Even Wright, who spent his time awake in a Cornwall bar playing pool and eating health food, recorded in his online diary that pixies and elves were dancing across his computer screen.

So even if prolonged sleep deprivation doesn't result in permanent psychosis, it does seem to produce a state of altered consciousness that can heighten feelings of paranoia and despair. For that reason, it has long been a standard "soft" torture technique, the Japanese and Russians using it to great effect during World War II. Unlike other interrogation methods, sleep deprivation leaves no telltale marks and yet is still brutally effective. Former Israeli prime minister Menachem Begin, in his memoir, *White Nights,* recalled his sleepless captivity in a Soviet prison: "In the head of the interrogated prisoner, a haze begins to form. His spirit is wearied to death, his legs are unsteady, and he has one sole desire: to sleep. . . . Anyone who has experienced this desire knows that not even hunger and thirst are comparable with it." More recently, the U.S. military used sleep-deprivation techniques at Guantánamo. In two programs known as Operation Sandman and Frequent Flier, they kept detainees awake by blaring loud music and by moving them every few hours to different locations.

Over the past decade, India's booming outsourcing industry has helped fuel a global economy increasingly dependent on cheap, sleep-deprived labor. In what is ironically known as "the Sunshine Sector," employees, taking advantage of the twelve-hour time difference between India and the United States, work through the night at call centers answering as many as 250 calls per shift. Most employees are between the ages of nineteen and twenty-one, and the attrition rate is high, with many burning out from the typical problems associated with night-shift work, such as insomnia and gastrointestinal issues. Consequently, Indian outsourcers are now beginning to outsource to China, where residents of the world's most populous nation are eager to demonstrate their willingness to compete in sleep-loss marathons. Not long ago, I read a review in *The New York Times* about a documentary titled *China Blue* that detailed life inside a Chinese blue-jeans factory. Young girls earning six cents an hour often work grueling twenty-hour shifts to make jeans for clients like Walmart and Levi Strauss. Facing stiff fines if they fall asleep, they've devised one method for battling fatigue that's a primitive version of the "eye clamp" technique in *A Clockwork Orange*. The accompanying photograph in the *Times* shows two girls propping open their eyes with clothespins. It's a terrifying image for multiple reasons. When you first look at the picture, you can't help feeling sorry for the factory girls; then you wonder if the clothespins hurt, and then you worry that with the increased pressure for all us to become "endurance artists," we'll soon be wearing invisible clothespins on our own eyes. In some ways, we already are.

Cephalon, the pharmaceutical company that put wake-promoting drugs on the map when they aggressively marketed Provigil, is located in Frazer, Pennsylvania, down the road from the Gunkle Spring Mill. The mill was built in 1793 and stands in sharp contrast to the modern glass cube that contains the company's headquarters and where, as if migrating into the future, a dozen geese are waddling toward the entrance. Outside, an American flag is flying next to one bearing the Cephalon logo. Walking into a large atrium decorated with towering trees and low furniture, I immediately smell coffee and can't figure out where it's coming from. Is Cephalon diffusing a special coffee scent through the air system to remind visitors of the importance of staying true to Provigil's slogan—"Alert, Aware, Awake!"?

The drug was approved for narcolepsy, a neurological disorder that causes severe and overwhelming daytime sleepiness, but it quickly caught on as an all-purpose elixir that could be used for jet lag, ADHD, cocaine addiction, and the fatigue associated with depression, MS, and Parkinson's. Students started taking it to cram for exams. Six U.S. track-and-field athletes were caught using it as a doping agent, and it's now on the United States Olympic Committee's list of banned stimulants. According to *The Washington Post,* it became the "entrepreneur's drug of choice" around Silicon Valley. So what is it? A stimulant? A wake promoter? A smart drug? And how did something that started out as a niche product emerge as the most controversial blockbuster of the decade?

I'm waiting to talk to Dr. Jeffry Vaught, executive vice president and chief scientific officer, but I'm early as usual. I've never had trouble being "Alert, Aware, Awake," so I sit on a couch and watch what I presume is a Provigil commercial on TV. It turns out to be a segment of CBS's *Up to the Minute,* in which Dr. Joyce Walsleben, an associate professor at New York University School of Medicine and a consultant to Cephalon, is discussing the drug's benefits with a reporter. Several months earlier I'd interviewed Walsleben, who told me that after the invention of CPAP for sleep apnea, Provigil was the next critical step in the evolution of sleep medicine. "If I'm on a highway, I'd rather know the trucker was on something than driving sleepy," she said.

The *Up to the Minute* segment is playing on a loop, and I watch it at least a half dozen times before a young PR assistant asks if I'd like some coffee. Following her through the building past dozens of employees clutching coffee cups, we arrive at the source of the overwhelming aroma: Starbucks. "We have our own right in the building," the assistant says. "I highly recommend the gingerbread latte. It's a favorite around here." Even at Cephalon, where Provigil accounts for nearly half the company's profits, coffee is still the stimulant of choice, as it is practically everywhere in the world. According to a Walter Reed Army Institute of Research study, caffeine (600 milligrams or six cups) was shown to be equally as effective as 200 and 400 milligrams of modafinil (Provigil's generic name) in maintaining alertness in sleep-deprived volunteers. So why pay two hundred dollars for a month's supply of a prescription drug when you can spend twelve dollars a pound for a roasted Starbucks blend? "Coffee makes you jittery, ruins your stomach, and keeps you up for hours," Walsleben told me. "Provigil is gone by nightfall, and with it, you can get a normal night's sleep. It's scary to think we could pharmacologically design both our sleep and our day, but I think that's where we're going."

Upstairs, Dr. Vaught is seated at a round table in a room that smells not like gingerbread but like plain old cafe Americano. Vaught, who is in his late fifties, has a salt-and-pepper beard and a laid-back style. "The drug was discovered in France in the late 1970s during an animal pharmacology study," he explains. "There were two boxes of mice, and the animals in one box were falling asleep, while the other guys treated with the experimental agent were awake and walking around and just happy."

In the early 1980s French scientist Michel Jouvet, who, along with Dement, is considered one of the founding fathers of sleep medicine, became very interested in the drug. Jouvet had conducted experiments on cats regarding muscle paralysis during REM sleep, which led to the discovery of "paradoxical sleep," so called because it "paradoxically" joined deep sleep and muscle paralysis with brain activity similar to that of the waking state. Jouvet was curious to see if the new compound might help narcoleptics battle their extreme daytime fatigue. "Jouvet said, 'Let me stick it in my cats,'" Vaught explains. "A few weeks later, he was ecstatic.

'I don't know what you've got,' he said, 'but my cats have been awake now for four days. But we're not seeing any signs that it's like an amphetamine. The cats' behavior is just normal.'" Jouvet went on to coin the term "eugregoric," or "good arousal," to describe what he believed would be a new class of vigilance-promoting drugs.

In 1993, Cephalon leased the rights to the chemical for six million dollars from the French pharmaceutical firm Lafon, which they later acquired. Their initial goal was to develop a drug for narcolepsy, but they harbored more ambitious plans. "I'd just come over from Johnson & Johnson, where they were very interested in the aging population," Vaught says. "With older people, you have a variety of sleep disorders, so I'm looking at this drug, thinking, 'Wow, if it really does what we think it does, it can go beyond narcolepsy to treat other sleep disorders.'" The company hired Hypnion's co-founder, Dale Edgar, who had previously determined how the brain maintains wakefulness, to conduct the pre-clinical trials, and eventually they came up with the term "wake promoter" to distinguish the drug from a "stimulant." "We weren't trying to be fancy," Vaught says, "but how do you describe something that isn't like an amphetamine, doesn't affect the cardiovascular system, and doesn't get you jazzed up? It just makes you happy and awake."

While that may sound too good to be true—who doesn't want to be happy?—Provigil wasn't thought to be habit-forming, as it didn't appear to engage the brain's dopamine system, which is linked to addiction. Cephalon tested it on experienced addicts who told investigators that compared with amphetamines or morphine it didn't get them high. In 2009, however, a study published in the *Journal of the American Medical Association* raised questions about the drug's addiction potential. Dr. Nora Volkow, director of the National Institute on Drug Abuse, scanned the brains of ten men after they received either a placebo or modafinil. Modafinil appeared to increase dopamine.

In 1998 the FDA approved Provigil for "excessive sleepiness associated with narcolepsy" under the Orphan Drug Act, which offers special incentives to companies developing drugs for the treatment of rare diseases. Since only about one in two thousand Americans suffer from narcolepsy, Cephalon's marketing strategy was targeted to the untold millions suffering from a broad but nebulous condition called excessive sleepiness, or ES. When Dr. Thomas Roth, head of the Sleep Disorders and Research Center at Henry Ford Health System in Detroit and a consultant to Cephalon, went before an FDA panel to offer his definition of ES, he described it as "the level of sleepiness that interferes with activities of daily living." By that definition, everyone should probably be taking Provigil, which might be the point. Cephalon began suggesting in its promotional materials that the drug could be used for such symptoms as sleepiness, tiredness, decreased activity, and fatigue. Provigil, it seemed, had become the Geritol of the twenty-first century. In 2002 the FDA sent the company a warning letter, reminding them that Provigil shouldn't be promoted as a daytime stimulant, although it was fairly obvious that something dubbed a "wake promoter" wasn't going to be confined to narcoleptics for long. While the company had hoped to get the drug approved for ES associated with all medical conditions, the FDA agreed in 2004 to expand the label to include obstructive sleep apnea and shift-work disorder. Not everybody agreed it was a wise idea. "With obstructive sleep apnea, sleepiness is an indication that something is wrong," says Dr. Charles Pollak at Weill Cornell. "Perhaps the patients aren't using CPAP as often as they claim. Treating sleepiness is such a minor benefit compared to the benefit of treating the underlying disorder." Vaught, however, explains that many people who are fully CPAP-compliant are still pathologically sleepy. "These people are almost as tired as narcoleptics," he says.

Provigil was shown to have only a "modest" benefit for people with shift-work disorder (SWD), and in an editorial accompanying the study, which was published in the *New England Journal of*

Medicine, Robert C. Basner, M.D., director of the Cardiopulmonary Sleep and Ventilatory Disorders Center at Columbia University Department of Medicine, wrote, "It is simplistic to consider that a pill alone could sufficiently modify the effects of this disorder." It's hard to know how many people actually have SWD, which results from an inability to adjust to a nontraditional schedule, although according to the *NEJM* study, it may affect between 5 and 10 percent of night-shift workers. "It's a legitimate disorder," Vaught says. "These people are sleepy all the time. Maybe they're operating heavy machinery or working as interns or residents in hospitals. We even had a streetwalker in our study. I don't know how she got in . . . but these are people who can't stay awake when they should be awake."

"If they're not biologically suited to shift work, maybe they should try to find another job," I say. "Wouldn't it be better than taking a pill?"

"The fact is, we're living in a twenty-four-hour society," he says. "I'm sure these people would love to find other jobs, but there may not be another one out there for them."

Vaught tells me that he's never taken Provigil and sticks to his story even after I give him a highly skeptical look. In 2002, Cephalon's president, Frank Baldino, came under some criticism after he admitted to a *New York Times* reporter that he had a prescription for it. While he didn't say for what purpose he was taking it, company employees claimed it was for jet lag. He wouldn't be alone there. One sleep doctor confided that she uses it regularly when she travels, as do many of her colleagues. Jet lag, however, can't begin to account for why over 80 percent of the drug's prescriptions are being written for non-approved uses. (While physicians can prescribe drugs "off-label," the law prohibits sales reps from promoting them for purposes beyond the FDA's indications.)

So how did Provigil become such a popular "off-label" drug? Vaught explains: "Physicians started using it, and they said, 'Gosh, based on what I'm seeing, I have other patients with excessive sleepiness associated with [other conditions] and maybe it will work there. Our reps weren't telling them what to do because they can't." In 2003, however, a former Cephalon sales representative in Ohio contacted the FDA over the company's illegal and potentially dangerous sales practices. In addition to promoting Provigil as an all-purpose wake promoter, the company allegedly marketed Actiq, an addictive narcotic used by cancer patients, as a general painkiller, and Gabitril, an epilepsy drug, for insomnia and anxiety. The sales rep agreed to wear a wire to a company sales conference to gather evidence for the government. After he was fired, he filed a lawsuit under the False Claims Act. He was later joined by three other whistleblowers, whose testimony led to Cephalon's 2008 agreement to pay $431 million in civil and criminal fines. The settlement—and Cephalon's guilty plea on a misdemeanor criminal charge—hasn't hurt Provigil, though. The genie is out of the bottle. The drug is now sold all over world under a variety of different names—Vigil, Modalert, Provake, Modiodal, Modavigil, and Alertec. In 2007, Cephalon launched Nuvigil, a longer-lasting version of Provigil; if everything goes according to the company's plans, it stands to become the first FDA-approved treatment for Jet Lag Disorder.

Cephalon has downplayed the benefits of using Provigil as a "smart drug" to improve mental functions, but a 2003 study published in *Psychopharmacology* suggested that it offered potential as a cognitive enhancer. In a 2008 poll conducted by the British science magazine *Nature,* one in five readers reported that they took drugs to boost brain power, with Provigil the second-most popular after the stimulant Adderall. On the Vaults of Erowid, an independent website that provides thousands of pages of information on psychoactive drugs, the "experience reports" on Provigil or modafinil are mostly positive, with headlines such as "Finally a Weapon to Slay the Fatigue Dragon," "That Extra Mental Edge," "Absolutely Amazing Stuff," and a "True Lifesaver." One male student, who has been regularly using a generic version from India for the past two years, started taking it in response to "increased pressure at school" and his "unfortunate habit of chronic procrastination." He writes: "Overall, I'm very happy that I have it as an option now for those times I need to go without sleep or I need a mental edge. . . . I imagine that one day it'll be deregulated and Coke will add it to their secret formula."

With the increased diagnosis of ADHD, most people already know somebody with Adderall or Ritalin in their medicine cabinet. A 2005 national study, led by a University of Michigan research team, found that 7 percent of college students have used prescription stimulants for nonmedical purposes over their lifetimes and 4 percent have used them in the past year. At one school, the figure was 25 percent, and other studies show even higher rates, with white males at highly competitive schools in the Northeast being among the most frequent users. In a sample of middle and high school students, the illicit use of stimulant medication was 4.5 percent. "People at school don't even bother selling the drugs," my sixteen-year-old godchild told me. "They just give them away." Since the drugs enhance focus and concentration for nearly everyone, whether or not they have ADHD, it begs the question: Are we heading toward a new normal? Anjan Chatterjee, a neurologist at the University of Pennsylvania, has coined the term "cosmetic neurology," drawing a parallel to the growing acceptance of cosmetic surgery. Just as Botox moved from Hollywood to the suburban mall, people may one day tweak their brains as nonchalantly as they now freeze their foreheads. They may also feel increasingly pressured to feed the drugs to their children. In the *Nature* survey, a majority of the fourteen hundred readers who responded said they didn't think smart drugs should be given to healthy children. However, if they learned that other parents were giving them to *their* kids, a third admitted they'd do the same.

Dr. Mary Carskadon, a professor of psychiatry and human behavior at Brown University and expert on adolescent sleep, fears the consequences of our increasingly technology-obsessed, stimulant-dependent society. "To be optimally alert, teenagers need nine and a quarter hours of sleep," she told me, "but they're sometimes getting as little as six and a half hours on school nights, so they're building up a huge sleep debt. As new technology has developed and been embraced, we've created a lot of problems we didn't have before. Kids in earlier times weren't up half the night on Facebook and Twitter." Carskadon's research suggests that changes occur in the biological clock during adolescence, with the result that teens fall asleep later and wake up later—a pattern that makes early-morning classes a real challenge. In 1998, Carskadon and a colleague studied the effect of changing school starting times from 8:25 A.M. to 7:20 A.M. By 8:30, half of the forty high school students were so "pathologically sleepy," their behavior mimicked narcolepsy. She suggests that excessive sleepiness may be partly responsible for the wave of depression in teenagers, who are then given antidepressants, which can worsen insomnia.

Even if kids don't take prescription stimulants to stay alert, they only need to go to their local grocery store to get wired. Since Red Bull first came on the market in 1997, energy drinks have moved from truck-stop coolers to the breakfast table to become a $3.7 billion business. With elaborate websites that advertise extreme sporting events and suggestive, hip-sounding names—Monster, Rock Star, Full Throttle—the market is geared primarily to young men and teenage boys. While it's not known precisely how energy drinks deliver their kick, they usually combine sugar, vitamin B, amino acids, herbal stimulants, and 50 to 550 milligrams of caffeine. (A six-ounce cup of coffee has 77 to 150 milligrams.) Among the two hundred or so brands, there is even one formulated for children aged four to eleven. In 2005, Advocare, whose motto is "We build champions," launched KickStart ·SPARK—"targeted nutrition especially for kids." It comes in two flavors—grape and green apple—and contains taurine, the key ingredient in Red Bull, as well as 60 milligrams of caffeine. According to the company's website, "Children today face many challenges and require a lot of energy to make it through the day." And if an energy drink doesn't provide the necessary kick, children now can have caffeinated foods, including Morning Spark instant oatmeal, NRG Phoenix Fury potato chips, and the Buzz donut, the brainchild of a molecular scientist named Dr. Robert Bohannon, who, when he's not dreaming of ways to inject caffeine into junk food, is working on rapid tests for anthrax and biowarfare agents.

While Buzz donuts aren't included in the military's standard rations, when it comes to keeping soldiers alert, nothing is too extreme. Sleep is a major factor in winning wars; without it, soldiers suffer lapses in attention, judgment, and memory that can lead to fatal mistakes. That's why humans are often described as the "weakest link" in warfare. While on special ops, soldiers often need to be awake for seventy-two hours straight; pilots may need to fly continuously for thirty hours or more. "In terms of pure survival, three hours of sleep is okay as long as your decisions aren't critical," Dr. Gregory Belenky told me. Once the top sleep researcher at the Walter Reed Army Institute of Research, he now directs the Sleep and Performance Research Center at Washington State University, Spokane. "Sleep deprivation doesn't impair physical strength, endurance, or coordination," he explained, "but to really be able to think and plan—the two areas most degraded by sleep deprivation—most people need eight hours."

While the Pentagon spends tens of billions of dollars on the most advanced weaponry, sleepy soldiers are still primarily dependent on the old military standbys: caffeine and amphetamines. In 2003 the military's use of Dexedrine or "go pills" came under scrutiny when two U.S. Air Force majors killed four Canadians in a friendly-fire incident in Tarnak Farm, near Kandahar, Afghanistan. During a pretrial hearing—the two air force majors faced court-martial—one of the defense lawyers claimed that the pilots had been pressured to take Dexedrine, which had impaired their judgment. Despite the drug's potential for abuse, Dr. John Caldwell, a former principal research psychologist for the U.S. Air Force's Warfighter Fatigue Countermeasures Group, has said that when it comes to a lengthy mission, "I'll fly with the guy on Dexedrine any day of the week."

Eager to find a stimulant with fewer side effects, the military has investigated the use of modafinil, which was given to French foreign legion troops during the first Gulf War and possibly to British troops—the British Ministry of Defense has been buying it since 1998. The U.S. Air Force has approved the drug for management of aircrew fatigue for some bomber missions, although it still prefers go pills. Given the relatively few options available, in 2002 the government initiated the Preventing Sleep Deprivation Program under the auspices of the Defense Advanced Research Projects Agency (DARPA), the Pentagon's premiere research division, whose mandate is to maintain technological superiority for the U.S. military. The agency was created in 1958 after the United States was caught off guard when the Soviets launched *Sputnik*. To make sure something like that never happened again, DARPA was encouraged to pursue cutting-edge science and technology. Along with such notable hits as the Internet, the Global Positioning System, the stealth aircraft, and night vision, the agency has had a number of bizarre failures, including the telepathic spy program that attempted to use psychics to carry out remote espionage and, more recently, a terrorism futures market in which speculators could bet on future assassinations and bombings in the Middle East. (It was canceled after politicians called it "ridiculous," "grotesque," and "unbelievably stupid.")

Some feared that the sleep program was as way-out as the terrorism futures market, especially after DARPA stated on its website that "the capability to operate effectively, without sleep, is no less than a 21st century revolution in military affairs." Was DARPA trying to create an army of "metabolically dominant" soldiers capable of fighting for days on end? To find out more, I contact

Dr. Yaakov Stern, a professor of clinical neuropsychology at Columbia University, who'd received one of the DARPA grants to help soldiers stay awake. He needs clearance from DARPA before he can talk to me. A week later, he tells me that I can interview him as long as I don't write about the sharks. Since I don't know anything about them, I immediately type "DARPA—sharks" into my computer and discover that the agency wants to implant electrodes into their brains and use them as underwater spies. "Okay," I say, "no sharks." Since Stern isn't involved with them anyway, it doesn't matter.

With his pale, elongated face and wispy white hair, Stern reminds me of the comedian Larry David. His expertise isn't even sleep—it's aging. "My main interest is in trying to discover why some people are more susceptible to the cognitive effects of aging and why some are not," he explains. "A DARPA projects manager contacted me and said, 'Look, I know what you're doing. I'd like you to do the same kind of thing for sleep deprivation.'"

Through Craigslist and by posting ads around campus, Stern found a group of volunteers who were willing to stay awake for forty-eight consecutive hours in a sleep lab. Using fMRI, Stern observed the volunteers as they performed memory tasks before and after sleep loss. After he isolated the areas of the brain responsible for the effects of sleep deprivation—he shows me two spots above the left ear—he wondered if he could stimulate that "brain network" to improve cognitive abilities after sleep loss. He turned to fellow researcher Dr. Sarah Lisanby, whose specialty is transcranial magnetic stimulation (TMS), a technique that uses magnetic fields to excite neurons electrically. "We found that by using TMS we could improve performance slightly," he says. "What's even cooler is that [Lisanby] found that the people who showed the most improvement were the people who had shown the most decline, so it was as if we were really treating this network."

"So what does this mean?" I ask Stern. "Tired soldiers can now zap themselves in the head with something like a stun gun?"

"No, no," he says. "It's like a big figure eight, and it's attached to a large cable that's connected to a machine." He goes over to his computer to show me a video demonstration, but it's not working properly. The images are blurry and pastel-colored; it's as if we're viewing a Martha Stewart Easter special wearing the wrong prescription eyeglasses. I make out a woman in the center of the screen; she's holding two white coils connected to something that resembles a gas pump.

Stern says he doubts the military will be using TMS anytime soon, although another scientist has been working on a helmet that would deliver jolts of high-intensity current to improve a soldier's coordination and thinking.

DARPA has recruited a number of other researchers in addition to Stern to come up with ways to combat the effects of sleep deprivation. With DARPA research money, Jerome Siegel has developed a nasal spray containing a naturally occurring brain hormone called orexin A. (Siegel discovered that the absence of orexin A appears to cause narcolepsy.) The nasal spray reversed the effects of sleep deprivation in monkeys, restoring their cognitive abilities, with no apparent side effects. Neuroscientist Giulio Tononi at the University of Wisconsin has managed to breed fruit flies that get by on a third the normal amount of sleep, and Sam Ridgway, the navy's "Dolphin Doctor," is studying dolphins to discern the mysteries of uni-hemispheric sleep—dolphins are believed to sleep with only one half of their brain at a time. Other scientists are looking into the migratory sleeplessness of the white-crowned sparrow. Flying at night while remaining active during the day, these songbirds don't appear to suffer any deficits in cognitive function.

Solving this mystery might one day help airborne humans cope with the rigors of flight. While sleep loss is a big problem on earth, it doesn't get any easier in outer space, where many astronauts use sleeping pills and Dexedrine. Confined to cramped quarters, they're subjected to constant noise, the absence of normal day and night cycles—the sun rises and sets every ninety minutes—and zero gravity. "Hitting the sack" means something entirely different when you're weightless. "When you get into your bed—they call it a bed, but it's really more like a hammock—you feel like you're falling out of it," astronaut Bryan O'Connor told me. O'Connor is NASA's chief safety and mission assurance officer and a veteran of two shuttle flights. "They give you a pillow that you have to strap to your head because there's no force to make your head fall back. My first night in space I slept maybe ninety minutes. On my second night, I slept really well. The third night was bad because my lower back was kind of bothering me. It had stretched out as a result of zero gravity, but I just took a Tylenol and tried to gut it out."

"We've always been very specific about astronauts' sleep/wake schedule," explained Dr. John B. Charles, project scientist for NASA's Human Research Program, "but they don't always follow our recommendations. Since they're working when they're awake, they often use their sleep time for sightseeing. We prize them for being intelligent and inquisitive, so they're hardly going to pass up looking out on the vista of the universe." Falling asleep in space, however, isn't like dozing at your desk. The environment is much less forgiving of error; one slipup could really mean staring into the void. "During the 1966 *Gemini* flight, Dick Gordon was doing a space walk while Pete Conrad was hanging on to his leg," Charles said. "At one point, Conrad realizes he's nodded off. He wakes up and looks over at Gordon and sees that he's hanging halfway out of the hatch—asleep. That was the first time we were really aware of the potential problem."

It's much worse for astronauts on long-duration missions, when severe sleep disruption erodes performance, diminishing concentration and reaction time. In 1997 astronaut Jerry Linenger, who was also a medical doctor, lived on the Russian space station Mir for five months. As part of an ongoing sleep study, he wore an electrode net on his head and kept a detailed diary, and from his experience, researchers concluded that after about ninety days the brain has difficulty controlling the body's sleep cycle when it isn't exposed to the earth's natural time cues. Linenger and his two Russian crew members were frequently exhausted, and some of the problems they encountered—an onboard fire that nearly burned through Mir's hull and a near collision with a resupply cargo ship— were later attributed to fatigue and sleep deprivation. "Russian controllers are less sensitive to the subtleties of sleep than we are," Charles told me. "It's like they have a job to do, and if they have to wake up the people on board to do it, that's fine with them. With space walks, for example, they can only be done at certain times. With the Russians, it was like, 'Okay, tomorrow we'll do it and you can stay up for twenty-four hours and then you can wake up in time for the space walk.' That's called 'slam-shifting.' We take a more gradual approach." Such was the culture clash that mission-control psychologists were reluctant to let Linenger and cosmonaut Vasily Tsibliev go on a space walk together for fear they might push each other off the station.

Within the next twenty to thirty years, NASA wants to send astronauts back to the moon and then eventually to Mars. Will astronauts be able to sleep 249 million miles away from home, on a planet with a gravitational force 38 percent as powerful as Earth's, in a cabin the size of a college-dorm suite? Not only is the Martian daylight a different color—yellowish brown as opposed to blue-green—but the length of day is twenty-four hours and thirty-nine minutes. How will that impact the human clock? What if they can't sleep and they really, really want to go home? Right now, astronauts on the International Space Station, which is 220 miles away from Earth, can hop aboard a Russian Soyuz space vehicle and be back home in a matter of a few hours. On Mars, astronauts will be stuck there for years.

To help astronauts cope with chronic sleep loss and other concerns, NASA has established the National Space Biomedical Research Institute, a consortium of university researchers, including Dr. David Dinges, a professor of psychology and chief of the

Division of Sleep and Chronobiology at the University of Pennsylvania School of Medicine. Over the past decade, Dinges has attempted to simulate the conditions of a long-duration space flight by turning his laboratory at Penn into an ersatz spaceship, where volunteers lived in cramped, dimly lit quarters, with limited social interaction. To test the effectiveness of naps, the volunteers submitted to continuous monitoring of their brain activity, heart rate, eye movement, muscle activity, body temperature, mood, and behavioral changes. Blood samples provided the levels of circadian-mediated hormones, such as melatonin, cortisol, and human growth hormone, most of which is released primarily during slow-wave sleep. (Growth hormone stimulates bone growth, and bone loss is one of the biggest medical concerns on extended missions.) More recently, Dinges has been collecting data on astronauts living in NASA's underwater lab, Aquarius, off the coast of Key Largo, Florida. He has created a self-assessment tool called the psychomotor vigilance test, a portable five-minute reaction-time task that allows crew members to monitor the daily effects of fatigue on their performance. In addition, the astronauts wear a waterproof wristwatch-sized device—the Actiwatch—that measures their sleep and wake cycles.

Dinges's expertise in fatigue management has given him an increasingly important role in a world that prizes wake over sleep. He is a consultant for Cephalon and has conducted studies on Provigil, which, as he told *The New Yorker*, "promises to satisfy our relentless desire to control time." It's not that he doesn't believe that sleep is important. He recognizes, rather, that in the twenty-first century, the focus has shifted from helping people sleep to keeping them awake. Even the moral argument against getting by on less sleep strikes him as a "twentieth-century thing." Government agencies don't give funding for the purposes of getting people to sleep more; they want to find a way for people to receive optimal benefit from sleeping *less*.

Dinges himself is a product of the new world order. I've planned a trip to Philadelphia to talk to him, but when I call to confirm, he tells me that it's a "bad time." He's in the midst of a technological meltdown—his computer has crashed or is in the process of crashing—and he sounds overworked and harried. I reschedule the interview, but when I call again several months later, he tells me he's confronting an even tighter time clock. "My problem is that my schedule is like speeding down a mountain in front of an avalanche," he says. "And it keeps getting worse. I'm in a cycle of twelve- to sixteen-hour days, seven days a week. In upcoming months, I've got ten trips, two European, Chinese, Australian—"

"Stop," I say. "You're giving me heart palpitations."

He tells me that he's very sorry, but that's just the way it is.

8

THE SELLING OF SLEEP

Natasha is a beautiful Indian psychic wearing a hot-pink sari and a sequined *bindi* marking her "third eye." She normally does her mystical readings in a quiet place, not in a simulated Bollywood bazaar with hundreds of shoppers milling about; but today, as part of ABC Carpet & Home's monthlong celebration of Indian culture, she is perched on a small balcony overlooking piles of marigold silk pillows, embroidered textiles from Rajasthan, and a stack of Kama Sutra books. I've never been to a psychic before. The closest I've ever gotten to dabbling in the occult was dressing up as a Gypsy fortune-teller for my eighth-grade Halloween party. But a friend suggested I see Natasha, which is convenient because I also need new bedding, and ABC, in its quest to attract customers while remaining one with the universe, is advertising "Om products for the home." It describes these ineffable items as "elements to move you, body and spirit, to an enlightened place."

Natasha's balcony is adjacent to a cordoned-off area reserved for ancient Indian beauty rituals. These include henna tattooing, hair removal through the "art of threading," and Ayurvedic facials customized to a person's *dosha*. According to Ayurveda, one of the world's oldest medical systems, there are three *doshas—vata, pitta,* and *kapha*—that determine our mind/body types, and they comprise two of the five basic elements: space, air, fire, water, and earth. A few years ago after filling out a lengthy questionnaire inside one of Deepak Chopra's books, I discovered that I was mainly *vata* (wind), with a mix of *pitta* (fire). An imbalance in a *dosha* can produce problems directly related to the characteristics of the *dosha,* and *vata* types are prone to anxiety and insomnia. While I never acted on this particular information, the concepts behind Ayurvedic medicine intrigued me, and I was especially drawn to two ideas: (1) that good health is related to a positive and wholesome interaction with one's immediate environment, and (2) that disease arises when a person is out of harmony with the universe.

Since palmistry and numerology fall outside the realm of traditional Ayurvedic medicine, I don't quite know what to expect from Natasha when she immediately requests my birth date and full name so she can do a few simple calculations. "Your special number is nine," she says, reading from a slip of paper, "and your gifts are understanding, communicating, and influencing." I'm impressed, until she lists my "challenges," which are "drifting, losing focus, and bad habits." Nobody likes to hear negative things, but these don't describe me at all. I'm almost too focused, and except for drinking a moderate amount of wine and buying too many shoes, I really don't have any bad habits. Natasha goes on to tell me that soon I'll be "attracted to someone or something to the point of distraction," and that I'll "suddenly lose my focus and switch professions." I've been a writer for most of my life. In the middle of writing a book, I'm going to change careers? I don't think so.

From numerology Natasha moves on to palm reading, studying the distinctive pattern of lines on my right hand. "Did you have a twin?" she asks. No. "Were you married and divorced twice?" No. She looks at my health line, warning me that I'd better take better care of myself or else risk "serious health implications." Since Natasha is really striking out, I try to make things a little easier for her. "I take really good care of my health," I say, "but I have insomnia."

She brightens up. "*You, too?* Ambien, Sonata . . . I've tried them all."

"You don't sleep either?"

"It's awful," she says, shaking her head.

"Did you find anything that works?"

"Not really, but you might want to remember the rules of sleep hygiene."

"I've already done that."

"Well, maybe you could light a lavender candle and pray to Nidra, the goddess of sleep." She writes down a mantra in Sanskrit and hands it to me. "Recite this three times before you go to bed," she says. As I'm about to leave, she reiterates her warning that I'm going to have a serious health issue unless I take better care of myself. "It's important for you to find serenity and sleep," she says.

"Natasha says something awful is going to happen if I don't find serenity and sleep," I tell Lee, who is waiting for me in the bedding department, standing next to an ornately carved Indian bed that bears the sign THE THREE FACES OF THE GODDESS.

"Maybe Nidra wants us to buy this bed," I say.

"You mean Natasha."

"No, Natasha's the psychic. Nidra's the goddess."

Lee looks at the $8,500 price tag and tells me I'd better come up with a cheaper alternative. Passing signs that read DREAMS AND AWAKENINGS, LINENS FOR FREE LIVING, and PEACE IS THE WAY, we stop by the Matteo boutique, where the tags on the vintage washed linens advertise the products as representing a "journey to preserve the planet." With collections named "Sack" and "Ticking," the linens speak to a simpler time when we lived off the land and sewed our own clothes. Across the way, as if a direct rebuke to

Matteo's "waste not, want not" sensibility, the Anichini display bed is so elaborately costumed it could be the centerpiece of *La Traviata*. Curious to get a price on the entire "ensemble," I ask the saleswoman to add up the various elements beginning with the headboard ($2,323). With calculator in hand, she moves on to the bedskirt ($815); slipcover ($995); top and bottom sheets ($1,220); duvet ($1,315); king shams ($330); cheaper king shams ($280); decorative pillow ($610); chinchilla throw ($1,685), and other items. With tax, everything adds up to $10,530, which is more than my father paid for the original House of Punk Sleep.

Prior to becoming a TV personality and style expert, Robert Verdi sold linens at ABC and once told *New York* magazine that he viewed a bed as an "aspirational" object, similar to a car or an apartment. "You spend what you want now," he said, "and, eventually, you trade up." Layers beget more layers, king pillows mate with queens, who give birth to boudoir or "baby" pillows. Blankets need blanket covers, or if one opts for a duvet, it should be made of the lightest and finest hand-selected Siberian goose down. No well-dressed bed is complete without a throw, preferably cashmere or fur.

My own bed is "accessorized" with an antique *suzani* that I bought in Istanbul. It originally came from Uzbekistan, where women traditionally embroidered textiles as part of their dowries, bringing the decorative pieces with them as they traveled from place to place. The man who sold it to me explained that since the women were nomads, they could sleep anywhere, and that if I used the *suzani* as a bedspread, I'd be able to sleep, too. So I carried the king-sized *suzani* back to New York, where in the bright light of my apartment it showed its true colors—and they were filthy. The textile was also badly torn at the seams, as if the bride, unhappy with her husband and her stressful nomadic life, had ripped it apart with her teeth in a fit of rage. Given the *suzani*'s tattered condition, I couldn't very well send it to a dry cleaner, so I gave it to a textile conservator, who, for a hefty fee, cleaned and repaired it. He advised me to be very careful with it and not to do things that might "stress it out." Even though it had been dragged around Uzbekistan for a hundred years, it was now apparently too fragile to be used as a bedspread. Not wanting to give it away or hang it on the wall, I now use it as a decorative bed "accent," forbidding anyone to touch it.

We demand a lot from our beds. We want them to be comfortable, but since we also spend each night dreaming on them, we expect them to be worthy of our fantasies. More than any other piece of furniture, they symbolize the arc of life; most of us were born in a bed, and we will probably die in one. As Anthony Burgess writes in *On Going to Bed*, "few people die in chairs unless they are electric." The Roman historian Tacitus, according to Burgess, recorded that the ancient Germanic tribes used to place babies as well as old men in cradles, offering little distinction between the birth and the death bed. When Howard Carter discovered Tutankhamen's tomb in 1922, he found numerous beds among the treasures, including one made of ebony with a woven string mattress and legs of inlaid ivory. The king had rested his head on curved pieces of lapis lazuli faïence and turquoise-blue glass. The ancient Romans had a bed for every purpose—sleeping, eating, studying, and lying in state, while the Persians created the first water-filled beds, made of goatskins. (The idea would reach fad status in the early 1970s, after a San Francisco design student created the "Pleasure Pit," filling a large vinyl bag with water.) Taking a homespun approach to their beds, the Saxons, after a day of farming, were happy to "hit the sack" in a sack. The phrase "making a bed" originates with them, for they would gather straw and then stuff it into a sack, making their bed from scratch every night. Depending on their social standing, they'd spread the sack on a table, a bench, or on the cold, drafty, rat-riddled floor.

Dating from around the twelfth century, European beds became increasingly comfortable, with mattresses made of feathers or filled with wool and rags. The royal French beds grew so large that as part of the nightly ritual a military guard had to whack the voluminous bedding with a "bed-staff" to make sure intruders or assassins weren't hiding in it. The *lit de parade*, or state bed, enjoyed near cult status. "Persons entering the bedchamber, even princesses of the blood, genuflected towards it as if it were an altar," writes Lawrence Wright in *Warm & Snug: The History of the Bed*. "Whether or not it had a protective balustrade around it, ordinary mortals would not approach. It had its own specially appointed guard." Trying to keep dogs away from the royal bed involved setting up giant wooden trellises or other types of "dog stoppers," although, as Wright tells us, puppies were sometimes allowed between the covers as "foot-warmers." In the seventeenth and eighteenth centuries, the decorative bed reached its zenith; wooden four-posters had ornately carved posts that were frequently lacquered or gilded, with canopies mimicking church steeples and draperies composed of heavy gold-thread brocade. The Industrial Revolution brought with it very industrial-style beds that were made of iron or brass, and by the beginning of the twentieth century, the extravagant "grand bed" had largely fallen out of vogue. Art Deco designers, such as Emile-Jacques Ruhlmann, redefined opulence with emphasis on exotic hardwoods, such as Macassar ebony, amboina, and rosewood.

In 1945, Mrs. Bernice Bowser, of the Bowser Service Corporation, who had previously campaigned for kitchen modernization after World War I, told *The New York Times* that she "condemned" rooms planned solely for sleeping. She called for "converting bedrooms to 24-hour-a-day duty to take care of numerous avocations and accommodate so wide a variety of handiwork as sewing, finger painting and designing airplanes." She'd probably be happy to see how the modern bedroom has evolved; while few of us design airplanes in our beds, we do practically everything else in them. The bedroom is no longer a private sanctum but a place where we eat our meals, watch TV, work on our laptops, check our email and BlackBerries, and play with our kids and pets. If "come to bed" is not the seductive phrase it used to be, it's possibly because the bed is no longer just an ordinary piece of furniture but a room of its own. To that end, Design Within Reach launched a bedding collection to address the bed's multipurpose status, creating not just linens and blankets but different-sized bolsters that can be used to support the neck, lumbar spine, and wrists to make working on a laptop in bed more comfortable. They also designed a variation on a saddle that hangs from the bedside and provides storage for cell phones, BlackBerries, eyeglasses, remote controls, and bottled water. But with or without saddles, beds are on the move these days, making the scene at restaurants, such as Manhattan's Duvet, where you can eat in a "dining boudoir" on one of thirty customized "dining beds" and drink Sweet Dream and Pillow Talk cocktails.

Choosing a mattress, which used to be a simple matter of soft versus firm, now includes such options as "viscoelastic temperature-sensitive memory cells." While there is little scientific evidence showing that mattress quality has much impact on our sleep, according to a Tempur-Pedic commercial, the "reason that people are so tired in the morning is that they are tossing and turning on an old mattress." The Better Sleep Council, a nonprofit organization supported by the mattress industry, claims that we should replace our mattresses every five to seven years because our bodies and technology are constantly in flux. The most popular style of mattress still uses a variation on the innerspring-coil invention that dates back to the late nineteenth century. The concept didn't fully catch on, however, until after World War II, when licensee groups, such as Sealy, Serta, and Simmons, took advantage of the increased demand for consumer goods, as well as the new TV exposure, advertising their products on programs such as *The Bob Hope Show* and *The Tonight Show*. If owning a home was the first step toward achieving the American Dream, one couldn't dream at all without a brand-name American mattress. It was even viewed as giving us the edge in the cold war. In 1956 the sales vice

president of Simmons, the makers of Beautyrest, traveled to the
Soviet Union to "gather evidence" to support his contention that
Russians don't sleep as well as their American counterparts. He
was later pictured in *The New York Times* next to two mattresses: an
extremely flimsy one he'd purchased in Kiev, and the Beautyrest—
"said to be far more comfortable."

Since innerspring mattresses were all basically the same, manufacturers began increasing the number and the weight of the springs
in order to sell higher-priced models. This gave rise to the popular
notion that firmer was the healthier option, an idea that persisted
until the late 1980s, when manufacturers began adding a softer
layer called a pillow top. As Americans grew increasingly obese,
mattresses expanded both horizontally and vertically, not only to
support our added girth but to fill up our larger bedrooms.
McMansions needed McMattresses. But while we were sleeping
large, we weren't, apparently, sleeping well, for with each new
improvement in design, the sleep epidemic appeared to worsen.

Common sense tells me that my mattress isn't my problem, but
what if it is? We leave ABC's linen department and go down to the
main floor to check out Hästens, one of the world's premiere mattress makers. Owned and operated by the same family in Sweden
since the mid-1800s, the company makes all its innerspring mattresses by hand, a laborious process that involves layers of cotton,
wool, flax, and the key ingredient: horsehair. (The name Hästens is
derived from the Swedish word for horse.) According to the company's 491-page deluxe catalogue, the horsehair, which is taken
from a horse's mane and tail, must "undergo a rigorous process
that includes washing, rinsing, washing again, boiling, another
rinse, steam cleaning, scorching, and storage." It is only after this
beautification process that the hair is deemed soft and voluminous
enough to become part of a Hästens bed.

A saleswoman points to a blue-and-white checkered mattress,

which she describes as the "most popular." Lee and I lie down on it, and we don't want to get up. The saleswoman presses my shoulder into the mattress to demonstrate how it "cushions." After five minutes on this bed, even though we're adjacent to an ersatz Indian bazaar, I could fall fast asleep. For comparison purposes, the saleswoman leads us over to a second model. It's perfectly fine, but we're in love with the popular one. How much is it? The woman pulls out a price list and, after highlighting our model in pink Magic Marker, shows it to us. No words are exchanged. I don't have my reading glasses with me, but the number looks like 21,057.

"Is that the price or the model number?" I ask.

"The price," she says, before telling me that the less popular model costs a mere $15,000. (The Hästens Vividus bed runs close to $60,000, but then it takes 160 hours to make and uses a far better grade of horsehair.)

I'm totally floored. My current mattress, the one I've now come to positively loathe, was $3,000, and I thought *that* was expensive.

"Twenty-one thousand dollars for a mattress?" I say. "At that price, do you sell many of them?"

"Lots," she says.

"To whom?"

"To people who really care about sleep and nature."

I care about sleep. I care about it so much I'm writing a book on it. As for nature, I recycle and always carry a reusable cloth bag to the supermarket and try in my daily life not to be wasteful of electricity. Since I also don't want to be wasteful of money, it seems totally crazy to spend nearly the equivalent of the per capita income of Sweden on a mattress made of coiffed Swedish horsehair.

A few weeks later, we walk several blocks to our local Sleepy's, where a gloomy-looking salesman in a black suit greets us with a somber "Welcome to Sleepy's, Home of the Mattress Professionals." The only other customer in the store is asleep on a bed, eyes shut, hands crossed over his chest. It's like being at an undertaker's. Before we can make a graceful exit, the salesman directs our attention to a Tempur-Pedic mattress, which he describes as "the only bed that's approved by NASA." Since I already know how badly astronauts sleep in space, that's not a major selling point, but the salesman is really keen on the NASA "memory foam." Originally developed in the 1960s as seat cushioning to help astronauts absorb G-forces, the formula eventually wound up in Sweden, where a foam company spent a decade trying to turn the material into a mattress. In 1992 they granted the North American distribution rights to a Kentucky horse breeder named Bob Trussell, who'd learned of the product through friends in the international horse-racing world. (Are all good mattresses connected to horses and Sweden?) With money raised through his horse connections, Trussell started Tempur-Pedic, eventually winning an award from NASA for transferring space-research technology into the private sector to "promote a better qualify of life for humankind."

The salesman urges us to take off our coats and shoes and lie down on the mattress. The foam's "memory cells" have the ability to conform to the body, remaining firm when cool, soft and pliable when warm. Rolling over on my side, I feel the foam pause for a few seconds, as if struggling to remember my body's contours. When I finally sink in, it feels wonderful, but then I shift positions and go through the same routine. Since I already think too much at night, I'm not sure I want a mattress with "memory cells." We move on to Kingsdown, with its BodyDiagnostics patented technology, which uses eighteen statistical measurements and more than a thousand calculations to establish the right surface best suited to one's body. "Is this like the Sleep Number bed?" I ask, remembering the commercials starring ex–Bionic Woman Lindsay Wagner. The Sleep Number bed comes with its own remote control that allows you to inflate your side of the mattress to match your "sleep number"—anywhere from 0 to 100. "No, it's nothing like that," he says, dismissing the competition. After Lee and I take turns on the diagnostic bed, it turns out I'm a soft, he's a firm. "So now what are we supposed to do?" I joke. "Flip a coin to see who gets the proper spinal support?"

"Well, he likes the soft one," the salesman says, pointing to the sleeping man.

"I don't think Kingsdown is for us," I say quickly. "Let's try something else." In doing research, I'd read about the Consumer Product Safety Commission's 2007 fire-safety guidelines that require mattresses to be coated with fire-retardant materials. Although the CPSC concluded that the amount of chemicals didn't come anywhere near close to being a health threat, the law set off a flurry of news reports on the dangers of "toxic mattresses." If I can help it, I'd rather not have chemicals such as antimony trioxide and boric acid in my bed. I ask the salesman if it's something I need to worry about, and he says, "Not really, but maybe you should look at the soy bed." Surely he's got to be kidding, but no, the Spanish company Spaldin sells "soy foam" mattresses made of natural soybean oil. "Why soy?" I ask, and he says, "Well, it's organic." The company's website claims that the "health properties of soy plants are transferred into Spaldin mattresses, improving our health." The Spaldin brochure goes a step further, promoting the brand almost as a vitamin supplement, with headings such as "Calcium and Strong Bones" and "Proteins to Get Up Plenty of Energy." While soy products, such as tofu, are high in protein and numerous studies have reported that soy protein, when added to one's diet, can moderately decrease total cholesterol, those studies involve people actually *eating* soy, not sleeping on it.

"Green" has become a key trend in bedding, with manufacturers tapping into a growing demand for eco-friendly products. Many lines now feature models made with soybeans, green tea, aloe vera, organic cotton, natural latex, and eco-friendly foam. Since no government agency regulates the labeling of mattresses as "organic" or "natural," and since manufacturers aren't required to label the list of fire-retardant chemicals, it's hard to know what's really inside them. Mark Strobel, who makes mattresses that can only be sold through prescription, has started an organization called People for Clean Beds. "If only fifteen percent of mattresses prove toxic," he writes on his website, "forty-five million people will die."

Toxicologist Stephen Safe of Texas A&M University doesn't believe that chemicals in mattresses pose a significant health threat to humans, although he does worry what happens to the environment when they end up in landfills, which gets me thinking that maybe I should keep my old mattress. That way I wouldn't be creating more waste, and since the mattress was made before the CPSC law came into effect, it doesn't have any flame-retardant chemicals. Then I happen to go into another Sleepy's in Connecticut, where I fall in love with a Vera Wang mattress that is so beautiful it almost looks like one of her wedding gowns. And did I mention that it's comfortable? Even Lee thinks so, although he does wonder how much Vera Wang actually knows about mattress design. But how much does a horse breeder or a Swede or NASA really know?

"What's the name of the mattress?" I ask the salesman.

"I think it's called Serenity," he says.

"*Serenity!* Natasha told me to find it—and I did," I tell Lee.

"So do you want this mattress?" he asks.

"I do!"

Americans spend $23.9 billion a year on goods and services related to sleep. But are we simply throwing money away? While many people have legitimate sleep disorders that need to be treated, many more have bought into the idea that our sleep system has become so polluted by the toxins of modern life that it's fast becoming an endangered biological process. Until very recently, most anthropologists avoided sleep as a research subject, leaving it to scientists to determine what is "normal." As a result, people whose behavior doesn't fit the norm are often viewed as having a disorder, which they can "fix" with medication or therapy or a new mattress.

Dr. James J. McKenna, director of the University of Notre Dame's Mother-Baby Behavioral Sleep Laboratory, was the first anthropologist to study sleep, specifically infant co-sleeping. "I've been watching the field for thirty years now," he told me, "and what we're seeing is sleep pathology on a massive scale. There's big money in sleep research, and when you define *pathology* broadly, you make everyone a patient." McKenna believes that when it comes to what constitutes "quality" sleep, we've got it totally wrong. "Right from the beginning, the first question always is, 'Is the baby sleeping through the night?' If the answer is yes, people say, 'What a good baby!' We're already making a moral judgment. Parents are presumed to be overly needy if they co-sleep. It's a reflection on the mother and father. It's the same with people who nap. They're seen as indolent or lazy. People who sleep differently are judged in harsh terms. We have a very unforgiving one-size-fits-all attitude, what George Williams has called the 'fallacy of medical normalcy.' What constitutes healthy sleep? It's what Americans have. But who's to say how many hours are 'good' or 'bad'? You have to take into account the person who is sleeping and what is going on in his or her life at the time. Just as human beings have varying personalities and temperaments, they have different sleep patterns. It's odd to think that for a species as complex as ours, every human being should spend basically the same number of hours asleep."

Matthew Wolf-Meyer, an assistant professor of anthropology at the University of California, Santa Cruz, focused his dissertation on sleep and capitalism, and like McKenna, he believes that sleep science has left no room for variations. "The explosion of interest in sleep has led to more drug and mattress advertising, which leads people to think more about symptoms than about causes," he explained. "They're not getting people to ask the right questions, such as 'Is your job keeping you up?' 'Are you spending long hours commuting back and forth?' People are being enticed just to spend more money. For the pharmaceutical companies it's been a movable feast—first depression, then erectile dysfunction, now sleep. We're throwing medications at people without viewing the larger problems. Right now, our model is the culture of exhaustion. We need to be exhausted before we can fall asleep, so we keep pushing and pushing ourselves. But if a society can't rest, how can it sleep? Yet we've come to believe that fatigue is necessary to consolidate sleep, but do we actually need to sleep straight through the night?"

In the early 1990s, Dr. Thomas Wehr at the National Institute of Mental Health conducted an important experiment in which he put a group of volunteers on a sleep schedule that attempted to duplicate what it was like before the invention of electricity or gas lights. Over a period of a month, they were left in the dark for fourteen consecutive hours; at first, the subjects slept an average of twelve hours a day, but by the fourth week, they were sleeping an average of eight hours and fifteen minutes. What is fascinating is that without light cues, the subjects drifted into a pattern of sleeping for a few hours, spending several hours in meditative wakefulness, and then falling back asleep again. One of the most interesting tidbits in A. Roger Ekirch's book *At Day's Close: Night in Times Past* is that preindustrial families experienced a similar "broken" pattern, splitting their slumber into "first" and "second" sleep. How they'd fill the hours in between depended on their personalities and economic status; some would pray, make love, perform chores, while others would use the cover of night to rob orchards or steal livestock. Still others used the time to engage in pleasant reverie or ponder their dreams. Ekirch writes: "There is every reason to believe that segmented sleep, such as many wild animals exhibit, had long been the natural pattern of our slumber before the modern age, with a provenance as old as humankind."

In an attempt to address the lack of globally oriented sleep research, Carol Worthman, an anthropologist at Emory University in Atlanta, interviewed a group of researchers who were familiar with the nighttime patterns of ten traditional non-Western populations. These included the Efe and !Kung hunter-gatherers in Africa, Ache foragers in Paraguay, the Swat Pathan herders in Pakistan, and Balinese farmers in Indonesia. From her in-depth interviews as well as her analysis of the limited anthropological literature on the subject, Worthman drew a picture of sleep that has little in common with the Western ideal. While we spend a fortune on bedding, most people in traditional societies recline on skins, mats, leaves, or perched between two logs. To protect against predators, they sleep in groups, in front of a fire, which further promotes a sense of security. In comparison with what Worthman calls our "lie down and die" model, in which we attempt to lie perfectly still for a solid eight-hour block, they have no specific "bedtime," drifting in and out of slumber depending on what's happening on any given night. They might get up to dance or sing or play a musical instrument, nodding off when they feel like it. Worthman speculates that interrupted or staggered sleep provided an advantage for these societies because someone was always awake and on guard.

By viewing sleepers as individuals and not as part of a social group, perhaps we've missed the obvious, that people at different times of their lives have different sleep needs and patterns. Wehr has even gone so far as to conjecture that some "sleep disorders" may simply be old patterns "breaking through." "What is defined as pathology may be, in fact, adaptation," McKenna told me. "When you look at the conditions under which humans evolved, it doesn't make sense that they'd basically go unconscious for eight hours in a row. There were too many pressures and predators to contend with. I maintain that our ancestors didn't sleep horizontally on the ground and that they probably constructed nests in the trees. This was before fire and before they had weapons to protect themselves. Babies can't cling to our bodies; they need to be secured. If you put those things together, it would seem that consolidated sleep wasn't a major feature. People haven't wanted to look at sleep as a social phenomenon. There was a lot of sleep variability, but today we're told that if we don't sleep eight hours, we're killing ourselves. People are sleeping less and living longer. How does that add up? A person walking around Manhattan during his or her lunch hour gets more stimuli than our ancestors ever did in a day. Why can't we accept that sleep will be integrated into other changes? Our bodies move toward adaptation, not pathology. Given the sensory context, our sleep is probably appropriate to the challenge."

It's a cold, blustery November afternoon and I'm standing outside the Empire State Building with a group of Japanese tourists who are pointing skyward and repeating the words *Sleepless in Seattle*. They're referring, of course, to the hit movie starring Tom Hanks, who plays an insomniac who presumably finds sleep after he meets Meg Ryan on the building's observation deck. I follow the tourists inside, and while they head for the eighty-sixth floor, I take the elevator to the twenty-second, entering a door that reads METRONAPS. The receptionist asks, "Can I help you?" and because I feel stupid saying, "I'm here to buy a nap," I tell her, "I'm just checking in." Presuming I'm a regular, she asks me if I have a series. Who'd buy a series? Who, in fact, would buy a nap? "No," I say, "just a single."

I can choose any number of naps from the menu, including the Coffee MetroNap, which involves drinking a cup of coffee prior to the nap and then sleeping while your body metabolizes the caffeine, so you'll be even more recharged when you wake up. I settle for the no-frills Midday MetroNap, at fourteen dollars for twenty minutes. It includes access to the Wake Station—a refrigerator stocked with energy drinks—and the Freshen-Up Station—a mirror, eyedrops, and breath spray.

The woman opens the door to the napping sanctuary, a dimly lit room, where six white EnergyPods glow like futuristic incubators built to hatch a new breed of Super Sleepers. The woman hands me a set of Bose headphones, and after I climb into one of the pods, she warns, "Don't touch this button!" To get my mind off the mysterious button, I stick my head out to see if I'm alone. There's someone sleeping two pods away. I assume it's a man because his exposed right hand is hairy. Like King Kong's. Suddenly the man's pod begins to vibrate, and after a light goes on inside it, he climbs out and walks out of the room. About ten minutes later, my own pod starts to shake and my nap is over.

"Power napping" is said to decrease stress and improve alertness and memory, but American culture has been slow to embrace the tradition, viewing it as tantamount to laziness. I wonder, though, whether power naps may soon supplement power lifting and Pilates, just as the three-martini lunch has given way to lunchtime workouts.

Arshad Chowdhury, the co-founder and CEO of MetroNaps, was quick to recognize the potential of selling specifically designed "pods" to enhance the nap experience. His initial plan was to set up MetroNap franchises all over the country, but when he discovered that people don't like to travel to take a nap, he refocused the business on selling the pods to corporations, such as Google, Cisco, and Proctor & Gamble.

With advances in telecommunications, the boundaries between home and work and between public and private space are being redefined so that one day soon it may seem perfectly normal to crawl into a pod instead of taking a coffee break. The Japanese have long practiced the art of napping in public. *Inemuri*, which in Japanese means "sleeping while present," isn't a cause for embarrassment but a source of pride, as it indicates that the person is overtired from hard work. For Latin Americans and southern Europeans, the siesta has been an integral part of their culture, allowing them to have lunch with their families before settling in for a nap. We experience a natural dip in alertness midafternoon, which is why many experts believe that humans, like many mammals, are biologically programmed to sleep midday. While Americans are slowly coming around to the idea of napping, Spain, which has been forced to align its schedule with the rest of Europe's, is moving away from the siesta. Instead of a three-hour lunch break, government employees can now take only an hour, with the result that Spaniards, who don't start dinner until after 9 P.M., are among the most sleep-deprived people in Europe. The stress, according to a spokeswoman for Pfizer, is "wreaking havoc with the Spanish male's libido." This has led to a Viagra "explosion," as well as $1.66 billion annual profits for the pharmaceutical company that sells it. Napping parlors have been cropping up in Spain, with naps usually sold in combination with a massage. Can the Viagra Café MetroNap be far behind?

While nap stores have yet to take off in the United States, napping rooms have become a feature at spas, and cosmetic companies are now touting the benefits of beauty products aimed at the sleep-deprived. Dr. Howard Murad launched Sleep Reform serum, featuring a "topical melatonin delivery system to deepen skin's nightly repair cycle," and the Sleep Reform dietary supplement, which is advertised as the "first supplement ever formulated to improve the depth and duration of sleep while supporting skin's cellular repair cycle." Basically, it's a melatonin pill mixed with glucosamine, vitamins, and something called Repair Enhancing Matrix or REM.

On a trip to L.A., I decide to experience the ultimate in beauty sleep by booking the "Jet Lag Therapy" at the Beverly Hills Hotel. After donning a terry-cloth robe and waiting in the reception area, I am led into one of the treatment rooms. My jet lag therapist, with his strapping build, thick brown hair, blindingly white teeth, and booming baritone, is a Disney prince come to life. He starts with a back and neck massage before moving on to foot reflexology. It feels good but no different from any other massage I've ever had.

"How does this help jet lag?" I ask.

"Frankly, I have no idea," he says. "It's just a name to sell the treatment."

Realizing he is being a little too candid, he backtracks a bit. "Well, massage is relaxing, and flying on a plane . . . isn't. So if this helps you relax, then I guess it helps jet lag."

"I was hoping I'd be more energized, because jet lag makes you sleepy."

"Are you sleepy?"

"Not really."

"Then it's working!"

After the Jet Lag Therapy, I go to a store called Doggie Styles, in Beverly Hills, where I'd read that they carry the high-priced Poochie Beds, the ultimate in canine comfort. With price tags as high as $1,700, they come with such glamorous names as Versailles, Nights of Arabia, and the Hepburn, a chenille chaise with crystal tufts and legs. When I tell the salesman I'm looking for a bed for my sister's poodles, he immediately pulls out several very plain circular styles.

"I was really thinking of something a little more elaborate, like the Versailles bed I'd seen online," I say.

"What are the dogs sleeping on now?"

"I think a ratty piece of carpet."

"Listen, dogs don't want Versailles. They want something small and comfortable . . . and in bisque."

"Dogs like bisque?" I ask.

"*Humans* like bisque. Dogs don't care. They'll sleep anywhere."

9

POLAR NIGHTS

Two days before Christmas, Lee and I are flying to the little town of Jukkasjärvi, 125 miles north of the Arctic Circle. I'd suggested to Lee that we spend a night in the Icehotel, telling him that I wanted to sleep in the world's largest igloo. There is, however, another reason I picked this remote place. In Lapland, reindeer outnumber people, and remembering my childhood fantasy, I had the idea that if I actually saw a reindeer on Christmas, I'd finally get the gift of sleep.

We arrive in Jukkasjärvi in the early afternoon as the light is already beginning to fade. Falling in the middle of the "polar nights," Christmas is the darkest time of year, with daylight lasting only a few hours. Off in the distance, I can see the Icehotel shimmering on the banks of the Torne River. I'd been expecting something fantastical, but the hotel's exterior is plain and primitive-looking, its simple shape reminding me of Newgrange, the prehistoric Irish passage tomb I visited when researching my Celtic roots. Newgrange, which predates the Pyramids, was built specifically so that the light of the rising sun on the winter solstice enters an opening on the roof, penetrating a passageway and illuminating the inner chamber. For the ancients, the winter solstice, which marks the

shortest day and the longest night of the year, was a time for
celebration, especially in those parts of the world that experienced
the bleak polar nights. Watching the sun sink lower and lower on
the horizon, people feared it might never return, plunging them
into permanent darkness. Passing the solstice signaled the return
of the sun, and people of all cultures commemorated the occasion
with feasts and bonfires. The Icehotel has honored the solstice in a
contemporary way by embedding lights in a wall of snow, captur-
ing the color and movement of the famous aurora borealis.

After we check in at reception we're given special snowsuits and
boots, the down parkas we'd purchased at our local sporting good
store deemed too flimsy. In our gigantic new clothes—they in-
stantly add fifty pounds—we meet up with our tour guide at the
entrance to the hotel. Dressed in a fanciful silk cape, she immediately scrambles up a steep mound of snow and briefs us on the
hotel's history. Each year since 1990, a team of artists has made the
pilgrimage to Jukkasjärvi to transform huge blocks of ice har-
vested from the Torne River into something both memorable and
evanescent. Come spring, when the midnight sun draws near, the
Icehotel, the ultimate nonpollutant, melts away, returning to its
source. While the hotel and an adjacent church are made entirely
of snow and ice, there are also heated cabins and chalets and two
restaurants. Entering a door covered in reindeer skin, she leads us
past the Absolut Icebar—sponsored by the vodka maker—and into
the main hallway, where a stunning ice chandelier dangles above
four petal-shaped chairs. Nothing about the exterior prepared me
for this. The guest rooms, off several long corridors, are the frozen
equivalent of Fabergé eggs, each one unique and exquisite. I like
the suite styled as an English gentlemen's club, with its overstuffed-
looking ice sofa and glowing fireplace, but not the Bubbleboil
Swamp Room, with its giant pulsing test tubes. The one that truly
terrifies me, however, is the Cyclic Vortex Room, which, according
to the artists, represents the circle of life, from seed to rebirth. On
a wall above the bed, there's a red, glowing, seemingly vast hole. I

imagine being sucked into it and, like Keir Dullea in *2001: A Space Odyssey*, waking up the next morning as a fetus, preventing me from going on the all-important reindeer ride we've scheduled.

We sign up for a dogsled excursion into "the wilderness," a term that isn't tossed around lightly here. In 1735 the French mathematician Pierre-Louis Moreau de Maupertuis made an expedition to the area to make geodetic measurements to support Newton's idea that the earth is flattened at the poles and not at the equator. Jukkasjärvi was considered then to be the end of the world, and even today, the dramatic landscape looks almost untouched, a tundra extending to infinity. The region is experiencing a warm spell, which means that instead of –15 Fahrenheit, it's 15 above. Still, it is cold. And before taking our places on the sleds, we have to wait for the drivers to untangle forty huskies. Sled dogs like to run, and when they're not running they bark and jump all over one another. Our Norwegian driver has brought along his eight-year-old daughter, who is piloting the sled she received last year for Christmas. With her two little huskies she rides beside us, her cheeks flushed pink. Despite the frigid weather, the whole experience is so exhilarating that for the rest of the ride I am that little girl.

That night we have dinner at the Icehotel Restaurant, which is inside a simple wooden building across the street. The all-white space is pretty, with orchids in the windows, but not very festive. Then I look outside at the falling snow and realize that anything more would be overkill. Nature, in its dazzling simplicity, is the main attraction here. The food, too, is a product of the landscape. I don't eat red meat, but I'm delighted with the fresh Arctic char and the delicious cloudberries and lingonberries from the nearby forest. I'm in heaven—until the waiter takes Lee's order.

"I'll have the fillet of reindeer," he says.

"You're ordering reindeer?" I ask. "On Christmas Eve?"

"It's the specialty."

The waiter nods. "We eat everything: the blood, intestines, stomach, hooves," he says.

When the dish arrives, Lee raves about it while I try not to look. The good news is that I've finally seen a reindeer. Unfortunately, it's on a plate with shiitake mushrooms and orange-braised onions.

After dinner we watch *It's a Wonderful Life* (with Swedish subtitles) in the warm room we've booked in case the frigid one turns out to be a bad idea. At 11 P.M. we walk over to the Icehotel, hoping to see the aurora borealis, but nature doesn't cooperate. In the warm cabin adjacent to the Icehotel, we're handed sleeping bags that were developed for the Swedish military's "survival unit." The man who gives them to us explains that after we return them in the morning, we'll be eligible for a diploma stating that we've spent a night in the Icehotel. Entering through a side door, we're hit with a blast of cold air. There are eighty-eight people staying here, but we're the only creatures still stirring, our moon boots crunching on the packed snow. The lights are dim and it's spooky. When we finally find our room, I'm relieved it's not Bubbleboil Swamp but Arctic Contrast, created by the Irish artist Dave Ruane. Behind our bed is a carving of the midnight sun; in front is Ruane's version of the northern lights. They're blinking. Brightly. We unfurl our sleeping bags and place them on the reindeer pelts covering the ice bed. Stripping down to our thermal underwear, we jump in and zip up. I say good night, and then, miraculously, I fall asleep. When I wake up, I ask Lee for the time.

"It's eleven-thirty," he says.

"In the morning? Wow!"

"Eleven-thirty P.M. You were asleep for five minutes."

I try to relax by staring at Ruane's northern lights. Though the temperature in the hotel is a constant 20 degrees Fahrenheit, Lee complains that his sleeping bag is hot and sticks his arms out. In a few minutes he's asleep—and snoring. I want to nudge him, but he's too far away. The northern lights are beginning to drive me crazy. I slither farther down into my bag, which smells weird. I hope they dry-cleaned it after the Swedish military used it. Finally

I call out, "Lee, Lee, we have to get out of here. We've got to . . . escape!"

"Huh?" he says groggily. "You mean we have to put on our clothes and leave?"

"We don't have to get dressed. We can hop out in our sleeping bags."

I try hopping but don't get very far, crashing into the midnight sun, nearly causing an avalanche. "This is ridiculous," Lee says. We throw on our clothes and before heading back to our warm cabin, we dutifully return our sleeping bags to the man behind the desk. "You don't have to tell me," I say. "No diploma."

On Christmas morning we wake up to a brilliant salmon-colored sky. After a carol service at the Ice Church, where the ice "stained glass" windows are etched with lilies, we take a walk down a deserted snowy road, winding up at a seventeenth-century wooden church famous for its primitive teak altarpiece. (One panel depicts a man returning a stolen reindeer in the presence of a looming Gauguin-style Christ.) When we return to our cabin, Lee gives me the Christmas present he's brought from New York. It is a special bound version of *Stories from Hans Christian Andersen,* with a picture of the Snow Queen tooled in leather on the front, the northern lights swirling behind her. Edmund Dulac did the illustrations, and the frontispiece depicts *The Real Princess,* otherwise known as the Princess and the Pea. It's a delightful picture of a huge canopied bed filled with a tower of feather mattresses that nearly reach the ceiling. At the top, there's a dark-haired woman, sitting upright, wide awake.

In the afternoon we go on a snowmobile safari to sample Sami culture. The Sami are the aboriginal people of Lapland; they once made their living as reindeer herders but now work mainly in mining or tourism. Our guide, Par-Stefan, is dressed in traditional costume—a navy tunic with leather pants and shoes made of reindeer hide. With his pale eyes and delicate features, he could be Legolas in *The Lord of the Rings.* We head into the woods just as the light is fading. We are an eclectic group: a pair of newlyweds from London, where the husband owns a "lad's magazine"; a couple in their late seventies from Shropshire; two women from Ireland with pierced noses and eyebrows; and a British family in court jester's hats. It takes about a half hour to reach the Sami campsite, where there are several *kotas,* which are tepeelike homes covered with skins. I'm listening to Par-Stefan describe how the nomadic Sami would dismantle their *kotas* and carry them when I notice a dozen hulking forms silhouetted against the snow. Reindeer!

As part of our "safari," we all get a chance to try *raidu,* or reindeer-sled driving. I had pictured sitting in a sleigh, covered in a fur wrap, like something out of Currier and Ives, but the sleds are literally sleds. We have to kneel on them—alone. These reindeer aren't tiny either. They weigh about four hundred pounds and stand nearly five feet tall, with massive antlers covered in furry skin known as "velvet." Though I realize this is probably the Sami equivalent of Santa's Lookout and that the reindeer have been going around the track forever, I'm still terrified.

I ask for a slow reindeer, and Par-Stefan gives me one that looks comatose. Lee goes first, with Par-Stefan running alongside shouting "Giddyap" in Sami. When it's my turn, I kneel and grab the reins. We're going at a comfortable clip until Lee snaps a picture of me. The flash spooks my reindeer, and it tries to overtake Lee's sled. I hope my reindeer has good spatial judgment because a tree is coming up and I'm not sure there's space for its antlers between the tree and Lee's sled. I scream, forcing Lee to take heroic action. Turning around, he smacks my reindeer on the snout, yelling, "Slow down!" The animal, in response, begins running for its life. Suddenly I'm in the chariot race from *Ben-Hur,* my sled bumping Lee's. Finally my reindeer pulls ahead and we're dashing away until we're nearly flying through the air, and I'm having the time of my life. Spotting Par-Stefan ahead, the reindeer begins to slow down and then stops precisely at the finish line. I climb off the sled and pat one of its furry antlers; I swear the animal winks at me.

After the *raidu,* we go into a *kota* to warm up and have something to eat. Par-Stefan builds a fire and then gives everybody a cup of hot lingonberry juice, while he places butter in a huge skillet and sautés chunks of reindeer meat. He rolls pieces of flatbread around the sizzling meat, creating the equivalent of reindeer falafel, and begins passing them around. Since there isn't a non-reindeer selection, I take the sandwich handed to me, immediately looking for ways to discard it. "This is really good," Lee says, digging into the sandwich. "Tastes just like caribou or elk."

The Sami have dozens of different words for "reindeer," reflecting the animal's important role in their culture, as a source of food, shelter, clothing, weaponry, and religious iconography. Beginning in the fifteenth century, the Sami turned to reindeer herding, following the animals as they roamed the wilderness in search of food. By the eighteenth century, however, industrialization threatened their nomadic existence, with factories, roads, and railways radically altering the landscape. Today, there are only between fifteen thousand and twenty thousand Sami in Sweden, with twenty-five hundred still tending their reindeer.

"The people of my father's generation had it the worst," Par-Stefan tells us. "The government didn't want them to continue with the Sami tradition and made them feel intellectually inferior. They took everything away—our land, our language." At the heart of the conflict was a profound culture clash between the Western view that nature exists to be conquered and the Sami's belief that the natural world is sacred. They believe that instead of existing apart from nature, they are inseparable from it. While the Western view is that time proceeds in a linear fashion, with days turning into weeks and months, for the Sami, time is cyclical, reflecting the migratory patterns of the reindeer. Living without fixed boundaries or rigid concepts of property rights, the Sami have struggled to retain rights to land they have walked on for generations. Their livelihood is in danger, too, for the reindeer population worldwide has plunged nearly 60 percent in the last three decades, the result of climate change and human encroachment. "If it continues the way it is going," Par-Stefan says, "we won't have any land at all, or reindeer."

Since the Sami have lived in direct contact with nature for so many generations, I figure Par-Stefan might have some valuable advice about sleep. "It must be awfully hard sleeping during the polar nights and midnight sun," I say. "How do you manage the two extremes? Don't you get depressed during the winter and manic during the summer?"

"It's really not a problem," he says. "When it's dark for twenty hours a day, I sleep about ten hours a night. When it's light, I sleep maybe four or five hours."

"Aren't you exhausted then?"

He shakes his head no. "It's all about keeping rhythm with nature. When the sun shines it gives us energy to keep going. When it doesn't, we go to bed. We don't think of nature as something separate. It's part of us and we're part of it."

Perhaps it's the extraordinary setting, in front of a campfire, in a forest filled with reindeer, but what he says makes more sense than most of the advice I've received. Before I get a chance to ask a follow-up question, the elderly woman from Shropshire starts up a conversation. She and her husband are wearing matching Nordic hats, and with their bright blue eyes and rosy cheeks they look like Mr. and Mrs. Claus. "Did you sleep in the Icehotel last night?" she asks. When I tell her yes, she goes on to tell me that she slept right through the night and that it was "marvelously invigorating."

"Was that your experience, too?" she asks.

"Not exactly. I slept for maybe a minute and then grabbed my sleeping bag and escaped."

When I tell her that we'll be staying in London for a few days, she says, "I hope you're seeing a musical." No, I say, we're seeing a Tom Stoppard play.

"You should really see a musical," she insists. "London does the best in the world."

I don't want to start an argument in a Sami *kota* at the end of the world, but I ask her if she's ever heard of Rodgers and Hammerstein, Lerner and Loewe, Stephen Sondheim?

"They do not in any way compare to Andrew Lloyd Webber," she states emphatically. "Have you seen *Cats* or *The Phantom of the Opera*?"

"Yes," I say. I want to tell her that not only have I seen them but that I've interviewed Andrew Lloyd Webber and that Michael Crawford, the original Phantom, once sang "Music of the Night" especially for me; however, that doesn't mean England produces better musicals. But now I'm starting to feel really stupid. There's Par-Stefan, whose culture has been decimated, and I'm going on about the superiority of the American musical.

"Are you a music critic?" the woman asks, and I tell her no, I'm actually writing a book on sleep.

"So you're a sleep critic."

"Of a sort. I'm trying to figure out why I don't sleep."

"Dear," she says, "have you ever thought about the possibility that you don't sleep because you're too critical of it?"

I have to admit she has a point. To show how totally openminded I can be, I pick up my reindeer sandwich and take a bite.

"It's good, isn't it?" the woman says.

"Best reindeer I've ever had," I say, wrapping the rest in a napkin and placing it in my knapsack.

Rudolph came home with me. I'd forgotten about the sandwich in my knapsack until I was back in New York, and it smelled just as you'd imagine it would after traversing two continents. At least now I know that reindeer really do know how to fly and can even elude airport security. It's probably just a coincidence, but after my trip to the Icehotel I begin to sleep much better. The atmosphere had been so serene that I try to carry that tranquil feeling with me, remembering what Par-Stefan said about keeping rhythm with nature.

Two weeks after the trip, I'm reveling in my newfound peace when I hear the Little Elephants upstairs. They're back from Europe, and after a burst of running, it turns dead quiet—a bad sign because it means they've gone to bed. Normally, I love it when they go to bed. I love it when they do anything that keeps their feet off the floor, but it's not even dinnertime yet, which means they'll be up when we're sound asleep. At 3 A.M., right on schedule, they begin running around the apartment, prompting Lee to phone upstairs. After about the fifteenth ring, the wife answers and says, "There's really nothing we can do. The children have jet lag."

The next day, Lee flies to L.A. on business, while I pack a bag and go to my mother-in-law's apartment to wait out the neighbors' jet lag. My mother-in-law is Italian and loves to cook, so my arrival is the perfect excuse to prepare a multicourse feast, which she insists I eat on a TV tray in the den so I can put up my feet and watch the evening news just as my late father-in-law used to do. Afterward, she serves freshly baked chocolate chip cookies and then asks if I want popcorn or a Valium. She's only half kidding about the Valium. In recent years, she has had terrible trouble sleeping but has learned to put her time awake at night to good advantage, methodically working her way through all the literary classics. She is now eighty-seven and has read nearly all of Trollope, Dickens, and Mann.

She is passionate about her new hobby but worries that her insomnia may be a sign of something more serious. So far, a variety of doctors have pronounced her perfectly healthy, although none bothered to explain to her the connection between sleep and the aging process. Just as our skin loses its suppleness and our joints begin to creak, our sleep architecture becomes increasingly more fragile with age. Both physiological and lifestyle changes contribute to the problems, from secreting lesser amounts of chemicals that play a critical role in the sleep/wake cycle to failing to get sufficient exercise and light. Some experts believe that seniors require just as much sleep as younger adults but simply aren't getting it, although a study at Brigham and Women's Hospital and the Harvard Medical School showed that seniors (aged sixty to seventy-six) needed 1.5 hours less sleep than their younger (eighteen-to-thirty-two) counterparts.

After eating one too many cookies, I wash up and go to bed in the spare room devoted to my late father-in-law's golf trophies. The bed is pretty comfortable, but the radiator makes loud clanging noises and just as I'm about to fall asleep I hear my brother-in-law banging around in the bathroom. He had a late dinner in the city, and instead of taking the train back to his house in Greenwich, he decided to stay with his mother. The next morning we meet in the hallway, where he tells me about the terrifying nightmare he had. Of the two brothers, he has always been more anxiety-prone, a trait he shares with his mother. "The world was about to end in a nuclear holocaust," he says. "I could see the flames and feel the heat, and everyone was going to get killed. But in the dream I set my watch back three hours so I'd be able to escape it." He looks at his watch. "Oh my God! My watch is three hours early! I must have actually reset it in the middle of the night. Do people actually do things like that in their sleep?"

"People do lots of weird things in their sleep," I say, telling him about a class of sleep disorders called parasomnias. These are defined as abnormal behaviors or emotional experiences that accompany sleep, with the two most common being disorders of arousal and REM behavior disorder or RBD. Disorders of arousal occur during deep sleep, after someone is partially aroused, by an outside noise or a bedmate's snoring, for example. The part of the brain that should be shut down in sleep is now turned on, causing the person to engage in activities, such as sleepwalking, that he or she will rarely remember the next morning. I still tease the Good Sleep Boyfriend about the time he jumped atop the mattress in the middle of the night and announced, "And NOW I'd like to introduce those famous monsters from the deep—the Lambrusco family!" (He had no memory of the incident, nor could he identify the renowned aquatic Lambruscos.) While that was a one-time event, many people experience one or two such episodes a month.

People with disorders of arousal not only walk and talk in their sleep, but they can also eat, operate machinery, and have sex. California neurologist David Rosenfeld coined the term "sleep sex" after a female patient came to him complaining that her husband was making love to her while he was asleep. "It was 1985 and there was no literature on it at all," he told me. "At first she kind of enjoyed it. Her husband was normally passive when they made love in the mornings, but at night he talked dirty and was more aggressive. She asked him to incorporate it into their normal routine. After a while, she didn't like it anymore. Knowing he was asleep, she felt it was a little like necrophilia. Afterward, he didn't remember anything."

The amnesia characteristic of such arousals has given way to a legal doctrine based on the concept of "non-insane automatism." In the first case to successfully use "sexsomnia" as a defense, in 2008, the Ontario Court of Appeal upheld the sexual-assault acquittal of a Toronto landscaper, who, after consuming twelve beers, four mixed drinks, and some "magic mushrooms," managed to put on a condom and then attempt to have intercourse with a woman at a summer croquet party. The landscaper testified at his trial that his memories of the incident were cloudy, comparing them to a "vision." The most famous case of non-insane automatism involves yet another Canadian, this one named Kenneth Parks, who in the spring of 1987 rose from his bed, drove fourteen miles to his in-laws' house, and removed a tire iron from the car. With no apparent motive, Parks proceeded to beat his mother-in-law to death and choke his father-in-law into unconsciousness. Although he was charged with murder, he was acquitted on the grounds that he had been asleep when he'd committed the crime and therefore wasn't fully aware.

A common misconception is that sleepwalkers or sexsomniacs are acting out their dreams, but that problem is associated not with disorders of arousal but with RBD (REM behavior disorder). REM sleep is usually characterized by muscle paralysis and brain activity that resembles wakefulness, but with RBD, the sleeping person doesn't lose motor inhibition and will act out dreams, sometimes becoming violent. At the sleep-disorders course in Las Vegas, I attended a lecture by Dr. Mark Mahowald, who, with his associate Dr. Carlos Schenck, identified RBD as a new parasomnia in the mid-1980s. Mahowald, a neurologist at the University of Minnesota and director of the Minnesota Regional Sleep Disorders Center, showed a collection of sleep-lab videos in which people appeared to be in the throes of demonic possession. In one famous case, a man who dreamt that he was trying to kill a deer by snapping its neck woke up to discover that he was actually trying to kill his wife. According to Mahowald, middle-aged men make up 87 percent of RBD cases, and in half the cases, they will later develop Parkinson's disease. It was once thought that people with RBD were mentally ill, but Mahowald told me after the lecture that strange, violent behaviors arising from sleep are actually quite common and are not usually related to psychiatric conditions.

"So do you think all those saints claiming they had visions, with angels piercing their flesh with swords, probably had RBD?" I ask him.

He smiles. "Probably, yes." He goes on to explain that we spend our existence in three states of being: wakefulness, sleeping, and dreaming. These states aren't mutually exclusive, and sometimes they overlap, creating a mixture of wakefulness and sleep, or wakefulness and dreams.

My brother-in-law resets his watch and gets ready for work, while I take the circular route home around the Central Park reservoir. That night at 9:15 P.M., I'm standing in a vacant lot between Fifty-third and Fifty-fourth Streets watching a gigantic Tilda Swinton climb out of bed as the sun sets on the exterior of the Museum of

Modern Art. Swinton is one of five characters in *Sleepwalkers*, Doug Aitken's video installation projected on the museum's steel-and-glass façades. Utilizing eight monumental screens, the film chronicles a night in the lives of five stylish New Yorkers as they shake off sleep and wend their way into the city to begin their workday. In addition to Swinton, who plays an office worker, the other actors include Donald Sutherland as an icy corporate chieftain, who, after colliding with a taxi, jumps on top of the hood and starts dancing, and the singer Cat Power as a postal worker, who spins ecstatically in a Sufi-like trance. Each individual narrative lasts thirteen minutes, and they play on a continuous loop with no beginning or end.

For the next forty-five minutes I circle the museum, watching the characters moving fluidly from sleep to wake to dreams. It's hard to keep track of the time; on the building's façade, the sun is constantly setting or rising, while the moon is shining over the museum. I pull the hood of my parka up over my head to keep warm. Why, I wonder, am I standing in a valley of skyscrapers with five enormous people who have co-opted the landscape, turning it into a wasteland of dysfunctional sleep? This can't be healthy.

In her book *The Power of Place,* Winifred Gallagher explores the various ways our surroundings influence our behavior, impacting everything from our creativity and fertility to our appetites, sleep patterns, and mood swings. With the Industrial Revolution, we turned away from the natural world, becoming creatures whose lives centered on indoor activities, in environments that were artificially lit, heated, and cooled. As society adapted to an indoor urban environment and we stopped looking to nature for our time cues, the increasing popularity of psychoanalysis drew us further inward. "Convinced of the therapeutic primacy of insight and inner change," she writes, "Freudians were skeptical of the idea that altering one's milieu, say, where one lived, might also have merit. That kind of thing was, they said, 'running away from your problems,' even though the people who ran away sometimes felt better."

Dr. Michael Terman, director of the Center for Light Treatment and Biological Rhythms at Columbia University Medical Center, has created the Pi-Square Dawn-Dusk Simulation System to help people with sleep-onset problems and SAD. By using the treatment, people can experience what it was like before the invention of electricity, when humans "awakened to the gradual coming of dawn" and then fell "asleep under the slow transition of dusk to starlight." A computerized timer the size of a clock radio gradually turns on a floor lamp with a diffuser that simulates a springtime dawn even in the middle of winter. While a thirty-minute session of bright-light therapy in the morning is still his treatment of choice, Terman told me that that his Dawn-Dusk Simulation System can still help sleep and have an antidepressant effect.

Instead of creating an artificial dawn, I wonder if for the sake of my sleep I should change my environment. Lee doesn't want to leave the city permanently, but maybe it's finally time to buy the country house we've been talking about. At 10 P.M., my cell phone rings. It's Lee, wondering where I am. "I'm standing in an alley watching Tilda Swinton brush her teeth," I say. "I think she's suffering from a circadian-rhythm disorder, or maybe she just needs a country house. In any event, she looks tired and totally miserable. Yeah, I know she's just an actress playing a part, but she needs the country. *Badly.*"

1 0

THE HOUSE OF RHYTHM AND BLUES

I've found my dream house. It's about eighty minutes from Manhattan and has a pool, an artist's studio, and an attached renovated silo. Who needs a Dawn-Dusk Simulation System when I can regulate my circadian rhythms by staring up at the sky through my own personal glass-domed silo? "Won't it be wonderful watching the moon and stars up here?" I say to Lee. "Maybe we can even set up our bedroom in the silo." Lee reminds me that the house is wildly out of our price range and asks me if I really need a silo. No, I guess I don't *need* a silo—I'm not in the grain-storage business—but it's certainly a nice bonus, one that will come in handy when I replace the House of Punk Sleep with the new and improved version—the House of Beautiful Dreams.

Sherry, our real estate agent, agrees that Silo House is on the pricy side, but maybe the seller will "come down." Though we've only known Sherry a short time, we've come to believe that sellers are inherently generous people who will drop their prices a half million dollars if we do the right thing and "throw in" a bid. "You never know until you try, right?" she says.

Sherry, who is dark-haired and very pretty, is endlessly upbeat—about real estate, about her flower and vegetable garden, about her third husband and their latest fabulous vacation, about her wonderful, brilliant, crazy kids. She would seem to lead a charmed existence, yet I've never met anybody who confronts major drama on such a regular basis. A good friend dies suddenly, a close relative develops a debilitating illness, civil war erupts at a family wedding, yet Sherry remains a model of resilience, even when she doesn't sleep well, which, given her 3 A.M. emailing habit, appears to be quite often. Having recently returned from visiting her oldest daughter, an award-winning film director, on the set of her new movie, Sherry tells me that her daughter isn't sleeping and she's worried about her health. Walking the grounds of Silo House, we discuss the downside of what appears to be a very glamorous industry but one that pushes people to work fifteen to eighteen hours a day, six days a week. In his documentary *Who Needs Sleep?* the renowned cinematographer Haskell Wexler focuses on the circumstances surrounding the 1997 death of a thirty-five-year-old cameraman, who, after nineteen hours on the set, fell asleep behind the wheel of his car and hit a utility pole. The eighty-seven-year-old Wexler has been working to curb excessive work hours in the film world, but the industry has yet to adopt concrete proposals, and with people just happy to get work, the answer to "Who needs sleep?" will, for the foreseeable future, probably be "Nobody."

Sherry and I debate the pros and cons of sleeping pills while discussing the pluses and minuses of Silo House. For me there aren't any minuses, save one: price. Knowing we can't afford it, I begin to fixate on its negligible flaws, starting with the bedroom mural, a copy of Georges Seurat's *A Sunday Afternoon on the Island of La Grande Jatte*. The seller, a congenial man whose two adorable children have been following us everywhere, tells us that the painting came with the house and he didn't have the heart to remove it. It's actually quite a good copy, right down to the thousands of tiny pointillist brushstrokes. However, I'm not sure pointillism is conducive to restful sleep, all those little dots like mosquito bites to the brain. We decide in the end not to place a bid, and somebody else buys the house. Sherry tells us not to worry. Something even more fabulous will show up.

Next on the list is a 1920s stone carriage house near Martha Stewart's Cantitoe Corners farms. I have nothing but deep admiration for Stewart, who built a multibillion-dollar empire and survived prison on only four hours of sleep a night, but having grown up with a mother whose favorite question was "What will the neighbors think?" I'm not sure I want the world's most famous domestic diva as my neighbor. What if I don't keep up appearances? Will Martha storm down the street and rap me on the knuckles with a trowel? Reading *Martha Stewart Living* is one thing, but living near Martha Stewart could be the mother of all nightmares. That, however, turns out to be the least of it, for the house abuts a beautiful estate that hosts concerts and weddings, raising the possibility that our summer nights will be filled with blaring music. "Too noisy, right?" Sherry says.

We move on to another property, which is away from Martha Stewart's and closer to Ralph Lauren's—not stylistically but geographically. It's next door. While the house needs to be painted and the shutters are falling off, the gorgeous kitchen reminds me of Diane Keaton's in *Something's Gotta Give*. "Isn't this the best?" I say to Lee, who is staring out the window, shaking his head.

"The house is too close to the road," he says. "And guess what road it happens to be? The one leading away from the music center! We'll get all the traffic at night, and since it's on a hill, the cars will be accelerating."

We look at the master bedroom. It's beautiful. It's also on the ground floor facing the road. We don't have to wait long wondering about the level of traffic noise because an antique car whizzes by. "I wonder if that was Ralph Lauren," I say. "I read somewhere that he keeps his huge collection of antique cars up here. Wouldn't it be ironic to live in the equivalent of a Ralph Lauren ad only to have the real Ralph Lauren ruin your sleep?"

Sherry takes us to another house, in another town, at the end of a quiet road. Built in 1775 and still bearing the original owner's name, it has a gabled roof and a large front porch, where I imagine sitting on a rocker drinking iced tea and reading Edith Wharton. It is indeed a tranquil place, but the interior looks as if Squeaky Fromme had decorated it, with sheets hanging on the wall and a spooky laundry room that could double as a torture chamber. In addition to an exorcism, the house needs a gut renovation, and even though Sherry tells us it can be done "over time," I don't want to trade my old problems in the city for new ones in the country. Barring a cemetery, aren't there any reasonably priced, quiet places that don't require lots of work and where a person can sleep peacefully?

"There are lots of other places to see," Sherry says brightly. "But all buyers make compromises. Even clients with ten million dollars to spend can always find something wrong." She urges us not to get discouraged. "Remember, guys, no house is perfect."

While I'm waiting to find my flawed dream house, a magazine-editor friend sends me an article about a unique method for treating insomnia called brain-music therapy. First developed in 1991 by Dr. Iakov Levine, a neurologist at Moscow Medical Academy, it was brought to the United States by a Russian colleague, Dr. Galina Mindlin, who works as a psychiatrist in New York. Having studied piano and voice, I am immediately drawn to the idea of using music as a healing agent and make an appointment to see Mindlin at her office near the Time Warner Center. After I fill out a sleep questionnaire, along with the Beck Depression Inventory, a multi-choice self-report that tries to gauge the level of depressive symptoms, she brings me into her office, which is decorated in chilly, monochrome colors. We sit opposite each other on matching off-white Barcelona chairs, and Mindlin, who has pale skin, long, dark hair, and a soft Russian accent, listens intently as I give her the rundown on my sleep. Music's ability to spark an emotional reaction in people was something she understood from an early age. Her mother sang at the Bolshoi Theater, and Mindlin was a dancer before studying neurology at Moscow Medical Academy. "I remember visiting my aunt on the Balkan Sea," she says. "She was a writer and yoga instructor, and I learned a lot about health from her. The rhythm of the waves made a big impression on me, and I began thinking about the universal harmony of nature and how all things are interconnected."

After we finish our brief therapy session, she records my brain waves on an EEG machine, placing a black rubber hairnet over my head to position the electrodes. She tells me to relax and think calming thoughts. Remembering my hypnosis tape, I picture myself on a deserted island, the waves lapping the shoreline, but soon I'm thinking about Mindlin's aunt doing yoga poses on the Balkan Sea, and then about something I hadn't thought of in years: When I was a teenager, my middle sister and I were walking along the New Hampshire shoreline when we spotted a dead body bobbing in the waves. It was that of a young man whom we'd seen earlier in the week drinking a beer and staring into the water. After five minutes Mindlin removes the hairnet. "Your brain waves were extremely active," she says, shaking her head. "I think you'll get a lot of benefit from this treatment. You can use it during the day when anything stresses you out."

Later, Mindlin will send my EEG results via computer to Dr. Levine in Moscow, where he'll use a complex series of algorithms to translate my brain activity into specific melodies and rhythms that can calm or energize. The treatment was originally developed for insomnia, but it has proven helpful for alleviating anxiety, depression, and stress, as well as for boosting concentration and productiveness. Mindlin points to several double-blind studies that have shown that subjects listening to their own brain music had better results than the group listening to a CD designed for someone else. The treatment appears to work by reinforcing brain waves that affect our autonomic nervous system, impacting heart rate, pulse, blood pressure, and muscle tension. To treat insomnia or anxiety, BMT helps electrical activity in the brain transition from the more active beta waves to the more relaxing alpha waves. To help energy and concentration, it enhances the beta waves.

Music therapy as a healing tool has been used by many different cultures for thousands of years. Pythagoras, the ancient-Greek mathematician, doctor, and musician, believed in the connection between musical and biological harmony, teaching his students that certain chords and melodies could aid in healing. In the Bible, David plays the harp to help alleviate King Saul's depression, and Oxford scholar Robert Burton, in his 1621 book *The Anatomy of Melancholy*, wrote that music "is a sovereign remedy against despair." In the United States, the modern era of music therapy began after World War II, when musicians went to veterans' hospitals to play for the thousands of soldiers suffering the physical and emotional effects of war. Today there have been numerous research studies supporting the physiological effects of music on the human body, and it is now used, in conjunction with other therapies, to treat Alzheimer's and Parkinson's diseases, chronic pain, autism, depression, anxiety, and substance abuse.

"What if I don't like my brain music?" I ask Mindlin, worried that it might sound like a Yoko Ono song.

"Too bad," she says. "Think of it as good for you."

Mindlin, who just returned from opening a franchise office in Beverly Hills, believes BMT is the perfect therapy for the twenty-first century. "It's instant medicine," she says. "You can have your brain waves in your pocket and carry them around with you."

While waiting for my CD to come from Moscow, I happen to mention the treatment to my hair colorist, George, who is married to a Russian woman. "Brain-music therapy?" he says. "That sounds exactly like what my wife and my in-laws do to get my kid to fall asleep." He pretends to rock a baby while singing something that sounds like a cross between a lullaby and a dirge. "Babies in Russia can't go to sleep without someone singing this annoying song."

"Aren't you exaggerating just a little?" I say.

He calls over three young Russian assistants, and without telling them about my new therapy asks them to describe what they do when they put their babies to bed at night. They all break into a similar song in the middle of the color room at the John Barrett Salon. "See!" George says triumphantly. "They could have recorded the CD and saved you the five hundred fifty bucks."

When I asked Mindlin if brain-music therapy grew out of the idea that Russians, in putting their children to bed, synchronize their own voices to a rocking movement, she said, "It's an interesting concept, but it's your idea, not mine." Three weeks later, when I receive the CD in the mail, I expect to hear George's lullaby, but the twelve-minute "calming" melody sounds like a digitized piano version of Stravinsky's "Song of the Volga Boatmen." I'm American, of Irish descent, so why should my brain music sound Russian? As for the "activating" music, it reminds me of something a Russian ice-skater would incorporate into her performance medley—perfect for building up speed before a triple loop or double Salchow. It is indeed energizing—once it even made my heart race—but I already have plenty of energy.

Following the instructions, I listen to the calming music twice before going to bed but still wake up in the middle of the night. After about a month I give up on BMT, which I suspect is more helpful for people who can't fall asleep than those who can't stay asleep. However, while it didn't help my insomnia, I did find it a useful tool for relieving stress. One evening, after I'd poured some of my mother-in-law's pasta sauce over a bowl of fettuccini and had settled in to watch HBO's *Rome,* the Little Elephants were making so much noise that I decided to call them up and ask them to stop. I'm not by nature an assertive person. Even without activating music, confrontations make me jittery, so when the husband answered I quickly apologized for bothering them and asked if they could keep it down. The husband replied, "They're chil-der-run," drawing out the syllables to emphasize the obvious. Following a long pause, he then said, "Twenty-two dollars," which I thought was a reasonable price to get the kids to stop, and just as I was about to race up the back stairs with the cash, I realized he was talking to a food-delivery man. When he got on the phone again he was surly and rude and the kids continued pounding. I grabbed my iPod and listened to the calming music. It worked.

I used the music before several other high-stress situations, and while it wasn't a magic charm, it did prove helpful. After a few months, however, it stopped working entirely. Mindlin had warned me that if I repeatedly listened to the CD, my brain waves might change and I'd no longer respond in the same way. If that happened, she recommended a "tune-up" in the form of a follow-up visit and a new EEG. Although she assured me that I wouldn't need to keep coming back, I was skeptical. Instead, I decided to refocus all my attention on finding a house.

My friend Alan is my unofficial real estate advisor, which has all the makings of a potential disaster, because with Alan things tend to go sideways, if not straight downhill. I've known him for thirty years, and I'm not sure if this particular dynamic is his problem or mine or ours together. Friends assure me that it's mostly his, and I tend to agree. Alan, who refers to me as "Ms. Morrisroe," is a big personality in an even bigger body that recently topped three hundred pounds. An outrageous flirt, an incorrigible prankster, a frustrated comedian, he is beneath it all a sweet, sensitive, needy guy who plays everything for laughs. I'm terribly fond of him, but I've also learned to keep him at a distance. He knows how I feel, and we even have a code word for it: *Carl.*

Carl was the name of the pilot who took us up in a four-seat Cessna for what was supposed to be a delightful aerial view of the autumn foliage. As our previous two expeditions to see the leaves had ended with Alan's vintage Jaguar breaking down and his boat nearly capsizing, getting into a plane with him was definitely asking for trouble, but Lee, a licensed glider pilot, was then taking commercial flying lessons and thought it would be fun. We'd arranged for an hour's ride, but after we were up in the air, Carl said he could only do twenty minutes. Alan was not happy and jokingly said, "Oh, maybe Lee will take over the controls"—this was before 9/11—and then behind Carl's back, he made a gesture as if wanting to strangle him. A few seconds later, Carl picked up the radio and said, "Emergency, emergency!"

"*Emergency?*" Lee said from the backseat. "What's wrong?"

"The engine's riding rough," Carl announced. "We've got to head back right away."

"This is it. We're going to be killed," I said to Lee, who, in his leather jacket and aviator glasses, looked more professional than Carl, who by then was visibly sweating. When we finally landed, I nearly fainted on the tarmac, while Carl, displaying a curious lack of interest in his passengers' well-being, made a beeline for the office. We later found out that he'd faked the emergency because he thought, thanks to Alan, that we were planning to hijack the plane. Lee, in his *Top Gun* gear, was singled out as the ringleader.

So then why would I want Alan anywhere near my dream house? I really don't, but Alan is a hard guy to shake, and he does have a big heart. When I was working regularly as a magazine writer, Alan's diverse résumé—entrepreneur, restauranteur, landlord, amateur pop singer—made him an ideal pinch-hitting interview subject. He landed in at least a half dozen articles, and when he didn't work out, he combed his extensive contact list for names and numbers. Now he thinks that if he helps me find a house, I'll have to put him in the book.

"C'mon, Ms. Morrisroe," he says, "it's important for my literary legacy."

"Well, do you have any sleep problems?"

"According to my girlfriends, I snore—loudly."

Though Alan has never married, he has never lacked for female company and is currently seeing a famous choreographer. How this happened I'm not sure, but he takes great pleasure in telling me how he's influencing the world of dance and how he recently met "Misha" Baryshnikov.

"Back to your snoring," I say. "Maybe you've got sleep apnea. You should get it checked out."

Alan assures me that he doesn't have it, but I'm not convinced; he's always been very cavalier about his health, and I recently heard through a mutual friend that he has type 2 diabetes. "I don't have apnea," he repeats. "I just snore, in between planning productions for ABT." Knowing how sensitive he is, I let it drop and we talk about "our" house. He first introduced me to the rural area in Westchester about twenty-five years ago, when he bought a small house on a magical piece of property across from a horse farm. For whatever crazy reason, he then switched houses with another person, trading the wonderful cottage for a big ugly modern one, and he wants to know if I'd like to rent that.

"I bet you'll sleep there," he says.

"Yes," I say, "isn't it pretty to think so?" We've been trading that line for at least two decades, when Alan, trying to impress a date, lied and told her he was passionate about Hemingway. When she asked him to recite the final line of *The Sun Also Rises,* he excused himself, called me on the phone, and asked if I knew it. "The answer is 'Yes, isn't it pretty to think so?'" I said. Along with "Carl," it's become part of our limited repertoire.

"No, I don't want to rent your house," I tell him, recognizing the possibility that it might come with Alan. He then asks if Sherry is single and if so, would I fix him up with her?

"No, she's married," I say, reminding him that he is already in a relationship. Alan replies, "But is she *happily* married?"

The next time we make an appointment to see Sherry I make sure Alan is staying at his apartment in the city. He has a way of cropping up where you least expect it, and Sherry has enough complications in her life. She takes us to a house that like everything else is too expensive and in need of extensive renovation—it was built in 1910—but has excellent bone structure. It's the Katharine Hepburn of houses, on one of the prettiest streets in the village, and I can really see myself sleeping here. (Alan totally agrees; somehow he got the address and has already seen it.) The owner, a retired TV producer, has an office on the ground floor, where he keeps his Emmy Awards and other memorabilia from the glory days of network television.

"This is a place I could grow old in," I tell Lee, who claims I'm only saying that because the house is old, but it's more than that. I really feel a connection to the place. The owner, however, won't budge on the price, and Sherry tells us the house needs too much work and to basically forget it. Alan calls to tell me the offer is still open for *his* house, and that if I rent it, he'll throw in a free plane ride with Carl.

A few weeks later, Sherry shows us a 1920s farmhouse near my friend Ira's renovated barn. Ira is also a friend of Alan's, but their relationship, to put it delicately, has always been complicated. Ira likes his space, and Alan, well, doesn't. Once when Alan looked at a house on the same street, Ira nearly died, picturing Alan showing up on a regular basis in his golf cart. The farmhouse is just a five-minute walk away, so Alan immediately hatches a plan for us to show up at Ira's one morning, in matching golf carts, to tee off on his lawn. "I don't know if we're even going to buy the house," I tell Alan, who replies, "Yes, but isn't it pretty to think so?"

The house has diamond-paned windows, a large stone hearth, a separate writer's studio, and a new pool on a rise overlooking acres of meadows. The only drawback is the shared driveway with the next house, which is so close you can practically see what the neighbors are watching on TV. The seller's agent, a woman named Muffin, assures Sherry that the people next door are exceptionally quiet, and on our second visit, we notice two Adirondack chairs at the end of their property. I immediately picture the neighbors as Jessica Tandy and Hume Cronyn, two lovely old people, not unlike my own lovely (and very quiet) parents.

We place a bid on Good Friday, but Muffin tells Sherry that it's the "full price or nothing" and that she'll be showing the house over the weekend. Other people are interested. We take the bait and offer the full asking price.

"We have a house!" I tell my sister Nancy after Lee and I drive up to Boston for the Easter weekend. We show her the pictures. She loves it. I call Alan, who says that he's buying us a golf cart as a housewarming present.

That night, at 3 A.M., I wake up with a major anxiety attack. "I'm not sure this house is right for us," I tell Lee. "It's got that shared driveway, and the people are so close by it's practically like living in the city. What if they have loud parties?" Lee reminds me that Muffin says they're a quiet couple without any children and tells me to calm down.

The next morning Sherry is on the phone. Jessica Tandy and Hume Cronyn are in their thirties, and Jessica is pregnant. Out with the Adirondack chairs, in with the jungle gym. On Easter, we pull the bid.

"Good move, Ms. Morrisroe," Alan says when I give him the update. *"Carl."*

"What do you mean? Carl, as in disaster?"

"No, I mean Carl as in neighbor. I think he lives next door."

We put house hunting on hold for a while, and then one morning, after searching through the real estate listings, I notice that Hepburn House has come down in price. It's still too expensive, but it's a start. We drive out to look at it again, and the seller's agent has laid out freshly baked cookies; wherever I go I smell the sweet, comforting scent of oatmeal raisin. "Oh, this smells just like home," I tell Lee. "I can picture Bumpa right here in the kitchen."

The agent tells us that the room currently used as an office was once an "egg room," where the previous owners would sell the eggs hatched by their chickens. "This is perfect," I whisper to Lee. "What better place to give birth to my ideas than an actual egg room!"

"When the house was built in 1910, it was named the 'ideal country house' by *Good Housekeeping* magazine," the agent tells us.

"Isn't that impressive," I say to Lee, who mutters something about how notions of "ideal" have changed considerably since before World War I. "The upstairs bedrooms are totally claustrophobic, and the windows are so small you can barely see out of them." The seller's agent tells us that we could probably put an extension over the garage, which would cost maybe $500,000 max. Sherry volunteers the name of an architect.

We tell Sherry we'll discuss it and get back to her. Meanwhile, I begin doing some research on the man who built the "ideal country house," give or take a century. It turns out that he was a famous architect named Alfred Hopkins, who specialized in building "farm groupings" on country estates in Long Island, such as the one owned by Louis Comfort Tiffany. I retrieve his obituary online, reading parts of it to Lee. "In addition to being an architect," I tell him, "he played the cello, violin, organ, and piano, and he composed several quartets. He was also greatly interested in the craft of bookbinding and wrote a magazine article on the methods of medieval bookbinders. So he was an author, too."

"What else did he write?"

"A book called *Planning for Sunshine and Fresh Air.*"

"Well, he didn't plan too well for it in the house. It feels totally closed in."

"Wait a minute," I say. "He also wrote *Prisons and Prison Buildings.*"

"That kind of explains it, doesn't it?"

"I guess he designed federal penitentiaries, too. You know the one at Lewisburg? That was his. And the ones at Terre Haute and

Wallkill. President Roosevelt thought so highly of him that he appointed him a delegate to the International Prison Conference at Berlin."

"And this is why you want the house?"

I can't explain why I want it. I just do, so I send Alan over to look at it again, and this time he has second thoughts. "I don't think it's for you," he says. "There's a horse farm next door, and horses can be very noisy." I don't trust his advice, however, because he's still pushing for us to rent *his* place.

Several weeks later, the owners of Hepburn House drop their price even lower. "It's fate," I tell Lee. "We've got to buy it." Lee agrees, not because he's changed his mind about the house—he still thinks it's a money pit—but because it happens to be within golf-cart range of his new tennis partner's state-of-the-art court.

After our bid is accepted, we meet the engineer for the home inspection, following him down into a basement that appears to be in its original 1910 condition. The floor is damp, with a six-inch watermark on the wall. "Obviously there's been flooding in the basement," Lee says. "How do you get the water out?" The engineer points to an old toilet in the corner. "You could, however, buy a sump pump," he says. "I guess they've just been pumping the water down that toilet." We move on to the electricity, which consists of a vast jumble of different-colored wires either tied together in clumps or hanging lose and exposed. "Are you handy?" the engineer asks Lee, who says, "I'm not a licensed electrician, if that's what you mean." The engineer checks out the sewage system— a hundred-year-old cast-iron pipe depositing water out onto the street. "You wouldn't want that to break," the engineer says, shaking his head. Walking back upstairs, Lee whispers, "Is this the kind of basement you'd ever want to step foot in? I think I saw a dead animal."

The engineer disappears into the attic, returning to tell us he found mold but that all we had to do was raise the roof a few inches for better air circulation. "All in all," he says, "the house is in pretty good shape for something this old."

"It was built by a famous architect," I volunteer.

"Would I know his work?" the engineer asks.

"Only if you've served time in a federal pen."

A few days later the engineer sends us the report. The house passes inspection, and we come up for another look, meeting the owners, who are planning to relocate full-time to Martha's Vineyard. While Lee talks to the husband, I sit on the breezeway with his wife, glancing at the pond across the way. "Isn't it idyllic here?" she says. "I'm really going to miss this place."

"It really feels like such a happy house," I say. "You must have such wonderful memories."

"Not all wonderful," she says. "We've had tragedies, too."

"I wish she hadn't said that part about tragedies," I tell Lee on the way home. "I wonder what kind of tragedies. I hope they weren't house-related ones."

"If they were," Lee says, "they probably occurred in the basement."

A few days later Alan calls and tells me he's got a quote for my book. "It's Plato," he announces. ("*Alan* knows Plato?" Ira said when I told him.) He then reads it to me: "How can you prove whether at this moment we are sleeping and all our thoughts are a dream; or whether or not we are awake and talking to one another in the waking state?"

"So we may be sleeping right now and not know it," I say.

"*Row, row, row your boat*," he sings. "*Gently down the stream. Merrily, merrily, merrily, merrily, Life is but a dream.*"

Not long afterward, Lee has a dream in which he's bound to a chair by electrical wire. Lee never remembers his dreams, or if he does, they're totally basic, such as about thugs chasing him. He's not prone to analyze either, so after he describes this particular dream he's ready to forget about it, but putting on my analyst's cap, I say, "Hmmm, do you remember anything else about the dream?"

"I think I'm in a basement somewhere."

"Oh."

"And someone is about to pull a switch," he adds.

"Like you're in an electric chair? Say, in Lewisburg Penitentiary."

"Could be."

"You don't want to buy this house, do you? You think it's totally wrong for us."

"I didn't say that."

"Yes, you did! Your subconscious said it, because you were too afraid to say it to me."

Once again, we pull the bid, making up a lame excuse to Sherry. A few weeks later, when my sister Nancy comes to visit, we take her on a drive, stopping by to look at the house. "I really feel a mysterious connection to it," I tell her.

"It's not such a mystery," she says. "It looks exactly like our old house."

"What do you mean?"

"It's the House of Punk Sleep. You know how they say you can never go home again? Well, not in your case."

When Alan calls for an update on the house and I tell him we're not getting it, he doesn't make jokes or do anything that might prompt me to utter the warning "Carl." He sounds tired and a little run-down, although he does manage to remind me that for old time's sake he really "should" be in my book. He emails me on my birthday, and then I don't hear from him for a while. Then one morning the Good Sleep Boyfriend calls to tell me some bad news. "Alan's dead," he says. He doesn't know all the details, but Alan's assistant found him in bed that morning. He'd apparently died of a heart attack in his sleep.

"In his *sleep*?" I repeat.

Several weeks later, I'm at Alan's memorial service at a club downtown, where friends pay tribute to his wonderful, horrible, endearing, annoying, joyful, neurotic personality. At the end of the service, his ex-girlfriend and former bandmate plays a tape of Alan singing one of the songs they'd performed together. As we file out of the club, Alan's music still in our brains, people mention that at least he died in his sleep and what a peaceful way to go. If Alan had been there I'm sure he'd have said, "Yes, isn't it pretty to think so?"

11

THE MAN FROM CON ED

On a chilly night in late winter, I stride into the 92nd Street Y wearing a black cashmere turtleneck and a pair of black leggings tucked into a pair of very tall riding boots. I'm here for a meditation course, and I'm wildly overdressed. For years people have been pushing me to meditate, but since some of them later wound up in rehab or as stars of their own reality shows, I'd usually tell them that writing was my meditation and leave it at that. Besides, if I *were* going to meditate, I'd do it properly and study with a guru in India. When I did go to India, however, I was too busy shopping and sightseeing, so meditation became something I planned to do the *next* time I happened to be in India. Realizing that wasn't going to be anytime soon, I signed up for the meditation course at the Y, which is right around the corner from my apartment.

There are twenty of us in the class, including a pair of newly-weds in matching track pants, a handsome young businessman carrying a briefcase, a woman with long blond hair in a pencil skirt and high heels, and a cute middle-aged couple, the wife in yoga pants and a Van Cleef & Arpels enamel-and-gold necklace. We all stand around pretending not to feel awkward, until the instructor, who looks like a combination of Denzel Washington and Lou Gossett, Jr., welcomes us inside.

"I'm Jan Childress," he says, "and I want you to take down my email in case you need to get in touch with me. You'll notice that I work for Con Ed, so don't go busting my chops about it, okay?"

At this point, I'm ready to leave. When it comes to whom you learn meditation from there's got to be a middle ground between an Indian guru and a guy who works for Con Ed. I look at my watch. Only fifty-five minutes to go.

The meditation room is used during the day for nursery school activities, the walls decorated with exuberant crayon renderings of cars, planes, boats, and trains. Jan tells us to get comfortable on the floor, which is partly covered in gray-green industrial carpet. Squeezed out of the carpeted area, I sit in back on the exposed concrete, near a bank of lockers.

"How many people have meditated before?" Jan asks.

Only one person raises a hand. Jan explains that he came to meditation primarily through the martial arts, winning several gold medals competing in international tai chi tournaments. Though in his late fifties, he's in fantastic shape and explains that along with meditation, he'll also be teaching qigong (pronounced "chee-gung"), which, like tai chi, is an ancient Chinese exercise system that combines meditation with a series of slow, flowing poses. Both qigong and tai chi are intended to promote health and relaxation by cultivating internal energy, or qi ("chee"). Jan defines qi as the "life force," but much like the soul, it is very hard to envision, and you basically have to take it on faith. Practitioners of Chinese medicine believe that all disease stems from an imbalance in the qi as it moves through twelve meridians of the body. Qigong is a way to balance qi.

"I thought this was a meditation class," one woman says.

"Qigong combines movement and meditation," Jan replies. "Not unlike yoga."

A man raises his hand. "Do we have to chant? I hate chanting. It's weird."

"No, we don't have to, but I think you'll grow to like it."

Jan's gaze is warm and direct, emitting a sense of authority that is both powerful and humble. He is someone to whom the phrase "comfortable in his own skin" applies. "When I first began meditating," he explains, "I'd combine it with yoga, spending a total of thirty to forty-five minutes on both. But as I became more acclimated to meditation and the idea of sitting still, I found the time just melting away. I might attempt to meditate for five minutes, and then forty minutes later I'd come out of it, so it got much easier. That's because there are a couple of very important benefits from meditation. One is self-awareness, the other is self-control. By sitting still, I began to see very clearly the agitations of the mind. If I had a negative thought, I could feel its strength build up like a tidal wave. If it was a happy thought, I could feel the euphoria. Either way, it wasn't beneficial. So I just learned through practice to detach myself and observe my thoughts without becoming engaged by them."

Jan tells us that he'll be offering a sampler of different techniques, such as mantra meditation, mindfulness meditation, and light meditation. What they all have in common is a singular goal: to increase the mind's ability to keep distracting thoughts at bay so we can become fully present in the moment. Jan suggests we start with the universal mantra "so-hum," which translates as "I-divine." "It's easy to use," he says, "because it mimics the sound of the breath." We sit in a cross-legged position, our hands resting on our knees, palms facing up, our forefingers and thumbs touching. He then tells us to breathe deeply into our *dantien,* which is located a few inches below the navel and is the center of qi. Beginning with the mantra "Om," the primordial sound from which everything is said to emanate, he repeats it twice and then tells us to silently say "so" as we inhale, "hum" as we exhale. When our attention wanders, we're to let these thoughts come and go without judging them before gently tugging the mind back to so-hum. I'm a judgmental person, so it's hard to let my thoughts come and go without commenting on them, especially when they involve Nancy Sinatra, who is singing "These Boots Are Made for Walking" in my head. As I gently pull her (by the hair) out of my thoughts, I realize that my own boots aren't made for meditating and they're digging into my ankles. After ten minutes of mental wrestling, I hear Jan chant "Om."

"All right now, why don't we get moving," he says, while we struggle to stand up. The woman in the Van Cleef necklace is massaging her toes, while two people are hopping around to regain the circulation in their legs. "Ouch," a man says, "my foot is asleep." I'd love to take off my boots but fear it would attract more attention, realizing that just as I've judged people by their clothing and accessories, I've distinguished myself as the Nancy Sinatra of meditation.

"You don't have to sit still to meditate," Jan tells us. "There's this whole notion of single-mindedness that is associated with Buddhism and is very much akin to meditation. It is the notion of being totally engaged in whatever it is you're doing. If you're walking, *walk,* and don't think about what happened last week and the movie that you're going to see this coming weekend. It's just being totally aware of what you're doing. To supplement meditation, I like to incorporate qigong, because it requires that same notion of single-mindedness in order to assume and to maintain the proper structure throughout the exercise."

While I am tall and thin and give the appearance of being coordinated, I'm more comfortable in my brain than in my body. I've never played sports—my tennis career ended in ninth grade when I accidentally hit my teacher in the eye with a ball. (He turned out to be okay, although I'll never forget watching him drop to the ground, screaming "My eye! My eye! I think you've blinded me!") I do Pilates but not yoga out of fear of winding up in a class filled with stealthily competitive people with awesome flexibility and sculpted arms. I'm wary of qigong. The newlyweds in track pants are bouncing up and down in their sneakers. The blonde takes off her heels.

First, we assume the "resting position," standing with our feet hip width apart and parallel, toes pointing straight forward, eyes open, lips parted, arms relaxed and hanging down at our sides. Jan tells us to breathe in and out as he goes around correcting our stances. Next he has us do a few simple exercises to circulate qi throughout the "microcosmic orbit." The qi apparently flows along two major meridians—the governor vessel and the conception vessel—but it's so confusing I can't follow him, which he says doesn't matter, because all we need to do is move and breathe. He demonstrates an exercise called White Crane Relaxes Wings, inhaling as he raises his hands palms up in front of his body, then lowers his hands palms down as he exhales. He tells us to think of our hands as picking up water in a bowl, lifting the water as we rise, then letting the water flow from our hands as we sink. We move on to other exercises with equally poetic names, such as Pressing the Heavens with Two Hands and Separating Heaven and Earth. While not difficult, they require practice and coordination, and some of us are better at them than others.

Jan ends the class with another brief meditation and then urges us to practice for ten minutes a day, staring at a lit candle with our eyes half-closed to help focus our concentration. "Next week you might want to bring a pillow to make it easier to sit," he says. "And you probably don't need to wear . . . shoes."

Walking home, I feel relaxed and happy, but instead of savoring the pleasant sensations, when I arrive I immediately jump on the computer to read about meditation and qigong. I need to know if and how they work. When Lee gets home, I bombard him with facts. "Did you know that during the early part of the twentieth century the Chinese government in its desire to modernize wanted nothing to do with the old traditional healing methods?"

"No, I did not."

"But then in the 1950s, Mao Tse-tung decided to celebrate ancient

Chinese medicine as a natural treasure. In the nineties, though, the communists made most forms of qigong illegal and began persecuting members of Falun Gong—they practice a form of qigong—so many of the great master teachers came here and—"

"Weren't you just in a meditation class?" he asks. "You don't seem very relaxed."

"It's a process. You don't change overnight."

The next morning, I begin reading about UCLA's Cousins Center for Psychoneuroimmunology, which is the study of how psychological processes interact with the nervous and immune systems. The center was named after Norman Cousins, the author of the 1979 bestseller *Anatomy of an Illness as Perceived by the Patient*, and an early proponent of mind-body medicine. In the mid-1960s, Cousins was diagnosed with a supposedly incurable disease of the connective tissues that left him nearly paralyzed. After researching the detrimental effects of stress on the immune system, he devised his own regimen that emphasized the power of positive emotions, including the importance of laughter, which he claimed relieved pain and helped him sleep.

I arrange a phone interview with Dr. Michael Irwin, Norman Cousins Professor of Psychiatry and Biobehavioral Sciences and director of the Cousins Center. Irwin has just completed a study that shows that the practice of tai chi significantly improved sleep quality in older adults. Irwin randomly assigned 112 patients into two groups, one practicing tai chi for twenty-five weeks, the other taking classes in healthy lifestyles, including sleep hygiene. The people in the tai chi group reported better sleep quality, less drowsiness, and increased concentration. "Stress affects every aspect of our health, but I consider it a key factor that contributes to the onset and perpetuation of poor sleep," he tells me. "Older adults are particularly prone to sleep problems, but sleeping pills can impact cognitive functioning and increase risk of falling.

Learning tai chi is all part of the idea of promoting healthy aging and instilling good habits before clinically severe sleep problems develop."

Most ancient healing practices, such as traditional Chinese medicine and Ayurvedic medicine, acknowledged the link between emotions and illness. In the West, however, doctors have tended to view the body and mind as distinct and separate entities; physical complaints had physical causes that could be ameliorated with the proper medicine or procedure.

But what of patients who still complained of symptoms even after medical tests failed to turn up something wrong? In *The Cure Within,* Harvard professor Anne Harrington explores the various ways we've tried to understand illness and suffering, from biblical narratives, through the "power of suggestion," to our more recent infatuation with the mystical East. Harrington dates the beginning of this eastward journey to the late 1960s, when the Beatles went to India to visit the Maharishi Mahesh Yogi, sparking the counterculture's fascination with Transcendental Meditation (TM).

Around the same time, Harvard Medical School cardiologist Herbert Benson was exploring the impact of stress on hypertension by teaching squirrel monkeys to either raise or lower their blood pressure by responding to colored lights. The monkeys who were "rewarded" for higher blood pressure ultimately developed hypertension. In a later study of TM practitioners, Benson found that they were able to lower their heart rate, blood pressure, and metabolism through meditation alone. In an attempt to dissociate his work from Transcendental Meditation and the counterculture, Benson labeled the effect "the relaxation response." Sixty years earlier, the Harvard physiologist Walter Cannon had discovered the "fight or flight response"—the body's evolutionary ability to react to stress by releasing certain hormones to prepare us to "fight" or "flee." According to Benson, our ancestors had passed down an equally important tool: "the ability to heal and rejuvenate our bodies." In 1975, he turned his Westernized version of TM into a bestseller, *The Relaxation Response.*

Throughout the 1970s, biofeedback, which was an outgrowth of psychologist Edmund Jacobson's progressive relaxation techniques, was making headway with people who wanted to learn how to relax without a mantra or the promise of transcendence. Aided by a machine that provided measurable feedback, patients could track changes in certain physiological processes, ultimately learning to bring them under some degree of voluntary control. In 1979, Jon Kabat-Zinn, who was schooled in both Buddhist meditation and molecular biology, set up a program at the University of Massachusetts Medical Center based on the Buddhist technique of mindfulness. Like Benson, he minimized its Eastern origins by referring to it as "stress reduction." In 1997, Kabat-Zinn collaborated with neuroscientist Richard Davidson in an experiment in which they recorded the brain waves of employees at a Wisconsin biotech company before and after the subjects completed an eight-week course in mindfulness meditation. What they discovered was that even a short program in meditation produced beneficial changes, with participants showing a significant increase in certain regions of the left prefrontal cortex, an area of the brain behind the left forehead that is associated with more positive emotions. This result was consistent with the collaborative work Davidson had done with Tibetan Buddhist monks, using brain-scanning technologies to gain insight into how the mind can be sculpted and shaped through regular meditation. At Harvard Medical School, Dr. Gregg Jacobs and Dr. Richard Friedman measured the effects of meditation-based relaxation techniques on brain-wave activity, showing that after six weeks, the subjects who practiced meditation, as opposed to a group listening to music, produced greater reductions in brain arousal as measured by slow-wave theta brain activity. (Theta is produced during the transition from wake to sleep.) Similar studies of insomnia treatments aimed at reducing arousal have also reported positive results, but everybody seems to agree that more research is needed.

The next week, I leave my boots at home and bring an old pillow I find stashed in the back of my closet. It's decorated with green cabbage roses, a remnant of my past life as chatelaine of an "English country" apartment. I stuff the pillow into an old canvas bag and carry it to class.

"Hey, that's a real collector's item," says the young businessman.

"Oh, I don't really think so. I mean, it's just a pillow."

"No," he says. "The bag."

The bag is badly stained from the time I spilled red wine on it during a picnic in Central Park before a production of *All's Well That Ends Well*. Up until recently, it has been in the trunk of our car, on top of a plaid blanket that a friend's dog had thrown up on. I honestly don't see how it could be a collector's item.

"See, right there," he says, pointing to the handles. "'Drexel Burnham '88.'"

Back in the eighties, Lee worked for Drexel Burnham Lambert, before the federal government indicted Mike Milken on federal racketeering and fraud charges. We were married two months before the firm went bankrupt, and when I recited "for richer or poorer," I couldn't stop laughing because I'd predicted Drexel's end was near. Since the minister had previously advised us *not* to get married on the basis of a lengthy "compatibility test" he'd administered, my cracking up during our solemn vows only reinforced his impression that we were a terrible fit: That was twenty years ago and we're still married and Drexel memorabilia is now apparently hot.

"You really should put that bag up on eBay," the man tells me.

"I've got a ton of this stuff at home."

"You could make a fortune."

Normally, I would have tossed the bag into the adjacent coatroom, but I bring it into the classroom with me in case someone recognizes its value as a highly prized collectible. We're a smaller group this time, but the newlyweds are here, along with the cute middle-aged couple, the wife wearing another pretty necklace, the blond businesswoman in sneakers instead of heels. We all sit together in a close circle, with Jan at twelve o'clock. I'm hoping he'll ask how our meditation practice has been progressing so I can boast that I've done it every day, but he begins talking about his guru, Sathya Sai Baba, who since the 1940s has been encouraging religious tolerance, urging his followers not to abandon their own religions but to cultivate truth, peace, and nonviolence through meditation and good works.

"In the West, meditation still has the connotation of spirituality / religion," Jan says. "We still haven't fully grasped the notion of those two things not being synonymous. So when we think about meditation, we often think about chanting, and for a lot of people, chanting is connected to religion. When I was twenty-two, I remember being out in San Francisco walking along Fisherman's Wharf and one of the members of the Hare Krishna movement came up to me and gave me a book with a picture of the god Krishna in it. He had blue skin. I'd been raised Protestant, and remembering the teachings of Christianity about worshipping false idols, I started thinking, 'You'll burn in hell for this!' I immediately put the book away. It fascinated me but at the same time frightened me, and that combination of awe and fear was the same approach that I had to meditation. I associated it with a religion that was different from the one in which I was raised. That's an obstacle for some people. But every road leads to the summit. When you're at the bottom of the mountain, you can't see across it to recognize that all religions have similarities, but the closer you get to the top, the more the mountain narrows and these differences recede."

He hands out a copy of the Gayatri Mantra, the ancient universal prayer recited before meditation. It's in Sanskrit, the classic lit-

erary language of India, and it looks unpronounceable. Jan recites
it for us in a singsong voice:

> *Om bhur bhuvah suvah*
> *Tat savitur varenyam*
> *Bhargo devasya dhimahi*
> *Dhiyo yo nah prachodayat*

We repeat the words after him, mangling them so badly that Jan
has difficulty keeping a straight face. He translates the prayer for
us: "O Mother who lives in the past, present, and future. In heaven,
earth, and below. And all the attributes. I pray to thee to illumine
my intellect. Just as the splendid sunlight dispels all darkness. I pray
to thee to make my intellect serene and bright and enlightened." It
reminds me of the Hail Mary, minus the emphasis on praying for
"us sinners." We repeat the Gayatri Mantra three times, the fluid
rhythm taking me back to my early churchgoing days, when Gre-
gorian chant was part of the Catholic liturgy. Afterward, we immediately go into a ten-minute meditation, and this time, propped on
my cabbage-rose pillow, in sweatpants and stocking feet, I am better prepared to focus on my breath and "so-hum." I do this successfully for all of two minutes, and then I start thinking of my
Drexel bag, picturing it as a rival to the Hermès Birkin. I begin cat-
aloguing all the other Drexel paraphernalia stashed in various
closets—the shoelaces, the T-shirts, the mugs. Then I remember
that I tossed everything out during a particularly aggressive spring
cleaning a few years ago, and now I'm filled with regret, not only
about the Drexel memorabilia but about all the college photo-
graphs my first serious boyfriend "lost," about the Art Deco furniture I should have kept instead of selling it back to the dealer at a
fraction of its original price; about the Central Park West apartment now worth fourteen million dollars that Lee's parents should
have bought instead of moving into a rental. Why can't people just
hold on to things?

"Om," Jan chants. I open my eyes. The ten minutes are up, and I'm mad at myself for thinking about holding on to things when I should be letting go. In my brief experience meditating I've revealed myself to be a totally shallow, materialistic person.

We begin doing some of the qigong exercises that Jan describes as the Eight Brocade, sometimes called the Eight Jewels or Eight Pieces of Silk as a way of signifying their precious status within Chinese medicine and the martial arts. Comprising a series of stretching and breathing routines, the Eight Brocade dates back to the fifth century A.D. and was designed to ensure health and longevity. Jan starts with Pressing the Heavens with Two Hands, which we learned last week, and then demonstrates Drawing the Bow and Letting the Arrow Fly. It requires a bit of coordination, but it's a great stretch, especially for someone who sits at a computer all day. We end with Bouncing on the Toes, and while it sounds easy, after doing it forty times we're all complaining about our aching calf muscles.

We sit back down on the floor while Jan leads us in "light meditation," telling us to visualize pure white light flowing down like water through the tops of our heads, down through our foreheads, illuminating every cell and atom. "Now imagine this pure white light flowing down your throats, illuminating your hearts and solar plexus," he says. "With every breath, imagine drawing in this white light, imagine it flowing down the front of our body, flowing down the front of your legs, pushing the cold air from your knees, bringing in warmth and light . . ."

When we open our eyes I am totally, utterly relaxed, although I do think it's somewhat funny that I'm doing light meditation with someone who works for a company that actually provides my electricity. After class I ask him if he thinks that meditation is beneficial to people with insomnia, and he tells me that in high school he had terrible sleep problems. "It was like playing an endless series of movie trailers over and over again in my mind," he says. "One of the things I've found with meditation is that it's a more powerful means of refreshing the mind and body than even sleep. With sleep, you are prone to dream, and sometimes you can wake up from those dreams feeling battered, as if you just ran a marathon. You're all caught up in the emotion of the dream. Meditation can give you a deeper feeling of peace."

For the next month I let nothing get in the way of meditation. Jan had given us a link to Sai Baba chanting the Gayatri Mantra, so after listening to it repeatedly, I've almost mastered the pronunciation. Sitting atop my cabbage-rose pillow, in front of a lavender candle that occasionally hisses and sends off sparks, I begin with the prayer and try to focus on my breathing. Even in the short time I've allocated—ten minutes to the exact second—I'm bombarded with thoughts and feelings. I hear the Little Elephants running overhead—anger. I worry about my elderly parents—fear. My stomach grumbles—hunger. My neck aches—pain.

One day, after fielding a barrage of worrisome, unpleasant thoughts, I start beating myself up for letting my mind act in such an untidy, undisciplined way. I call myself names; I picture myself at my own throat. I can't imagine how anyone would consider meditation relaxing because it's not. It's hellish. I try to remember to breathe but feel as if I'm drowning, my own brain waves crashing over my head. And then suddenly a voice says, "Be kinder to yourself." The voice is coming from deep inside me, from a place I didn't even know existed. Tears spring to my eyes and roll down my cheeks. I'm not someone who cries easily, and in all my years of therapy I've only twice pulled tissues from the box my therapist keeps handy, but now I'm sobbing. Feeling ridiculous sitting cross-legged while weeping convulsively, I lie down on the floor and cry into my pillow. When I realize the strange voice I heard was actually mine, I cry even harder.

When Lee comes home he immediately wants to know why I'm so upset. "Your eyes are all swollen," he says. "Did something bad happen today?"

"No, actually something good happened," I say, telling him about the voice. "I just hope I can hear it again."

Over the past few weeks, the class has grown increasingly smaller, and tonight it's just the hard-core regulars. Even though we've been sitting in a circle with our eyes closed for the past two months, I don't know any of the other students' names and still think of them as "Woman in Necklace" or "Guy Who Covets Drexel Bag." As he does every week, Jan talks for a few minutes before we meditate, and this time he returns to the idea of the importance of regular practice.

"Meditation is truly a discipline," he says. "If I'm not meditating regularly, I tend to multitask and imitate the 'monkey mind'—that is, I'll do one thing and then another, like a mind out of control. Ideally, the best time to meditate is predawn, when the body is refreshed from sleep and the responsibilities of the day haven't already weighed upon you. But it's probably just as important to be consistent." He tells us that through meditation he was able to withstand having a tooth pulled without any anesthetic. While that's not one of my personal goals, I could certainly use some help ignoring the flickering fluorescent light and the incessant hallway noise. Don't people know we're meditating in here? After we practice the Gayatri Mantra, which I'm pleased to report I've totally nailed, he gives us a new one—the Asathoma Prayer, which we're supposed to recite after meditation. We repeat after him:

> Asatho maa sad gamaya
> Thamaso maa jyothir gamaya
> Mrithyor maa amritham gamaya

We end with "Shanti," the Sanskrit word for "peace." "This mantra has different meanings," Jan explains. "Some are more complicated than others, but I like to think of it as 'Lead me from untruth to truth. Lead me from darkness to light. Lead me from death to immortality.'"

This time when we begin meditating I'm better able to block out the hallway noise, but I'm a little disappointed that my "voice" has gone silent. Not that I expected to turn into Joan of Arc, but having experienced such a catharsis, it's a letdown to realize that meditation doesn't always yield such rich insights. After class I confess to Jan that I've stalled out. "Oh, that happens to everyone," he says, smiling. "You've just got to stick with it. You'll see."

If the Sisters of Notre Dame inculcated one thing in my brain, it was the importance of being disciplined, so I do stick with it, and over the next month of regular practice I begin to notice a sense of greater calm. I imagine it's like what a novice marathon runner experiences when she goes that extra mile without feeling so winded. After three months of daily meditation, I'm beginning to feel more rooted. I'm also sleeping much better. Perhaps it's because I feel calmer, or maybe it's the placebo effect. I don't know, but it seems to be working.

Over the next six weeks, Jan covers a lot of territory, introducing us to the seven major chakras, a word derived from Sanskrit, meaning "wheel." He explains how the body has seven energy centers that resemble spinning wheels; they are located along the line of the spinal column, on both the front and back of the body, and they regulate the flow of energy through it. "Everything—our emotions, our experiences, our states of awareness—is divided into seven categories, each associated with a particular chakra," he explains. "Let's say you're feeling tense or emotionally upset about something. It will disturb the energy balance in the chakra associated with the part of the physical body linked to that chakra—your stomach or lungs, for example."

Jan gives us a handout depicting a man with different-colored chakras running up and down his body. "Each chakra is associated with one of the seven colors of the rainbow," he explains. I'm trying to keep an open mind, but Jan is losing me here. I think he sounds ridiculous. He has us close our eyes while we "activate" our chakras, imagining red at the base of the spine, orange at the *dantien*, yellow at the solar plexus, green at the heart, blue at the base of the throat, purple at the third eye, and pink at the crown. As he leads us through it, though, I actually enjoy it; when we "move" the lights from the back up the front, the colors blend together, as if I'm actually creating my own rainbow. Later, we'll learn a corresponding chant; the chakras are associated not only with color and light but also with sound and vibration.

Another week Jan explains "working with intention," a central concept of most religious traditions, in which "intent" is viewed as the force behind free will, directing it toward good or evil. More recently, however, the idea was taken up by Wayne Dyer, who, in his book *The Power of Intention* writes that intention is not something we "do" but an invisible field of energy that we connect to with our inner awareness. As Jan talks about this energy, I begin thinking of the universe as a vast utility company with powers we've yet to tap into. He explains that before an important meeting he states his intention in the positive, visualizing the outcome he'd like to achieve and then acting upon the inner picture. "More often than not," he says, "it works." Except for the "invisible field of energy," the idea is not far off from Norman Vincent's Peale's *The Power of Positive Thinking*. I decide to try it before going to bed, visualizing sleeping through the night and waking up refreshed. I find that it's an effective method, although since I'm also meditating and doing the qigong exercises, it may simply have to do with my overall reduced stress.

At the end of the twelve-week session, I am so pleased with my progress that I decide to sign up for the summer course. Jan assures me that it will be a continuation of what we've already learned, and when I arrive at Room S104, I'm relieved that it's a tiny class and that Woman in Necklace and her husband are there. Without having to go into a lengthy explanation, Jan begins with light meditation, and very quickly I'm able to tune out the distractions and become absorbed in the process. At some point, however, I'm jolted back into awareness by a man shouting, *"The people from the class were sent to the wrong place. They're outside!"* Seconds later, a dozen disgruntled people troop into the classroom, where Jan invites them to sit down. It's suddenly very crowded and I feel myself tensing up.

"You expect me to actually sit *cross-legged?*" a woman says in a loud voice. "I'm seventy-four. *Seventy-four!* I can't get into this position. I thought we were going to meditate in chairs."

While someone goes to get the woman a chair, I glance around at the new people. I immediately don't like them. There's a woman in big sunglasses and a ton of jewelry that jangles every time she moves and a man who keeps snapping his suspenders as if he's Gordon Gekko. The others have no distinguishing characteristics except for their sour faces. "This is what you get when you take a summer course in New York," I tell myself. "Anybody who is anybody is out of town." But then I realize *I'm* here. I'm in town. As I try to be kinder to myself, I'm trying to be kinder to others. But it's hard, especially today.

Jan goes through a brief introduction, talking about some of the Sanskrit prayers he'll be introducing. The seventy-four-year-old woman, who is now sitting in a chair, shouts, "San—*what?* You've got to speak louder. I can't hear you. I'm seventy-four!" She moans and groans throughout our next meditation, and afterward Jan explains how we can use the white light to form a protective barrier around us—a cocoon of light, as it were. As he talks, I feel as if he is directing his comments at me, but I want to meditate, not build a fort. When we start doing the qigong exercises, the seventy-four-year-old woman has a near fit. "What?" she says. "We have to move? I just sat down." The woman wearing all the bracelets is making a terrible racket as she begins Pressing the Heavens with Two Hands. I tell myself there's no sense getting overly agitated because I'm never coming back here. That's it. I'm done.

At the end of class Jan announces that he won't be here the following week and that he's looking for someone to take over. He appears to be staring at me. Is he insane? I'm not leading the class. I'm *leaving* it. When I don't volunteer, he looks over at Woman in Necklace, suggesting "Maybe you both can split it." She immediately agrees. I'm trapped.

"Didn't you die when all those people started streaming in and they were all so noisy?" I say to her on the way out.

"Yeah," she says, "but you know what? It's nice to share what we've learned. By the way, my name is Rachel."

"*You're* leading a meditation class?" my sister Nancy says when I tell her what happened. "That's hysterical!"

"Why?"

"I don't know, because it's *you*."

The class is only a day away, and I'm starting to get nervous. To make sure I remember how to do the qigong exercises, I go on YouTube, watching someone who appears to be doing them in prison. The night of the class I meet Rachel a few minutes beforehand to go over the plan. We agree that I'll do light meditation, she'll do chakras, and we'll split the Eight Brocade. I'm up first, and as Jan did before every class, I talk about my own relatively brief experience with meditation and how it's been very helpful with my insomnia.

"I don't sleep either," the older woman says. "I've never slept. I'm a composer, and all night long I'm hearing songs in my head."

As I lead the meditation, I begin riffing on the concept of the white light as a cocoon. "Just imagine these bands of white light wrapping around you," I say, "encasing you in a cocoon of light, a harmonious, restful cocoon . . ."

In a repeat of the previous week, I hear someone walking into the room and I open one eye. A middle-aged woman, with short gray hair and glasses, is standing before me, and she looks mad.

Why is everyone coming into the room angry? Now that I've wrapped the class in bands of white light, turning them into glowing mummies, there is no way I'm breaking the spell. When I finish, she's still there, still mad.

"I was sent to the wrong room," she says. "Plus I have a bad knee and I can't sit down."

"Use a chair!" the older woman shouts. "That's what I do."

Someone gets the new woman a chair while I begin Pressing the Heavens with Two Hands. The woman immediately objects. "I didn't know there were exercises involved. The catalogue didn't say that. Why wouldn't the catalogue make that clear?"

"Honestly, I have no idea. I'm not the real teacher. He's off today."

"Who are you?"

"I'm just a student."

I return to the exercises, opting for Punching with Angry Eyes, which involves squinting like a gunslinger and jabbing the air with both fists. I move on to the second-most aggressive exercise in the Eight Brocade, Drawing the Bow and Letting the Arrow Fly.

"Listen here, I'm an old woman!" the seventy-four-year-old shouts. "I can't do these exercises. They're much too hard."

"Older people in China have been doing these exercises for centuries," I say.

"But I don't live in China."

"Okay, I'll help you," I say, guiding her arm as she pulls the invisible bow. We do it together until she finally gets the knack of it. That night I sleep a full eight hours. The next morning, before my annual physical, I meditate for ten minutes in the waiting room. When the nurse takes my blood pressure, which is normally 120/80, it's 100/70. "Wow, that's low," she says.

At the next class, people are coming in late again in the middle of meditation. The middle-aged woman who needs a chair decides she wants a different chair, and after she drags one out of the room, she drags another in. Three more people come in and sit down. I open my eyes and look across at another man, who makes a gesture as if to say, "What the hell is going on here?" Next, someone's cell phone rings. At this point, even Jan opens his eyes. "We can't control the outside," he says. "We can only control how we react to things. We should only hope that someone interrupts us, because then we can put that to the test. It's relatively easy to meditate in a quiet room with a candle. The trick is to create that same quiet, peaceful place even in the middle of chaos."

We start working with the chakras, with Jan explaining how important it is to activate the green chakra in order to open up our hearts. "I want you to send out love, not only to your friends and loved ones but to people you may not like," he says.

"I've suffered from anxiety and depression since I was in my mother's womb," the older woman volunteers. "If I send the green light to my son, will he feel it and call me?"

"I'm going on a job interview tomorrow," says a young man, who has spent the past three classes diligently taking notes on a yellow pad. "What if I send the green light to the person interviewing me?"

Jan tells him about the power of intention, then suggests that before the interview he meditate for at least ten minutes to clear his mind.

"How do you spell *om?*" the man asks. He writes "OM" in big letters on his pad, and then when Jan tells him he should repeat it three times, he writes "OMx3."

Suddenly the woman with the noisy bracelets lets out a scream. "Oh my God! I think I saw a mouse. I'm terrified of mice." She starts screaming again. "I think it ran under the radiator! I can't believe it! I think I'm going to faint. I may have to leave."

"Oh, well, it's gone now," Jan says. "Don't worry, it won't hurt you."

At the end of class, Jan tells us that he has to be away next week for his job and asks Rachel and me to substitute for him. Following the same formula, Rachel takes the chakras and we split the Eight

Brocade, but this time I teach the Gayatri Mantra and the Asath-oma Prayer, writing everything down phonetically on a piece of paper and passing it around. Then I sing it and they follow along. I haven't done any singing in a long time, and even though it's in an ancient language I don't understand and the music is atonal, it feels good to use my voice again. After we meditate, I teach the class Wise Owl Gazes Backwards, in which we slowly turn our heads in each direction, looking over our shoulders. "When doing the exercise, pick a fixed spot and really look at it," I say. "Pretend you're an owl sighting its prey."

The woman in the bangles screams, *"It's the mouse!"*

I'm thinking, "Lady, you don't have to be dramatic in your visualization," but then I notice a little brown furry thing scurrying in a corner. The woman keeps screaming, "It's the mouse! It's the mouse!" She grabs her sneakers and runs out of the room. Another woman follows her. The class is almost over anyway, so I say, "I guess that's it."

"You forgot to say 'om,'" says the young man, reading from his yellow pad.

"Ommmmm."

12

SPIRIT OF THE DREAM

Five months after my first meditation class, I have the following
dream: I'm standing at the gated entrance to a road leading to a
lush primeval forest. On my right, there's a sign that reads QUIET,
SILENT RETREAT IN PROGRESS, on my left, a row of tall bamboo trees.
I open the gate, and just as I'm taking a few tentative steps, guards
in black robes rush toward me, one holding a snarling pit bull by a
leash. The dog is wearing a spiked collar made of Popsicles. The
guards yell, "Get out! You're trespassing!" but I push them aside
and begin walking along the new path. Up ahead, the forest looks
beautiful and I am totally at peace.

Since the dream was fairly straightforward, without quick-
cutting scenes and obscure imagery, I was able to interpret it quite
easily. With meditation, I'd connected to a part of myself that I'd
suppressed, equating spirituality with my painful memories of
Catholic school. In the dream, I want to take what I've learned in
meditation class and walk along a new road—but the guards (read:
nuns) are warning me not to "trespass." In taking this new path,
I'm pitted against church *dog*ma, which ingeniously reveals itself as
a pit bull. It took me a while to figure out why the dog was wearing Popsicles, but then I realized that *pop* was shorthand for *pope* or

the Holy Father, and that *sicle* referred to the papal message known as an en*cyclical*. So basically the nuns were going to "sic" the pope on me if I dared trespass against the church. Instead of turning back, however, I move forward, beginning my own journey.

The dream fills me with hope, and immediately afterward, things begin to fall into place. Having grown discouraged by our house-hunting experience, we temporarily sidelined our real estate search, but in looking through the new listings, I notice what appears to be a lovely property in our price range. I call Sherry and we make an appointment, meeting her at her real estate office the following Saturday. She is happy to see us, calling us her "favorite clients," although since the market is beginning to slow down I wonder if "favorite" is agent-speak for "only." Nevertheless, we climb into her car and drive to the adjacent town, which isn't quite as "horsy" as the Martha Stewart/Ralph Lauren town we'd been looking in but is suitably countrified. Driving down a long driveway, we approach a pale yellow house sitting catty-corner on a hill, with views of both a pond and a lake. The house itself is small but has a living room with a large hearth and wall-to-wall bookshelves, a screened-in porch, and a pool by the lake.

"What's the name of the lake?" I ask the seller's agent, a friendly, exuberant man with a head of thick, highlighted hair.

"Robin Hood," he says.

"Did you hear that?" I say to Lee. "The lake is named after your favorite movie."

"And there's Sherwood Road over there," the agent says, pointing across the lake.

We walk around the property, admiring the mature rhododendron bushes and ancient oak trees, the boughs hanging protectively over the roof, giving the house the feeling of a fairy-tale hideaway. "I could sleep happily ever after here," I tell Lee.

I'm ready to put in a bid, but Lee thinks we should wait, so we make an appointment to see the house again the next day. That night I have a dream about the Good Sleep Boyfriend's deceased father, an international lawyer and avowed atheist, who lost his wife of forty years to a sudden heart attack while he was in the midst of battling cancer. He was then in his eighties, and my ex-boyfriend was afraid he wouldn't have the will to live. Not only did he survive cancer, he began dating a much younger woman and lived for the next decade. In my dream, I'm worried that I won't have enough furniture to fill the new house, but my boyfriend's father shows up as my interior decorator and tells me, "Fill your house with Swedenborg angels." Emanuel Swedenborg was a seventeenth-century Swedish scientist and philosopher who, at the age of fifty-six, began having a series of dreams that led to a spiritual awakening. Prior to my own dream, however, I had no recollection of ever hearing or reading about Swedenborg.

"I think it's a sign," I tell Lee on the way up to look at the house again. "I mean, I never heard of Swedenborg, and he's in my dream."

"You may have heard of him and filed away the information," he says.

"Possibly, but I'm not so sure."

When we arrive at the house, we meet one of the owners—a young architect with two small boys and an older husband who is seriously ill. They've decided to move out of state to be closer to relatives. While it's clearly a stressful time for them, the wife is almost heartbreakingly upbeat. It's a beautiful sunny day, the window boxes overflowing with yellow pansies. The house is light and airy, and although the bathrooms are small and the kitchen's a mess, we know from experience that nothing is perfect. We return to Sherry's office to talk about placing a bid, while the seller's agent gets a pedicure at the nail salon next door. We arrive at a suitable price before all his toes are done, and by the end of the afternoon we have a house. Before returning to the city, we decide to take a little tour of our new neighborhood, driving down a long winding road opposite a golf course. Glancing to my left, I catch sight of a wall of bamboo trees and tell Lee to pull over so I can get a better look at what turns out to be the entrance to a Zen Buddhist religious complex.

"It's the same as in the dream," I say, getting out of the car. "Look, there's the gate and the road and the sign that reads QUIET, SILENT RETREAT IN PROGRESS. And up there, there's the forest. It's all here!"

"I'm sure we've gone down this road before," Lee says.

"Maybe, but do you remember this particular spot?"

"No. I don't think I've ever seen it before."

"Well, I swear I've *never* seen it. So how could I dream about it? It's like I've been here before. I know this place."

"I can't explain it," Lee says. "Weird things happen."

"How can you prove whether at this moment we are sleeping and all our thoughts are a dream," I say, "or whether or not we are awake and talking to one another in the waking state? Alan sent me that quote right before he died. It's Plato."

"*Alan* knew Plato?"

"That's not the point! There are more things in heaven and earth, *Lee,* than are dreamt of in your philosophy."

"Can't argue with that."

The International Association for the Study of Dreams is a non-profit organization dedicated to the "pure and applied investigation of dreams and dreaming." Its members come from all over the world, representing a variety of different disciplines, including psychology and psychiatry, anthropology, theology, philosophy, and the arts. Every summer IASD holds a five-day annual conference, and this year I've joined them for "The Spirit of the Dream," at Sonoma State University, in the heart of California wine country. At the registration table I'm handed a map of the campus, where everything is named after wine varietals. I'll be staying in Sauvignon Village, in the Grenache building, not far from Fumé Blanc, Burgundy, and Sirah.

My room is what you'd expect from a college dorm—small, with twin beds and bad acoustics. I can hear the Italian man next door talking loudly on his cell phone. *Buona notte! Ciao!* I've made a terrible mistake coming here. After finally getting a grip on my insomnia, I'm going to destroy all my good progress by sleeping in a flimsy dorm room named after a wine I've never heard of. I hope it's not red. Red keeps me up at night. I remind myself to take a deep breath and calm down. It will be okay.

I missed last night's opening reception, where newcomers had a chance to meet "like-minded dreamers" and hobnob with "dream luminaries," but I'm hoping to catch up with some of them today. The New York psychologist Ross Levin warned me that some of the people at the IASD conference might appear a little "flaky." He was a member of the organization but quit seven years ago. "People who are attracted to dreams are very different types than those attracted to science," he said. "They tend to be interested in their own experiences, but when you have phenomenal experiences without method, it just adds up to a lot of New Age drumming, get-in-touch-with-your-inner-shaman kind of stuff."

Since dreams can't be studied directly—only the dreamer "sees" the dream—they've often been associated with the mystical. The ancient Greeks believed they were messages from the gods; in biblical times, they were prophesies. Modern-day dream science began with Freud, who in 1899 published *The Interpretation of Dreams,* in which he proposed that dreams are the guardians, not the disturbers, of sleep. Dr. Margaret Gilmore, a psychoanalyst who teaches dream analysis at the New York Psychoanalytic Society and Institute, explained it to me this way: "In his book, Freud writes about eating salty foods before going to bed, and then having a dream about drinking a tall glass of cool water. By translating the wishful thought into a dream in which the wish is satisfied, sleep is therefore 'protected.'"

With the discovery of REM in the fifties, dreams dominated sleep research with the hope that the new "dream laboratories," with their state-of-the-art equipment, would finally uncover the mystery of why we dream. When that didn't happen, many sleep researchers abandoned the field, pouring their efforts into studying narcolepsy and other diseases. Dream research peaked in the late 1960s and then began a slow decline. The next significant development came in 1977, when two Harvard neurophysiologists, Allan Hobson and Robert McCarley, proposed the "activation-synthesis model of dream production." It was a full frontal attack on Freud. Hobson and McCarley argued that the primary motive for dreaming wasn't psychological but physiological, describing dreams as reactions to random nervous-system stimuli originating in the pons, a structure in the brain stem responsible for REM. (It was widely assumed that REM sleep and dreaming were interchangeable, although investigators had reported evidence of NREM—or non-REM—dreams as early as 1960.) According to Hobson and McCarley, dreams result when the brain "synthesizes" this meaningless nerve activation, attempting to organize it into a coherent story. Hobson described Freud's dream theory as the "most fanciful, delicious, absurd theory that anyone's taken seriously for 100 years." In 1983, Francis Crick and the mathematician Graeme Mitchison proposed that REM sleep was the brain's way of discarding useless data, asserting that "we dream in order to forget." They subsequently amended that catchy slogan to "We dream to reduce fantasy" or "We dream to reduce obsession."

Since then, the public debate has tended to pit those who dismiss dreams as little more than mental fireworks—the Hobsonians—against those who believe that they are deeply meaningful—the Freudians. While this is an oversimplification—for several years Hobson himself kept a dream journal—the either/or story line has persisted, with Mark Solms, a South African neuropsychoanalyst, the most recent Hobson antagonist. After studying a group of people who could no longer achieve REM sleep as a result of damage to the pons, he discovered that they were still having dreams. Further research led him to locate the origins of dream content not in the stem but in the "higher" parts of the brain that energize our drive for food, water, and sex, lending credence to Freud's theory that dreams are disguised wishes. Solms and Hobson took their disagreement to *Scientific American,* with Solms's article titled "Freud Returns" and Hobson's response "Like a Bad Dream."

Robert Stickgold, who has spent his career studying dreams, sometimes in collaboration with Hobson, believes that dreams foster learning by building associations between different memories. In one study, Stickgold had twenty-seven subjects play the videogame Tetris before going to sleep. Upon awakening, seventeen subjects reported seeing the same images of the falling, rotating Tetris blocks. What's interesting is that five of the subjects were amnesiacs, who had no memory of playing the game but still dreamt of the blocks. This indicated to Stickgold that the brain employs vast associative networks not just to remember images but to make sense of them.

Over the past forty years, G. William Domhoff, a psychology professor at the University of California, Santa Cruz, has catalogued more than twenty-two thousand dreams. (All are available on the website DreamBank.net.) His research has led him to conclude that "dreams have meaning but no purpose." While people over the centuries have developed many uses for them—in religious or healing ceremonies, for example—he believes that they serve no biological function. Children under the age of six almost never dream, he says, and adults with certain brain injuries that prevent them from dreaming still report sound sleep. In addition, people recall only a small fraction of their dreams, which rarely contain solutions to problems.

All these are merely theories, though, and since we still haven't figured out why we sleep, why should dreaming be any different? After unpacking my bag, I race across campus to my first symposium on psi dreams—dreams that manifest varieties of ESP, such as telepathy or precognition. Over the years I've had several such dreams and have never been able to make sense of them. One involved a woman I met through the Good Sleep Boyfriend; at one time we'd been quite close but over the years we lost touch. I kept meaning to call her, but I somehow never did. In the dream, she's sitting at the deathbed of her mother-in-law, a woman I knew only slightly, and I'm looking down from above. When I woke up the next morning, I mentioned the dream to Lee, speculating that it was about my desire to reconnect with something that was dead to me—in this case, my friendship. An hour later, the GSB called to let me know that my friend's mother-in-law had died. My friend had been at her bedside, just as in the dream.

It turns out that such dreams happen with great frequency, according to Rita Dwyer, who is chairing the symposium. In 1959 she was nearly burned to death when rocket fuel exploded in the aerospace laboratory where she was working as a research chemist. For weeks beforehand, a co-worker had been having nightmares of a similar accident in which he'd rescued her from flames, and these "dream rehearsals" served as practice for the real explosion. The event changed Dwyer's life. In trying to make sense of her own experience, she eventually left the aerospace industry, "trading outer space for inner space," and started a dream group outside Washington, D.C. The group has been meeting for nearly thirty years, and after listening to hundreds of dreams, Dwyer believes that if we all keep a "dream journal," we'll see evidence of "psi phenomena" that will alert us to illness, death, and natural disasters. "Dreams are much more than they were once thought to be," she says, "and we as dreamers are much more than we thought ourselves to be."

I've always thought of myself as a prolific and creative dreamer, but in listening to the other three speakers, I realize that I'm a rank amateur. Writer and researcher Judy Gardiner relates a "cosmic dream," in which her mother was a simile for Mother Earth, the kitchen floor for the earth's crust, dinner plates for tectonic plates, and urine for uranium. "Ultimately, the dream fragments joined to sound an ecological warning to mankind," she says, going on to explain that the logic of cosmic dreaming doesn't follow the same range of emotion found in personal dreaming. "Concern for species survival outweighs concern for self." Robert Hoss, the founding director of the DreamScience Foundation, wonders if such dreams that transcend personal experience, which Carl Jung called "big dreams," are a "foretelling of things to come for earth and mankind, or are they simply picturing an ego shattering (earth shattering) transformation of one's own personal psyche?" Reading from *The Portable Jung,* he explains the psychiatrist's concept of the "collective unconscious" as something that "unites all humanity," containing the "whole spiritual heritage of mankind's evolution." The collective unconscious is apparent in archetypal dream imagery that transcends the individual to "reveal a truth at a cosmic level," as well as revealing important truths "in the transformation of the dreamer."

Maybe I'm too selfish, but I've never had a dream in which anything symbolized a tectonic plate or sounded an ecological warning. My dreams tend to relate to my emotional life, but perhaps I'm thinking too small. Ed Kellogg, who holds a Ph.D. in biochemistry from Duke University but who lists his occupation as "phenomenologist," has recorded twenty thousand of his own dreams, and he estimates that in 80 percent of them his "dream Self" is different from his "waking Self." Sometimes he's a different age, race, or gender. In response to the question "Why do we dream?" Kellogg believes the purpose is to reconnect to our "greater Selves," allowing a "therapeutic release from the constraints of a time space-bound existence."

After "Cosmic Dream Connections," I'm ready for something a little more down-to-earth, so I attend a workshop on "dream collage." The workshop's leader, Emily Anderson, is a multimedia artist and teacher who believes that visual imagery can help convey the essence of dreams that are sometimes "beyond words." She's brought dozens of magazines with her, and we grab a stack, then sit down at one of six tables. Before we begin cutting and pasting, we're supposed to first share a dream with the others at our table so that we can later examine the subconscious material that presents itself through the artwork. My two table mates are cancer survivors, having recently undergone mastectomies and hysterectomies; their bond is immediate, and instead of sharing dreams, they trade stories of personal struggle. I'm the third wheel, so I just listen. Having never done collage before, I randomly rip pages from magazines, cutting out any pictures that appeal to me. There's no method at all to what I'm doing. It's just rip, cut, and paste. When we're finished, we're told to go out into the hallway so we can get a better look at everybody else's work. Many of the collages are beautiful and extremely accomplished, some folding out like accordions. Mine is easily the most basic, without apparent theme or specific design.

During the lunch break, I sit outside on the lawn eating a yogurt, studying the afternoon's schedule. Pulling a bottle of water from my bag, I spill a few drops on the collage, where it makes a mark on the central image, that of Ruth Bernhard's famous photograph "In the Box, Horizontal." It's of a sleeping woman stretched in a rectangular box. I'd picked that image because I have another photograph from that series in my office. Looking more closely at the collage, I see that I'd pasted a picture of a knight over the woman's shoulder. The other images that stand out include a grandfather clock; a waterfall; a 1950s bride and groom; and a Robert Mapplethorpe self-portrait, in which he holds a death's head cane. Having written Mapplethorpe's biography, I knew the image well, and although he was then in his early forties, he was dying and looked like an old man. My collage, it seemed, was about death—not surprising, as I'd been sitting with two cancer survivors, but was there something else? The woman was sleeping in a confined space. Could it be a kind of crib? There was a knight standing guard. Was *knight* a play on *night*? Staring at the grandfather clock, I begin to recall an incident that happened in my parents' first apartment (picture of the 1950s bride and groom) when I shared a room with Bumpa. I was two years old and sleeping in a bed with the sides pulled up. (The box.) I'd woken Bumpa to ask for a drink of water, and carrying me downstairs, he'd slipped on the first step. We tumbled down the entire flight, Bumpa holding me tight so I wouldn't get hurt. (Waterfall.) He was unconscious for a time, and I was terrified that he was dead. My mother called the doctor, and even though I was very young, I have a distinct memory of her being very angry with me. "If you hadn't wanted the water," she said, "he wouldn't have gotten hurt."

Bumpa was ultimately okay, but I carried the guilt with me for the rest of my life, burying it so deep that it only now surfaced in a collage, and then only when I actually spilled water on it. Remembering more of the incident, I began to realize the effect it had on my sleep patterns. Getting up in the middle of the night to use the bathroom, I always walk very tentatively, as if I'm afraid of falling downstairs. By the time I get back into bed, I'm conditioned to be anxious, especially as the concept of "falling to sleep" evokes guilt over my grandfather's fall. That's why I've been telling doctors that if I can remain in the "cocoon of sleep" I'm fine, but if I "fall" out of it, I'm in trouble. While I realize this insight won't "cure" my sleep problems and probably points to only one of several contributing factors, it helps explain why meditation has been so beneficial to me. It helps curb my anxiety.

At 10:30 P.M., after dinner, I walk across the campus to attend a "full-moon sound circle." The leader of the event is a local multi-percussionist named Kim Atkinson, who first discovered African drumming in the early 1970s and later became interested in the metaphysical links between sounds and healing. He now leads classes and workshops, acting as a "facilitator" in drum circles, which are designed as "gatherings" in which everyone participates. There are about eighty people in the circle, and we've all been given percussion instruments, such as shakers, seedpods, gongs, and rain sticks. Atkinson begins drumming, and within minutes we've all joined in, the music growing louder and louder, the rhythm more intense. Encircling the perimeter, a dozen women—old women, young women, short, tall, plain, pretty—start dancing. We could be anywhere, in any period of time, and I'm sad when the music ends, because the communal spirit is uplifting. Walking back to my dorm, I forget to worry that in the twin bed with an awful mattress I won't sleep, and I wake up the next morning having had a surprisingly restful night. I immediately go outside to meditate, feeling a little foolish to be sitting cross-legged on the lawn in full view of people, but if I can't meditate here, in the land of Greater Selves and Cosmic Dreams, where can I?

Over the next few days I'm overwhelmed by the sheer diversity of courses. Where else in the same afternoon could you listen to a lecture on the dreams of Islamic militant jihadists and the nightmares of people with sleep apnea? Eager to meet a bona fide "dream luminary," I take a workshop with Jeremy Taylor, a Unitarian minister and co-founder of the organization that is now IASD. For the past forty years, Taylor has been doing dream work in schools, hospitals, prisons, residential treatment centers, and corporate boardrooms. His experience has led him to believe that dreams have multiple meanings and layers of significance, and today he's here to give us a little taste of what it's like to share dreams in a group setting. A balding, bearded Friar Tuck of a man, he has a kind face and a preacher's charisma. "There is no such thing as a bad dream," he tells us. "There are only dreams that sometimes take a dramatically negative form in order to grab our attention." He speaks of the wordless "aha!" moment of recognition, which he believes is the "only reliable touchstone of dream work." In his dream workshops, Taylor sets certain rules, such as: When addressing others about their dreams it's important to preface any remarks with "if it were my dream." He asks if anybody wants to read from their dream diaries. Many of the workshop participants are already members of local dream groups, and dozens of hands shoot up. Taylor picks a woman whose dream is titled "Suicide in Space." She describes being on a space voyage with her husband and a close friend. Realizing that they'll never reach home, she drinks cyanide. "I feel drugged but I'm not sure it worked," she says.

"If this were my dream," a man says, "I'd wonder why there were three of us on this voyage."

"If this were my dream," a woman says, "I'd wonder about my relationship with my close friend."

Taylor asks when she had the dream, and she tells him it was on June 21. "You had it on the summer solstice," he says. "So, it's a midsummer night's dream. If that were my dream, I'd say that it was very hopeful, that I was growing and changing. I'd say that my death or suicide indicates a desire for transformation—for a new person to emerge."

Taylor's workshop makes me want to join a dream group. Having discussed my dreams in therapy with the same person over the years, I can see the benefit of listening to other perspectives, especially when dealing with Jungian-style "big dreams." When I was twenty-five, I had a dream that haunts me to this day. Bumpa had just died, and after attending his funeral in Andover, I was back in my small studio apartment on the Upper East Side. The tenants had staged a rent strike, and the landlord had retaliated by turning off the heat and hot water. It was December, it was freezing, and I was totally miserable. Bumpa was the first person I'd ever lost, so bereavement was new to me, and I couldn't fully grasp the concept that I'd never see him again. He'd once made a promise that he'd make one final appearance before he moved on to the afterlife, and ten days after he died, I was asleep when I suddenly heard my grandfather's voice saying, "Good night, dear." I sat up in bed and turned on the lights. The voice was so strong and clear I was convinced that he was in the room with me. There was something else, too. Bumpa wore Aqua Velva aftershave, and suddenly the whole room smelled of it. I got out of bed and walked into the bathroom to make sure I wasn't dreaming. I still smelled his after-shave. "Good night, Bumpa," I said. The smell lingered for a few minutes and then drifted away. The dream gave me enormous comfort, and while I still missed him, I no longer grieved in the same heart-wrenching way.

Listening to Kevin Erik Kovelant present his paper "The Experience of Felt Sense in Visitation Dreams of the Dead," I begin to understand that such dreams are common throughout history and across cultures. "With sleep and death so closely linked," he says, "is it any wonder that we dream of the dead?" He has collected "felt sense" dreams from a variety of people, and many of them show similar features. "Could something be going on beyond simple grief of bereavement?" he asks. While he realizes that it's difficult to know whether the deceased person in the dream may actually have been the deceased person or a wishful projection, he thinks it's important for people who've experienced such dreams to learn from them, especially since the process of grieving has little place in modern American culture.

Deborah Coupey, Kovelant's co-presenter, goes on to discuss Patricia Garfield's seminal book on the topic, *The Dream Messenger,* in which she sets out nine steps for receiving a message from the dead, from "the Announcement" to "the Gift of the Dream Messenger." These "dream gifts" can come in the form of something concrete, such as a bowl or a vase or a brooch, or they can be more subtle. In listening to Coupey, I think of what my grandfather said to me in the dream, not goodbye, but good *night.* Coupey discusses the concept of "lucid dreams"—a state in which a person knows that he is dreaming and may even be able to influence the course of events. She cites the experience of a German psychologist who, in a lucid dream, confronted his deceased father instead of running away; at the end of the dream, the two men shook hands. "If one is talented in becoming lucid in dreams," she says, "you might have an advantage of incubating dreams from the dead."

To learn more about the process, I attend the panel "Exploring

Inner Space: Adventures in Lucid Dreaming." In the eighties, psychologist Stephen LaBerge demonstrated the scientific validity of lucid dreaming while a student at Stanford; he later founded the Lucidity Institute in Palo Alto, where he conducts dream research and training programs. Panelist Beverly D'Urso worked with LaBerge at Stanford and describes herself as an "extraordinary" lucid dreamer who believes that dreams have the power to heal. She tells of trying to help a young boy with a degenerative disease by pointing her index and middle fingers at his body and chanting the Harry Potter spell, "Scourgify." Afterward, the boy's condition improved, and while D'Urso doesn't necessarily take credit for the result, she says she was "pleased" to have tried to help. She then discusses the ethical implications of lucid dream healing, such as whether we need permission to heal people. What about our pets? Or people who have died? Can we heal our country? She lists the kinds of props we can use, such as sparks shooting from fingertips, hands-on manipulation, chants, affirmations, potions, alternative selves. At this point, I write in my notes, *"Is she crazy?"*

Robert Waggoner, author and lucid-dream expert, tells us that in 1975 he "taught" himself to dream, finding it a revolutionary psychological tool, in that he is now able to interact with "dream figures" that represent various parts of him. "I don't like to call them dream 'characters,' because I feel it denigrates them," he explains. "In your interactions with the figures, you're receiving cognitive information in a dream state." He passes out a set of "Ten Rules for More Successful Conversations with Dream Figures," including "Do not insult" them. Ed Kellogg, who is wearing a T-shirt that reads I WEAR MY POWERS FOR GOOD, describes a dream in which he'd tuned in to the afterlife of a "disincarnate man, trapped in an earthbound limbo, who had just woken up twenty-nine years after his murder." There's probably a lot more to the dream, but I sneak out of class. I need a coffee break.

My final workshop is David Jenkins's "Dreamwork: The Rashomon Approach," in which he uses Kurosawa's famous film as a way of working with dreams in a group setting. "In *Rashomon,* each person remembers a series of events very differently," he explains. "In a dream group, everyone hears the same dream from their own perspective. Rather than try to agree on a single 'correct' meaning of the dream, we encourage divergent accounts and allow them to flourish."

Jenkins, a handsome gray-haired man with a goatee, teaches classes on dreams and conducts dream groups in Berkeley. His Ph.D. study was on Emanuel Swedenborg. Before we begin, he tells us to take off our shoes—"oppression begins with the feet!" There are twenty-seven women in the workshop, along with a ponytailed man who sits quietly doing needlework. The woman next to me has a strange, exotic look; when she tells everybody that her favorite movie is *Waterworld,* in which Kevin Costner plays a sci-fi fisherman with webbed toes and gills behind his ears, I am not altogether surprised.

Jenkins picks a serious-looking woman across from me to begin the process by telling a recent dream. "Don't make eye contact with her," he says. "Eye contact is consensus building. Looking away helps you stay with *your* account."

The woman describes being in a parking lot with a friend, and they're staring at a building where she sees artistic activity going on through the windows. Her friend says, "I want to bring that to orphans." In the next scene, the woman is in a park, surrounded by homeless people. One puts his face right against hers. The woman starts crying—in real life, not in the dream—and while I know I'm not supposed to look at her, I can't help it. Others in the room are now crying, too. I'm the only one who isn't crying. What's wrong with me? Am I insufficiently in touch with my feelings? The woman then cuts to a third scene, in which people are celebrating, and she feels tremendous joy. She sees a tea bag descending from the sky, and she reaches up for it, and now she's crying again and the other people are crying, and I'm still not crying.

Now Jenkins directs people to tell the story from the perspective of the homeless man or the woman's friend. When it's my turn, he says, "I want you to tell the story from the perspective of a lady in the tea bag."

"You want me to be a lady . . . *in a tea bag?*" I say, thinking it's a pretty good description of someone with insomnia. "Well, without water, she's just a bunch of tea leaves, so I guess she needs to be activated." My dream quickly turns political, about the role of the artist in society, with the homeless man asking, "What have you done for me?" When I get to the celebratory part of the dream, I say it feels hollow, because how can we celebrate when there's so much poverty, hunger, and inequality in the world? I'm not sure why I've suddenly jumped on the soapbox; I'm not exactly Nelson Mandela in real life.

The next dream comes from a pretty woman with gray-streaked brown hair. In the dream, a friend brings her to visit her new house, which is large and white, with shiny marble floors. When the friend shows off her new baby, the woman realizes it's the one she gave up. Now she wants her baby back but realizes that her friend's husband, a wealthy Arab, will never agree. Ultimately, they work out an arrangement that allows her to be the weekend babysitter. Throughout her dream narration, the exotic-looking woman next to me has been snoring loudly. She suddenly wakes up, explaining that she has narcolepsy and that she was dreaming of her mother. "When I was a little girl," she says, "my mother had a nervous breakdown and left me. She tied me to a chair so I wouldn't run after her. My grandmother raised me. Eventually my mother came back and my grandmother let her babysit. In the dream, I realize my mother did the best she could."

I find it amazing that the woman would be having a parallel dream. Her story is so painful that everybody starts crying again. When it's time for an older woman to retell the dream from the perspective of the woman who lost the baby, she begins touching her breasts, mourning her inability to nurse it. This sets off another round of tears. I'm uncomfortable with this outward display of emotion, so when Jenkins tells me to relate the dream from the viewpoint of the house, I turn it into the White House, where Prince Bandar, the former Saudi ambassador to the United States, is visiting George Bush. The loss of the baby symbolizes lives lost in Iraq. My account is about as impersonal as it gets, and I realize that the story has touched a raw nerve, and that I purposely distanced myself from it. When Jenkins goes around the room and asks what actor we'd choose to play us in the dream, I say Emma Thompson, presumably for her stiff upper lip. The woman next to me picks an alien in a *Star Trek* episode.

At the end of the afternoon, Lee, who's been in San Francisco, joins me for a two-hour "dream hike" through a local state park. Alan Siegel, an assistant clinical professor in the psychology department at University of California, Berkeley, and a hiker and naturalist, leads a group of twenty, including four very fair-skinned psychologists from Wales and a Russian psychiatrist in heels. Though it's already 4 P.M., it's brutally hot and the Welsh contingent is growing pinker by the minute. As part of the plan, we're supposed to stop midway to share our recurring dreams, but after sitting in classrooms all day, everybody just wants to walk. A hawk comes swooping down. The Russian woman takes a picture of it. Siegel goes around plucking wildflowers, berries, and plants. "Here, this is mugwort," he says. "Place it under your pillow tonight, and you'll dream of your next lover." A woman wearing a long-sleeved shirt and a big hat introduces herself to me as a "birder and a poet."

We seem to be walking around in circles, and Lee is getting a little annoyed. "It's hot," he says. "I wish I had a Diet Coke." The Russian woman scrambles up ahead in her high heels, taking pictures of every little insect and vine. The Welsh group, who remind me of the characters in *Four Weddings and a Funeral*, are laughing and joking, eating raspberries and blackberries off bushes. One woman suggests we look at the creek, and the birder/poet seconds the motion. They both say it's a very special place. "It better be,"

Lee says. We walk for at least another half hour, and it soon becomes clear that the woman doesn't know where the creek is. Neither does the birder/poet. It's like a bad dream where you're walking around in circles and never get to your destination. Finally, the woman shouts, "I found the creek!"

It's totally dry. There's nothing there but a bunch of rocks.

"Aren't the rocks beautiful?" the birder/poet says. People gather around the rocks, admiring the colors and different shapes. The Russian woman takes pictures of the rocks, while the salmon-colored Brits look on.

"I don't get it," Lee whispers. "Am I missing something?"

"Dreamers are a different breed," I say.

The "Dream Ball" is the highlight and final event of the conference. We're supposed to come dressed or disguised as a character from one of our dreams. I ordered a Robin Hood outfit for Lee from an online costume store and a fairy costume for myself. When reading the name of the conference—"The Spirit of the Dream"—I'd thought it said "The *Sprite* of the Dream," and thinking of the stories my grandfather used to tell me about the sleep sprite, and how she used to lull little girls to sleep, I figured it was the perfect costume. "I hope other people are going to be wearing costumes," I say, wriggling into a powder-blue tutu and slipping on enormous sparkly wings.

Lee is parading around the room in brown breeches, a "microsuede" tunic, lace-up shirt, and a pointed hat with a feather. "Don't you think I look a little like Errol Flynn?" he asks. I'm about to say, "Not really," but in the spirit of the dream, I say, "As a matter of fact, you do." It's the perfect summer night—clear, with a slight breeze. Walking across campus to the commons, I wonder why nobody else I see is in costume. We run into several real-life college students who give us the kind of looks reserved for drunken alumnae whooping it up at their fortieth reunion. "We've got to turn back," I say. "We look ridiculous." As we get closer to the commons, however, I see another fairy, and then a Tin Man and a wizard. Inside, with a band named the Poyntlyss Sistars playing the best of the seventies, several hundred people, all dressed as their dream selves, are grooving away with total abandon. There's the goddess Parvati, in a slinky sequined gown, next to a garden slug. "Suicide in Space" has come as a belly dancer; Beverly d'Urso, the lucid dreamer, is wearing gigantic prosthetic breasts. The Goddess of Spring fans herself to combat global warming. Dr. Faustus dances with the Devil. When the band plays "Get Off of My Cloud," Lee begins doing the Mick Jagger impersonation that I've forbidden him to do in public, but since we're in the private realm of dreams, he can do anything he wants. As I dance, my wings keep bumping into people. Nobody seems to mind. I feel incredibly light, almost weightless. When the band takes a break, I spot the woman from the Rashomon workshop and tell her how touched I was by the story she told about her mother. After she thanks me, she asks, "Who are you supposed to be?" When I tell her, she says, "You make a lovely sleep sprite."

Thunk, thunk, thunk . . .

We're spending our first night at the new house. It's the height of the fall foliage season, and I haven't seen autumn leaves outside of Central Park in years. Things are good. I've now been meditating every day for the past eight months, and for me it's been an unqualified success. I'm sleeping very well, and even when I have an off night, I'm no longer panicky about it. Meditation is the best thing I've ever done for myself, and I can't imagine life without it. I'm also happy with the house and with the prospect of escaping the Little Elephants on weekends. But what's the thunking noise?

"Did you hear that?" I ask Lee, who replies, "How could I not?" He checks the clock. It's 2 A.M. The thunking continues.

"Do you think it's some kind of animal on the roof?" I say. "Like squirrels?"

"Try to go back to sleep."

"Do you think the house is haunted?"

He places the pillow over his head and eventually falls back asleep, while I stay up and count thunks. The next morning, I walk outside and notice that the ground is covered with acorns, the boughs extending over the roof attached to several imposing oak trees. "Come down quickly," I call to Lee. "Trees are making the noise!" After we're kept up the following night, we make an appointment with a company called SavATree to talk about killing trees. The SavATree man is understandably reluctant, telling us that while the boughs may appear to be dangerous, dangling as they do over the entire length of the roof, it would be a shame to destroy several ancient oak trees all because of a few thousand acorns. "But my wife can't sleep," Lee says. The man says it's a particularly bad year for acorns and that it will get better.

A few weeks later, I open the front door one morning and find myself face-to-face with two Canada geese. After the geese dig up our lawn and deposit their droppings everywhere, we realize that maybe we need to do something, so we go to the hardware store, where a salesman says, "Yeah, Canada geese are a nuisance." He suggests learning to live with them. Maybe there's a lesson in all of this, but right now I hate the geese and want to extradite them to Montreal. Lee goes online and finds a product called AwayWith-Geese—a flashing light enclosed in a weatherproof float that we're supposed to position in the center of the "afflicted" pond. The light blinks at night and disturbs the geese, forcing them to move on.

"Apparently geese are particularly vulnerable to sleep deprivation," Lee says.

I can't do it. There's no way I'm going to cause geese to lose sleep. "Maybe it will get better," I say.

And it does. We learn to live with the geese. The following autumn, the oak trees produce far fewer acorns. A skunk encounters the groundhog living beneath our porch and sprays it at 3 A.M., the smell wafting up to our bedroom, but that's hardly a sleep crisis. I continue to meditate and attempt to stay calm. One night, getting up for a glass of water, I worry that I must have left the porch light on because it appears to be daylight outside. Going downstairs, I look out the window to see a full moon shining on the pond. Surrounded by so many buildings in Manhattan, I hadn't seen one in a long time and had forgotten how dazzling it could be. I throw on a coat and sit on the swing in our screened-in porch. It's 4 A.M. and I'm not asleep, but who cares? Sometimes even the moon is wide awake, and it is splendid company.

ACKNOWLEDGMENTS

A book, unlike sleep, is a collaborative effort. Many people helped along the way. I'm extremely grateful to my editor, Cindy Spiegel, for her smart and sensitive editing. I'd also like to thank her talented team: Hana Landes, Beth Pearson, Margaret Wimberger, Greg Mollica, Rodrigo Corral, and Kristina Miller. A special thanks to my agent, Mark Reiter, for finding the book a good home.

Among the many people who shared their knowledge and insights with me, I'm grateful to Dan Adams, Dr. Nisha Aurora, Dr. Gregory Belenky, David Blaine, Dr. Daniel Buysse, Dr. Mary Carskadon, Dr. John Charles, Jan Childress, Dr. William Dement, Dr. Matthew Ebben, Dr. Dale Edgar, Dr. Steven Ellman, Dr. Michael Gelb, Dr. Anne Germain, Dr. Margaret Gilmore, Dr. Paul Glovinsky, Dr. Michael Irwin, Dr. Neil Harrison, Dr. Daniel Kripke, Dr. Ross Levin, Dr. Mark Mahowald, Dr. James McKenna, Dr. Galina Mindlin, Christina Molfetta, Tracy Nasca, Bryan O'Connor, Dr. Mel Pohl, Dr. Charles Pollak, Dr. David Rosenfeld, Richard Rutherford-Moore, Dr. Jerome Siegel, Dr. Arthur Spielman, Dr. Yaakov Stern, Dr. Richard Strobel, Dr. Michael Terman, Dr. Robert Troell, Dr. Michael Twery, Dr. Jeffry Vaught, Dr. Joyce Walsleben, Dr. Daniel

Williams, Matthew Wolf-Meyer, Dr. Steven Woloshin, Dr. Gary Zammit, and Dan Ziff.

I am indebted to Kenton Kroker, whose book *The Sleep of Others* provided me with a crash course in sleep history. Boris Dubrovsky and Arthur Klausner read and commented on portions of the book and their help at a critical period was very important. Thanks also to Richard David Story, who published a portion of "Polar Nights" in *Departures*.

I'd like to thank Ira Resnick for my author photo and his friendship; Chris Fogel for her graphic wizardry; and Dr. Clarice Kestenbaum for her wisdom and guidance. I am grateful as well to Jamie and Jenny Delson, Glynnis O'Connor, Robin Sherman, James Danziger, Aimee Troyan, and Dorothy Stern. A special thank-you to my wonderful parents; my sister Nancy; my niece Isabel, and, of course, Bumpa, who inspired me with his Shakespearean Kleenex.

Most of all, I am deeply grateful to my husband, Lee, for listening to me these Eight Thousand and One Nights. I couldn't imagine this tale without him.

NOTES

INTRODUCTION

5 **One "sleep eater" claimed:** Stephanie Saul, "Study Links Ambien Use to Unconscious Food Forays," *New York Times,* March 14, 2006.

5 **ABC reported:** "'Sleep Violence' Sufferer Attacked Wife Nightly," ABC News, April 30, 2006.

5 **a startling story:** Graham Lawton, "Get Ready for 24-Hour Living," *New Scientist,* February 18, 2006.

6 **"golden age of sleep research":** Chip Brown, "The Man Who Mistook His Wife for a Deer," *New York Times Magazine,* February 2, 2003.

7 **Once the recession:** Denise Gellene, "Sleeping Pill Use Grows as Economy Keeps People Up at Night," *Los Angeles Times,* March 30, 2009.

1: THE HOUSE OF PUNK SLEEP

20 **"A medium is not something":** "Marshall McLuhan, Author, Dies; Declared 'Medium Is the Message,'" *New York Times,* January 1, 1981.

2: LADY IN THE DARK

28 **In 1975:** *ADVANCE for Respiratory Care and Sleep Medicine,* American Academy of Sleep Medicine, http://respiratory-care-sleep-medicine .advanceweb.com/Editorial/Content.

28 **today there are:** American Academy of Sleep Medicine, August 2009.

28 **You can't read about:** Allan Rechtschaffen et al., "Sleep Deprivation in the Rat: X. Integration and Discussion of the Findings," *SLEEP* 12 (1989): 168–87.

32 **I hope I don't do something:** Chip Brown, "The Man Who Mistook His Wife for a Deer," *New York Times Magazine,* February 2, 2003.

33 **In 1974:** "A Science Odyssey: People and Discoveries: Johanson Finds 3.2 Million-Year-Old Lucy," www.pbs.org/wgbh/aso/databank/ entries/do74lu.html.

34 **"To the best of our knowledge":** Coren, *Sleep Thieves,* p. 38.

34 **As Rechtschaffen once said:** Ibid., p. 36.

35 **Like Rechtschaffen with his rats:** Kroker, *Sleep of Others,* p. 174.

36 **Beginning in 1917:** Ibid., p. 201.

36 **One of its most famous victims:** "Medicine: Sleeping Sickness," *Time,* April 4, 1927.

36 **A major breakthrough:** Kroker, *Sleep of Others,* p. 11.

36 **In the mid-1930s:** Alfred L. Loomis, E. Newton Harvey, and Garret A. Hobart, "Cerebral States During Sleep as Studied by Human Brain Potentials," *Journal of Experimental Psychology* 21, no. 2 (August 1937): 127–44.

36 **In the mid-1950s:** Dement and Vaughn, *Promise of Sleep,* p. 32.

39 **In 1968, Allan Rechtschaffen:** Michael H. Silber et al., "The Visual Scoring of Sleep in Adults," *Journal of Clinical Sleep Medicine* 3, no. 2 (2007).

3: ARE SLEEPING PILLS MORE DANGEROUS THAN AL QAEDA?

42 **In 1981, a four-hundred-square-foot cavity:** "Giant Fla. Sinkhole Expanding, Filling with Water," *Washington Post,* May 11, 1981.

44   **Prior to my visit:** "Lilly Completes Hypnion Purchase," *Boston Globe*, April 3, 2007.

45   **Americans spend:** Stephanie Saul, "Sleep Drugs Found Only Mildly Effective, but Wildly Popular," *New York Times*, October 23, 2007.

46   **"we published our findings":** Dale M. Edgar, William C. Dement, and Charles A. Fuller, "Effect of SCN Lesions on Sleep in Squirrel Monkeys: Evidence for Opponent Processes in Sleep-Wake Regulation," *Journal of Neuroscience* 13, no. 3 (March 1993): 1065–69.

47   **Rats dream:** Natalie Angier, "Smart, Curious, Ticklish Rats?" *New York Times*, July 24, 2007.

50   **In 1998:** Daniel F. Kripke et al., "Mortality Hazard Associated with Prescription Hynotics," *Biological Psychiatry* 43, no. 9 (May 1, 1998): 687–93.

51   **In 2008 Kripke did a study:** Daniel F. Kripke, "Possibility That Certain Hypnotics Might Cause Cancer in Skin," *Journal of Sleep Research*, September 17, 2008: 245–50.

51   **As part of Kripke's analysis:** Daniel F. Kripke et al., "Mortality Associated with Sleep Duration and Insomnia," *Archives of General Psychiatry* 59 (February 15, 2002): 131–36.

52   **According to Paul L. Schiff, Jr.:** Paul L. Schiff, Jr., "Opium and Its Alkaloids," *American Journal of Pharmaceutical Education*, Summer 2002.

53   **When Edith Wharton:** Charles McGrath, "The House of Mirth: Wharton Letter Reopens a Mystery," *New York Times*, November 21, 2007.

53   **She, too, had died:** "Anna Nicole Smith Autopsy Released," Smoking Gun (thesmokinggun.com), March 26, 2007.

53   **Chloral hydrate:** "Consumers Union Report on Licit and Illicit Drugs," www.druglibrary.org/schaffer/library/studies/cu/cu28.htm.

53   **As David Healy:** Healy, *Creation of Psychopharmacology*, p. 44.

53   **In 1948 the output:** "Grave Peril Seen in Sleeping Pills," *New York Times*, December 16, 1951.

53   **In 1951 barbiturates:** "Insanity Peril in Sleep Pills Told," *Los Angeles Times*, December 16, 1952.

54 **Similar stories were published:** "Sleeping Pills: Doorway to Doom," *Coronet,* January 1951.

54 **In 1962, President Kennedy signed:** www.fda.gov/AboutFDA/ WhatWeDo/History/CentennialofFDA/CentennialEditionofFDA Consumer/ucm093787.htm.

54 **The 1970s saw a shift:** "Your Prescriptions," *Los Angeles Times,* February 28, 1978.

54 **Leo Sternbach:** "Leo Sternbach, 97, Valium Creator, Dies," *New York Times,* October 1, 2005.

54 **The BZDs were considered safer:** R. Jeffrey Smith, "Study Finds Sleeping Pills Overprescribed," *Science* 204 (1979): 287–88.

54 **Dalmane drew the most fire:** Ibid.

55 **"Perhaps this is not":** Ibid.

55 **In 1979, twenty-eight years:** "U.S. Study of Sleep Drugs Finds Risks and Overuse," *New York Times,* April 5, 1979.

55 **Doctors began writing:** Ibid.

55 **Since its debut:** Geoffrey Cowley and Doris Iarovici, "Sweet Dreams or Nightmare? The Most Popular Sleeping Pill in the World Faces a Mounting Challenge Over Its Safety," *Newsweek,* August 19, 1991.

55 **The FDA's medical-review officer:** Ibid.

55 **In 1989 a Utah woman:** Ibid.

55 **At the same time, William Styron:** Styron, *Darkness Visible,* p. 49.

55 **"very dangerous drug":** Cowley and Iarovici, "Sweet Dreams or Nightmare?"

55 **Ultimately, Britain banned Halcion:** Elisabeth Rosenthal, "U.S. Not Planning to Ban Sleeping Pill," *New York Times,* October 3, 1991.

56 **No stranger to controversy:** Melanie Warner, "The Lowdown on Sweet?" *New York Times,* February 12, 2006.

56 **Needing a legitimate way:** Edelman 2006 corporate brochure.

56 **To coincide with the NSF's official launch:** "Health Groups' Funding Faulted," *Sacramento Bee,* June 29, 2005.

56 **The public, however, didn't know:** Ibid.56

56 **extensive ties with drug companies:** "Editorial Board Medscape: Neu-

rology & Neurosurgery," www.medscape.com/pages/public/bios/ed-neurology.

57 **In June 1993, Congress established:** *Wake Up America: A National Sleep Alert, 1993,* Report of the National Commission on Sleep Disorders Research.

57 **generated more articles:** Jane E. Brody, "America's Falling Asleep," *New York Times,* April 24, 1994.

57 **William Dement:** Kroker, *Sleep of Others,* p. 420.

57 **a "national emergency":** *Wake Up America.*

57 **This was good news:** Julie M. Donohue, Marisa Cevasco, and Meredith B. Rosenthal, "A Decade of Direct-to-Consumer Advertising of Prescription Drugs," *New England Journal of Medicine* 357, no. 7 (August 16, 2007): 673–81.

57 **According to IMS Health:** "Sleeping Pill Competition May Spur Ad War," ABC News, http://abcnews.go.com/Health/print?id=1784559.

57 **During the first eleven months:** Stephanie Saul, "Record Sales of Sleeping Pills Are Causing Worries," *New York Times,* February 7, 2006.

58 **The Sleep Disorders Institute and Clinilabs:** Gary Zammit, interview by author, New York City, January 4, 2007.

58 **At one time Zammit:** "Rozerem Expedites Experts' Dreams: Honoria," Pharma Marketing Blog, October 25, 2007, http://pharmamkting.blogspot.com/2007/10/rozerem-expedites-experts-dreams.html.

58 **Zammit has received:** Gary Zammit et al., "Evaluation of the Efficacy and Safety of Ramelteon in Subjects with Chronic Insomnia," *Journal of Clinical Sleep Medicine* 3, no. 5 (2007).

59 **They remain profitable:** Stephanie Saul, "Sleep Drugs Found Only Mildly Effective, but Wildly Popular," *New York Times,* October 23, 2007.

60 **While Sonata has been shown:** Drugs@FDA, "Sonata, Label and Approval History," www.accessdata.fda.gov/scripts/cder/drugsatfda/index.cfm.

61 **I've tried Ambien:** Stephanie Saul, "Study Links Ambien Use to Unconscious Food Forays," *New York Times,* March 14, 2006.

61   **Since I can fall asleep:** Drugs@FDA, "Ambien CR, Statistical Review and Evaluation Clinical Studies," 2005, p. 52.

62   **Trying Rozerem isn't really an option:** Drugs@FDA, Rozerem, Label, Indications and Usage.

62   **an article in the *New England Journal of Medicine*:** Roni Caryn Rabin, "Vital Facts May Be Missing on Drug Labels," *New York Times*, November 3, 2009.

4: EXTERMINATING ANGELS

64   **"spreading like a swarm":** "Just Try to Sleep Tight: The Bedbugs Are Back," *New York Times*, November 27, 2005.

64   **No one is safe:** Rush and Molloy, "Side Dish: Bill Clinton's Bedbug Battle," August 23, 2009.

64   **And it's no better overseas:** Arthur Martin, "Bedbug Epidemic That's Turning Great Britain into Great Bitten," *Daily Mail*, September 30, 2007.

64   **Entomologists and exterminators:** Sewell Chan, "Another Reason the City Never Sleeps: More Bedbugs," *New York Times*, September 19, 2006.

64   **"To keep gnats at bay":** Ekirch, *At Day's Close*, p. 270.

65   **A 2009 study:** Charles M. Morin et al., "Cognitive Behavioral Therapy, Singly and Combined with Medication, for Persistent Insomnia: A Randomized Controlled Trial," *Journal of the American Medical Association* 301, no. 19 (May 20, 2009): 2005–15.

66   **Eric Nofzinger:** Eric Nofzinger, "What Can Neuroimaging Findings Tell Us About Sleep Disorders?" *Sleep Medicine*, June 2004, 1:S16–22.

66   **A 2008 study:** John W. Winkelman et al., "Reduced Brain GABA in Primary Insomnia: Preliminary Data from 4T Proton Magnetic Resonance Spectroscopy," *SLEEP* 31, no. 11 (November 1, 2008): 1499–506.

67   **stimulus-control "tools":** Richard R. Bootzin, "Stimulus Control Treatment for Insomnia," Programs and Abstracts of the 80th Annual Convention of the American Psychological Association, September 2, 1972.

70   **The method was developed by Dr. Edmund Jacobson:** Kenton Kroker, *Studies in History and Philosophy of Biological and Biomedical Sciences* 34 (2003): 77–108.

71   **"It is physically impossible":** Jacobson, *You Must Relax*, p. 85.

71   **chronic insomniacs:** Daniel E. Ford and Douglas B. Kamerow, "Epidemiologic Study of Sleep Disturbances and Psychiatric Disorders: An Opportunity for Prevention?" *Journal of the American Medical Association* 262, no. 11 (September 15, 1989): 1479–84.

72   **An 1888 article:** "Victims of Insomnia," *Washington Post,* November 18, 1888.

72   **One way for insomnia sufferers:** Advertisement, *Washington Post,* January 27, 1900.

72   **"American nervousness":** George M. Beard, *American Nervousness: Its Causes and Consequences.* New York: G. P. Putnam's Sons, 1881.

73   **National Institutes of Health convened a consensus conference:** "Drugs and Insomnia: The Use of Medications to Promote Sleep," NIH Consensus Statement Online 4, no. 10 (November 5–17, 1983): 1–19.

73   **By the time the NIH held its second insomnia conference:** http://consensus.nih.gov/2005/2005InsomniaSOS026html.htm.

80   **Exercise raises body temperature:** Glovinsky and Spielman, *The Insomnia Answer,* p. 137.

81   **Many scientists believe that SAD:** Jane E. Brody, "New Tack Promising on Winter Depression," *New York Times,* March 31, 1998.

82   **Invented by Spielman:** Arthur Spielman, Paul Saskin, Michael Thorpy, "Treatment of Chronic Insomnia by Restriction of Time in Bed," *SLEEP* 10 (1987): 45–56.

5: ASTEROID LAS VEGAS

87   **Las Vegas glows so brightly:** "Lightscape/Night Sky," www.nps .gov/grba/naturescience/lightscape.htm.

87   **The city is so invested:** "Las Vegas Welcomes Asteroid Named in Its Honor," www.lasvegas2005.org/news/asteroid.html.

87   **Due to its reputation:** Ibid.

87   **In his book *Neon Metropolis*:** Rothman, *Neon Metropolis*, p. xxvii.

88   **The American Medical Association:** John W. Shepard et al., "History of the Development of Sleep Medicine in the United States," *Journal of Clinical Sleep Medicine* 1, no. 1 (2005).

88   **drug companies finance:** Duff Wilson, "Steps to Greater Accountability in Medical Education," *New York Times*, October 20, 2009.

89   **Jim Horne, the director:** Horne, *Sleepfaring*, p. 186.

90   **According to some reports:** Robert Barnes, "Exxon Oil Spill Case May Get Closure," *Washington Post*, February 24, 2008.

94   **Christina Molfetta:** "Winning in Las Vegas," *Sleep Review Magazine*, September 2006.

94   **In 2005, SDI Future Health was indicted:** "Diagnostic Laboratory Indicted for Fraud and Illegal Kickbacks to Nevada Physicians," www.usdoj.gov/usao/nv/home/pressrelease/march2005/sdi030305.htm.

94   **According to a recent Burt Sperling/Centrum study:** "The Unhealthiest Cities in America," http://health.msn.com/fitness/articlepage.aspx?cp-documentid=100104950.

94   **A Sperling/Ambien poll:** "Sleep in the City: Best and Worst Places for Sleep," www.bestplaces.net/docs/studies/Sleep.aspx.

95   **Of the approximately 860,000:** Nevada Department of Employment, Training and Rehabilitation, September 2009, detr.state.nv.us.

95   **In addition to the "master clock":** "Sleep Deprived Pay the Price for Shift Work," *Los Angeles Times*, March 24, 2008; Shin Yamazaki et al., "Resetting Central and Peripheral Circadian Oscillators in Transgenic Rats," *Science* 288 (2000): 682–85.

95   **In 2007 the International Agency for Research:** Acacia Aguirre and Martin Moore-Ede, "Does Shiftwork Cause Cancer?" Circadian 24/7 Workforce Solutions, www.circadian.com.

95   **Six out of the eight studies:** Ibid.

96   **Approximately 8.6 million Americans:** Alan Mozes, "Night Shift Work Hard on the Heart," *U.S. News & World Report*, March 3, 2009.

97   **one in every twenty weddings:** American Experience, Las Vegas: An Unconventional History, http://pbs.org/wgbh/amex/lasvegas/sfeature/sf_weddingstories.html.

97   **Adolescents are often:** "Adolescents in Adult City: Often from Else-where, and Going Nowhere," *New York Times*, June 1, 2004.

98   **Turek led an important study:** Fred W. Turek et al., "Obesity and Metabolic Syndrome in Circadian Clock Mutant Mice," *Science* 308 (May 13, 2005): 1043–45.

99   **Her laboratory produced:** Karine Spiegel et al., "Sleep Curtailment in Healthy Young Men Is Associated with Decreased Leptin Levels, Elevated Ghrelin Levels, and Increased Hunger and Appetite," *Annals of Internal Medicine* 141, no. 11 (December 7, 2004): 846–50.

99   **However, a 2008 review:** Nathaniel S. Marshall, Nick Glozier, and Ronald R. Grunstein, "Is Sleep Duration Related to Obesity? A Criti-cal Review of the Epidemiological Evidence," *Sleep Medicine Reviews* 12, no. 4 (August 2008): 289–98.

102   **Another doctor brings up Libby Zion:** "A Life-Changing Case for Doctors in Training," *New York Times*, March 3, 2009.

102   **While an eighty-hour week:** "Napping During Hospital Shifts," edi-torial, *New York Times*, December, 9, 2008.

103   **Jim Horne believes:** Horne, *Sleepfaring*, p. 79.

103   **This pattern of risky behavior:** Vinod Venkatraman et al., "Sleep Dep-rivation Elevates Expectation of Gains and Attenuates Response to Losses Following Risky Decisions," *SLEEP* 30, no. 5 (May 1, 2007): 603–9.

103   **In 2007 the Mayo Clinic:** Maja Tippmann-Peikert et al., "Pathologic Gambling in Patients with Restless Legs Syndrome Treated with Dopaminergic Agonists," *Neurology* 68, no. 4 (January 23, 2007): 301–3.

104   **While the Mayo Clinic study:** M. Leann Dodd et al., "Pathological Gambling Caused by Drugs Used to Treat Parkinson Disease," *Archives of Neurology* 62, no. 9 (September 2005): 1377–81; J. Michael Bostwick et al., "Frequency of New-Onset Pathologic Compulsive Gambling or Hypersexuality After Drug Treatment of Idiopathic Parkinson Disease," *Mayo Clinic Proceedings* 84, no. 4 (April 2009): 310–16.

104   **The real-life Fossey:** Alex Shoumatoff, "Fatal Obsession: The Jungle Death of Dian Fossey," *Vanity Fair*, September 1986.

6: BREATHLESS

108 **A growing body of research suggests:** American Society of Clinical Hypnosis, www.asch.net.

108 **Several studies published:** Allan Staib and D. R. Logan, "Hypnotic Stimulation of Breast Growth," *American Journal of Clinical Hypnosis,* 4 (1977): 201–8; R. D. Willard, "Breast Enlargement Through Visual Imagery and Hypnosis," Ibid., 195–200.

108 **In A.D. 167:** John Bartlett, *Familiar Quotations,* 10th ed.

108 **The modern age of hypnotism:** Sanders, *Clinical Self-Hypnosis,* p. 30.

109 **Another Scottish surgeon:** Alan Gauld, *A History of Hypnotism.* Cambridge: Cambridge University Press, 1992, p. 222.

109 **To make sure patients were suitably:** Ibid.

109 **French neurologist Jean-Martin Charcot:** Sanders, *Clinical Self-Hypnosis,* p. 35.

109 **Freud studied with Charcot:** Ibid.

109 **The role of hypnosis in modern medicine:** James H. Stewart, "Hypnosis in Contemporary Medicine," *Mayo Clinic Proceedings* 80, no. 4 (April 2005): 511–24.

109 **In 1958 the American Medical Association:** "Hypnosis Still Provokes Some Skeptics," *New York Times,* March 31, 1987; "NIH Technology Assessment Panel on Integration of Behavioral and Relaxation Approaches into the Treatment of Chronic Pain and Insomnia," *Journal of the American Medical Association* 276 (1996): 313–18.

110 **Several studies using PET scans:** "Altered States," *Newsweek,* September 7, 2004.

112 **Dream Quilts:** www.talkaboutsleep.com.

114 **Before apnea came into vogue:** Kroker, *The Sleep of Others,* p. 401.

114 **Robert Macnish:** Ibid., p. 402.

115 **It wasn't until the early 1980s:** Ibid., p. 414.

115 **It looks like a small vacuum cleaner:** www.sleepapnea.org/ resources/pubs/pioneer.html.

116 **POS can predispose:** Alexandros N. Vgontzas et al., "Polycystic Ovary Syndrome Is Associated with Obstructive Sleep Apnea and

Daytime Sleepiness: Role of Insulin Resistance," *Journal of Clinical Endocrinology & Metabolism* 86, no. 2 (February 2001): 517–20.

120 **The American Academy of Sleep Medicine recommends:** "Practice Parameters for the Treatment of Snoring and Obstructive Sleep Apnea with Oral Appliances," *SLEEP* 18 (1995): 501–10.

7: ALERT! AWARE! AWAKE!

125 **He'd just spent a week:** Kenneth Silverman, "When the City Was Magical," *New York Times,* May 13, 2006.

125 **When he did "Frozen in Time":** "Weak from His 62 Hours in Ice, Ice Man Exits to an Ambulance," *New York Times,* November 30, 2000.

126 *Guinness World Records:* "Man Who Stayed Up for 266 Hours Awakes to Bad News," www.timesonline.co.uk/tol/news/uk/health/article1842716.ece.

126 **In 2007, Tony Wright:** Ibid.

126 **Six years earlier, Dement:** Dement and Vaughn, *The Promise of Sleep,* p. 244.

126 **one of the first scientific studies:** Ibid.

126 **Tripp's symptoms:** Stanley Coren, "Sleep Deprivation, Psychosis and Mental Efficiency," *Psychiatric Times* 15, no. 3 (March 1, 1998), www.psychiatrictimes.com/p980301b.html.

126 **After his ordeal:** Paul Martin, *Counting Sheep,* p. 69.

127 **Dement had initially interpreted:** Dement and Vaughn, *The Promise of Sleep,* p. 43.

127 **After observing Gardner:** Ibid., p. 247.

127 **Looking back on the Tripp episode:** Ibid., p. 45.

127 **Yet Gardner wasn't taking any stimulants:** Coren, "Sleep Deprivation."

127 **Even Wright:** "How Man Pushed Sleepless Limits," news.bbc.co.uk/1/hi/england/cornwall/6690485.stm.

127 **For that reason:** Rebecca Lemov, "The Birth of Soft Torture," *Slate,* November 16, 2005.

127 **Former Israeli prime minister:** "The Real Victims of Sleep Deprivation," news.bbc.co.uk/1/hi/magazine/3376951.stm.

127 **More recently, the U.S. military:** "Guantanamo Records Reveal

Another Case in Which U.S. Used Sleep Deprivation," *Associated Press,* July 15, 2008.

128 **Most employees:** "Indian Call Centers: Not a Bed of Roses," http://indiacurrents.com/news/view_article.html?article_id =2ba79f90c71d60e.

128 **Consequently, Indian outsourcers:** "Where Do India's Outsourcers Outsource?" www.forbes.com/2007/05/21/outsourcing-india -destination-biz-cx_rd_0529india.html.

128 **a review in *The New York Times*:** "Film in Review, China Blue," *New York Times,* January 26, 2007.

129 **The drug was approved:** Andrew Pollack, "A Biotech Outcast Awakens," *New York Times,* October 20, 2002.

129 **Six U.S. track-and-field athletes:** "USOC Lists Failed Drug Tests," *USA Today,* December 30, 2003.

129 **According to *The Washington Post*:** Michael Arrington, "How Many Silicon Valley Startup Executives Are Hopped Up on Provigil?" *Washington Post,* July 14, 2008, www.washingtonpost.com/wp-dyn/ content/article/2008/07/15/AR2008071500261.html.

130 **According to a Walter Reed Army Institute:** Nancy J. Wesensten et al., "Maintaining Alertness and Performance During Sleep Deprivation: Modafinil Versus Caffeine," *Psychopharmacology* 159 (January 2002): 238–47.

130 **Jouvet had conducted experiments:** Jouvet, *The Paradox of Sleep,* p. 34.

131 **Jouvet went on to coin:** Norton Milgram, "Adrafinil: A Novel Vigilance Promoting Agent," *CNS Drug Reviews* 5, no. 3 (1999): 193–212.

131 **In 1993, Cephalon:** Pollack, "Biotech Outcast Awakens."

131 **the drug's addiction potential:** Nora D. Volkow et al., "Effects of Modafinil on Dopamine and Dopamine Transporters in the Male Human Brain: Clinical Implications," *Journal of the American Medical Association* 301, no. 11 (March 18, 2009): 1148–54.

132 **Since only about one in two thousand:** www.ninds.nih.gov/ disorders/narcolepsy/narcolepsy.htm.

132 **When Dr. Thomas Roth:** www.fda.gov/ohrms/dockets/ac/03/transcripts/3979T2.htm.

132 **Cephalon began suggesting:** www.pharmcast.com/WarningLetters/Yr2002/Jan2002/Cephalon0102.htm.

132 **In 2002 the FDA sent:** Ibid.

132 **the FDA agreed in 2004:** www.apneanet.org/pressreleases/provigil.htm.

132 **Provigil was shown:** Charles A. Czeisler, James K. Walsh, and Thomas Roth, "Modafinil for Excessive Sleepiness Associated with Shift-Work Sleep Disorder," *New England Journal of Medicine* 353, no. 5 (2005): 476–86.

133 **It's hard to know:** Ibid.

133 **after he admitted:** Pollack, "Biotech Outcast Awakens."

133 **80 percent of the drug's prescriptions:** Ibid.

134 **Cephalon's 2008 agreement:** http://online.wsj.com/public/resources/documents/cephalonplea.pdf.

134 **a 2003 study:** D.C. Turner et al., "Cognitive Enhancing Effects of Modafinil in Healthy Volunteers," *Psychopharmacology* 165, no. 3 (January 2003): 260–69.

134 **In a 2008 poll:** www.nature.com/news/2008/080409/full/452674a.html.

135 **A 2005 national study:** www.umich.edu/news/index.html?Releases/2005/Jan05/r010605.

135 **In a sample of middle:** Sean Esteban McCabe, Christian J. Teter, and Carol J. Boyd, "The Use, Misuse and Diversion of Prescription Stimulants Among Middle and High School Students," *Substance Use & Misuse* 39, no. 7 (June 2004): 1095–116.

135 **"cosmetic neurology":** Anjan Chatterjee, "Cosmetic Neurology: The Controversy Over Enhancing Movement, Mentation, and Mood," *Neurology* 63 (2004): 968–74.

136 **In 1998, Carskadon:** Mary A. Carskadon et al., "Adolescent Sleep Patterns, Circadian Timing, and Sleepiness at a Transition to Early School Days," *SLEEP* 21, no. 8 (1998): 871–81.

136 **Since Red Bull:** Michael Mason, "The Energy-Drink Buzz Is Unmistakable," *New York Times,* December 12, 2006.

136 **While it's not known:** Ibid.

136 **In 2005, Advocare:** Duff Wilson, "A Sports Drink for Children Is Jangling Some Nerves," *New York Times,* September 25, 2005.

136 **According to the company's website:** www.advocare.com.

137 **the brainchild of a molecular scientist:** www.buzzdonuts.com.

137 **In 2003 the military's use:** Thom Shanker with Mary Duennald, "Bombing Error Puts a Spotlight on Pilots' Pills," *New York Times,* January 19, 2003.

138 **"I'll fly with the guy":** "Sleepy Soldiers Face Serious Dangers in Iraq," *Dallas Morning News,* March 25, 2003.

138 **given to French foreign legion troops:** Richard Martin, "It's Wake-Up Time," *Wired,* November 2003.

138 **British Ministry of Defense:** "U.K. Army Tested 'Stay Awake' Pills," BBC News, October 26, 2006.

138 **The U.S. Air Force has approved:** "Modafinil and Management of Aircrew Fatigue," Memorandum from the Department of the Air Force, December 2, 2003.

138 **Preventing Sleep Deprivation Program:** Jonathan D. Moreno, "Juicing the Brain," *Scientific American,* November 29, 2006.

138 **The agency was created:** "DARPA History," www.darpa.mil.

138 **Along with such notable hits:** Charles Filler, "Army of Extreme Thinkers," *Los Angeles Times,* August 14, 2003.

138 **It was canceled:** Ibid.

138 **"metabolically dominant" soldiers:** www.darpa.mil/darpatech2002/presentations/dso_pdf/speeches/GOLDBLAT.pdf.

140 **Jerome Siegel has developed:** "DARPA Develops Brain Chemical to Replace Sleep," Reuters, January 4, 2006.

140 **Neuroscientist Giulio Tononi:** www.darpa.mil/Docs/PSD_info_paper_Oct07_200807180945043.pdf.

140 **Sam Ridgway:** Noah Shachtman, "Darpa: Dolphins Stay Alert for 5 Days Straight: Could Soldiers Do the Same?" *Wired,* October 7, 2008.

140 **Other scientists:** Niels C. Rattenborg et al., "Migratory Sleeplessness

in the White-Crowned Sparrow," *PLoS Biology* 2, no. 7 (July 2004), www.ncbi.nlm.nih.gov/pubmed/15252455.

140 **many astronauts use sleeping pills:** NASA website, http://space flight.nasa.gov/shuttle/archives/sts-95/factsheets/fs1998 _09_010jsc.html.

141 **In 1997 astronaut Jerry Linenger:** "University of Pennsylvania Researchers Find Potential Sleep Problems," www.eurekalert.org/ pub_releases/2001-11/uopm-uop111501.php.

142 **Linenger and his two Russian:** William Speed Weed, "Can We Go to Mars Without Going Crazy?" *Discover,* May 2001.

142 **Such was the culture clash:** Jerry Linenger, *Off the Planet: Surviving Five Perilous Months Aboard the Space Station Mir.* New York: McGraw-Hill, 2000, p. 129.

143 **To test the effectiveness of naps:** NASA website, http://science .nasa.gov/headlines/y2005/03jun_naps.htm.

143 **Dinges has been collecting data:** "NEEMO: Astronauts Under Water," www.eurekalert.org/pub_releases/2006-05/nsbr-iuh050906.php.

143 **"promises to satisfy":** Jerome Groopman. "Eyes Wide Open," *New Yorker,* December 3, 2001.

143 **a "twentieth-century thing":** "Waking Up to Sleep Conference," Science Network at the Salk Institute, 2007.

8: THE SELLING OF SLEEP

148 **"You spend what you want now":** Shyema Patel, "Make Your Bed," *New York,* July 19, 1999.

149 **As Anthony Burgess writes:** Burgess, *On Going to Bed,* book flap.

149 **The Roman historian Tacitus:** Ibid., p. 8.

149 **When Howard Carter discovered:** Wright, *Warm & Snug,* p. 4.

149 **The ancient Romans:** Ibid., p. 11.

149 **while the Persians:** David Derbyshire, "Bad News for Playboys," *Telegraph* (U.K.), October 20, 2004.

149 **The idea would reach:** David Maurer, "Comfort of Water Is Not Really New," *Charlottesville Daily Progress,* May 4, 2008.

149 **The phrase "making a bed":** Wright, *Warm & Snug*, p. 18.

149 **The royal French beds:** Ibid., p. 54.

150 **"Persons entering the bedchamber":** Ibid., p 58.

150 **In the seventeenth and eighteenth centuries:** Von Furstenberg, *Beds*, p. 114.

150 **In 1945, Mrs. Bernice Bowser:** "Change Is Urged in Bedroom Design," *New York Times,* July 7, 1945.

151 **Design Within Reach launched:** "The Bed, Remade," *New York Times,* April 27, 2006.

151 **In 1956 the sales vice president:** "One of Simmons' Inner Springs," *New York Times,* November 25, 1956.

154 **Originally developed in the 1960s:** www.tempurpedic.com/about/history_heritage.

154 **In 1992 they granted:** Arlene Weintraub, "Sweet Dreams Are Made of Foam," *BusinessWeek,* August 15, 2005.

154 **"promote a better quality of life":** www.tempurpedic.com/about/history_heritage.

155 **the law set off a flurry:** "What Might Be in Your Mattress," CBS Chicago, September 24, 2007; "Sleeping with Danger," ABC Cincinnati, May 5, 2008.

156 **Toxicologist Stephen Safe:** Julie Scelfo, "The Stuffing Dreams Are Made Of?" *New York Times,* January 17, 2009.

156 **Americans spend $23.9 billion:** Lesley Alderman, "Cost-Effective Ways to Fight Insomnia," *New York Times,* June 6, 2009.

158 **In the early 1990s, Dr. Thomas Wehr:** Thomas A. Wehr, "In Short Photoperiods, Human Sleep Is Biphasic," *Journal of Sleep Research* 1, no. 2 (June 1992): 103–7.

158 **"There is every reason":** Ekirch, *At Day's Close,* p. 303.

159 **Carol Worthman:** Carol M. Worthman and Melissa K. Melby, "Toward a Comparative Developmental Ecology of Human Sleep," webdrive.service.emory.edu/groups/research/lchb/PUBLICATIONSWorthman/PUBLICATIONS CMW 2002/Ecology of Human Sleep.pdf.

159 **"lie down and die":** Ibid., p. 108.

159 **old patterns "breaking through":** Roger Ekirch, "Dreams Deferred," *New York Times,* Op-Ed, February 19, 2006.

161 **Arshad Chowdhury:** Elwin Green, "Carnegie Mellon Graduate's Idea for Sleep Salon Evolves into Nap at Work Business," *Pittsburg Post-Gazette,* January 14, 2008.

161 **The Japanese have long practiced:** Summers-Bremner, *Insomnia,* p. 141.

161 **We experience a natural dip:** Mednick and Ehrman, *Take a Nap!,* p. 5.

162 **moving away from the siesta:** Daniel Woolls, "Comfy Chair: Niche for Serving Siesta-Deprived," *Los Angeles Times,* June 13, 1999.

162 **Instead of a three-hour lunch break:** Leslie Crawford, "Spaniards Wake Up to the End of the Siesta," *Financial Times,* December 27, 2005.

162 **"wreaking havoc":** Dan Bilefsky, "Spain Says Adiós Siesta and Hola Viagra," *New York Times,* February 11, 2007.

162 **Napping parlors:** Richard Boudreaux, "Spaniards Are Missing Their Naps," *Los Angeles Times,* March 28, 2000.

9: POLAR NIGHTS

164 **Newgrange:** www.nd.edu/~ikuijt/Ireland/Sites/jstah/detail.htm.

166 **Pierre-Louis Moreau de Maupertuis:** www.encyclopedia.com/doc/1E1-Maupertu.html.

170 **Beginning in the fifteenth century:** "Sami Culture," www.utexas.edu/courses/sami/diehtu/newera/samiculturenordic.htm.

170 **between fifteen thousand and twenty thousand Sami:** "UNESCO in Action Culture: Anna's Quest," http://portal.unesco.org/en/ev.php-URL_ID=10411&URL_DO=DO_TOPIC&URL_SECTIO.

170 **the reindeer population worldwide has plunged:** www.livescience.com/environment/090611-reindeer-populations-plunge.com.

173 **our sleep architecture:** National Heart Lung and Blood Institute, www.nhlbi.nih.gov/health/prof/sleep/res_plan/section4/section4c.html.

174 **a study at Brigham and Women's:** Elizabeth B. Klerman and Derk-

Jan Dijk, "Age-Related Reduction in the Maximal Capacity for Sleep: Implications for Insomnia," *Current Biology* 5, no. 15 (August 5, 2008): 1118–23.

175 **California neurologist David Rosenfeld:** David S. Rosenfeld and Antoine J. Elhajjar, "Sleepsex: A Variant of Sleepwalking," *Archives of Sexual Behavior* 3 (June 27, 1998): 69–78.

175 **"sexsomnia" as a defense:** "Court Upholds 'Sexsomnia' Rape Defense," United Press International, February 8, 2008, www.upi .com/Top_News/2008/02/08/Court-upholds-sexsomnia-rape -defense/.

175 **Kenneth Parks:** Paul Martin, *Counting Sheep,* p. 273.

176 **identified RBD as a new parasomnia:** Carlos H. Schenck, Thomas D. Hurwitz, and Mark W. Mahowald, "REM Sleep Behavior Disorder," *American Journal of Psychiatry* 145, no. 5 (May 1988): 652.

177 **"Convinced of the therapeutic primacy":** Gallagher, *The Power of Place,* p. 14.

178 **Pi-Square Dawn-Dusk Simulation System:** Center for Environmental Therapeutics, www.cet.org.

10: THE HOUSE OF RHYTHM AND BLUES

182 **First developed in 1991:** "In Session with Galina Mindlin, MD, PhD," *Psychiatry Weekly,* www.psychweekly.com/aspx/article/ArticleDetail .aspx?articleid=215.

183 **several double-blind studies:** Leonid Kayumov et al., "Brain Music Therapy for Treatment of Insomnia and Anxiety," www .brainmusictreatment.com/popup_sleep.html.

184 **Pythagoras:** Christoph Reidwig and Steven Rendall, *Pythagoras: His Life, Teaching, and Influence.* New York: Cornell University Press, 2008, p. 30.

184 **In the Bible:** 1 Samuel 16:23.

184 **Oxford scholar Robert Burton:** James Le Fanu, "Mood Music," *Globe and Mail* (Canada), February 23, 2008.

184 **modern era of music therapy:** Ibid.

184 **numerous research studies:** www.amc-music.org.

11: THE MAN FROM CON ED

197 **Qigong:** Jahnke, *The Healing Promise of Qi.*

201 **Irwin has just completed:** "Improving Sleep Quality in Older Adults with Moderate Sleep Complaints: A Randomized Controlled Trial of Tai Chi Chih," *SLEEP* 31, no. 7 (July 1, 2008): 1001–8.

202 **Harrington dates the beginning:** Harrington, *The Cure Within,* p. 210.

202 **teaching squirrel monkeys:** Benson, *The Relaxation Response,* p. 7.

202 **Harvard physiologist Walter Cannon:** Ibid., p. 8.

202 **"the ability to heal":** Ibid., p. 9.

203 **In 1979, Jon Kabat-Zinn:** Stephen S. Hall, "Is Buddhism Good for Your Health?" *New York Times,* July 23, 2009.

203 **At Harvard Medical School:** Gregg D. Jacobs and Richard Friedman, "EEG Spectral Analysis of Relaxation Techniques," *Applied Psychophysiology and Feedback* 29, no. 4 (December 2004): 245–54.

12: SPIRIT OF THE DREAM

221 **dreams are the guardians:** Freud, *The Interpretation of Dreams,* p. 128.

222 **Dream research peaked:** Tore A. Nielsen and Anne Germain, "Publication Patterns in Dreaming," *Journal of the Association for the Study of Dreams,* vol. 8(2) (June 1998): pp. 47–58.

222 **"activation-synthesis model of dream production":** J. Allan Hobson and Robert W. McCarley, "The Brain as a Dream State Generator: An Activation-Synthesis Hypothesis of the Dream Process," *American Journal of Psychiatry* 134, no. 12 (December 1977): 1335–48.

222 **It was widely assumed:** Van de Castle, *Our Dreaming Mind,* p. 265.

222 **"most fanciful, delicious":** Lisa Birk, "Dream Warriors," *Boston Phoenix,* January 21–28, 1999.

222 **In 1983, Francis Crick:** Van de Castle, *Our Dreaming Mind,* p. 275.

222 **Since then, the public debate:** G. William Domhoff, "Dream Research in the Mass Media: Where Journalists Go Wrong on Dreams," *Scientific Review of Mental Health Practice* 4, no. 2: 74–78.

222   **After studying a group of people:** Mark Solms, *The Neuropsychology of Dreams: A Clinico-Anatomical Study,* www.psychoanalysis.org.uk/solms4.htm.

223   **Solms and Hobson:** Mark Solms, "Freud Returns," *Scientific American,* May 2004.

223   **Robert Stickgold:** Kristin Leutwyler, "Tetris Dreams," *Scientific American,* October 16, 2000, www.scientificamerican.com/article.cfm?id=tetris-dreams.

223   **Over the past forty years:** "Dreams: The Purpose of Dreams," http://psych.ucsc.edu/dreams/Articles/purpose.html; www.dreambank.net.

231   **psychologist Stephen LaBerge:** Lucidity Institute website, www.lucidity.com.

BIBLIOGRAPHY

Angell, Marcia. *The Truth About the Drug Companies: How They Deceive Us and What to Do About It*. New York: Random House, 2004.

Barrett, Deidre. *The Committee of Sleep: How Artists, Scientists, and Athletes Use Dreams for Creative Problem-Solving—and How You Can Too*. New York: Crown, 2001.

Benson, Herbert. *The Relaxation Response*. New York: William Morrow, 1975.

Burgess, Anthony. *On Going to Bed*. New York: Abbeville, 1982.

Chopra, Deepak. *Restful Sleep*. New York: Three Rivers Press, 1994.

Coren, Stanley. *Sleep Thieves: An Eye-Opening Exploration into the Science and Mysteries of Sleep*. New York: Simon & Schuster, 1996.

Dement, William C., and Christopher Vaughn. *The Promise of Sleep*. New York: Delacorte, 1999.

Dyer, Wayne W. *The Power of Intention*. Carlsbad, Calif.: Hay House, 2004.

Ekirch, A. Roger. *At Day's Close: Night in Times Past*. New York: W. W. Norton, 2005.

Ellman, Steven J., and John S. Antrobus. *The Mind in Sleep*. New York: John Wiley & Sons, 1991.

Flanagan, Owen. *Dreaming Souls: Sleep, Dreams, and the Evolution of the Conscious Mind*. New York: Oxford University Press, 2000.

Freud, Sigmund. *The Interpretation of Dreams.* Charlotte, N.C.: IAP, 2009.

Gallagher, Winifred. *The Power of Place: How Our Surroundings Shape Our Thoughts, Emotions, and Actions.* New York: Poseidon Press, 1993.

Gay, Peter. *Freud: A Life for Our Time.* New York: W. W. Norton, 1998.

Glovinsky, Paul, and Arthur Spielman. *The Insomnia Answer: Breakthrough Solutions for Getting to Sleep, Staying Asleep, Broken Sleep.* New York: Berkley, 2006.

Greene, Gayle. *Insomniac.* Berkeley: University of California Press, 2008.

Harrington, Anne. *The Cure Within: A History of Mind-Body Medicine.* New York: W. W. Norton, 2009.

Hayes, Bill. *Sleep Demons: An Insomniac's Memoir.* New York: Washington Square Press, 2001.

Healy David. *The Creation of Psychopharmacology.* Cambridge, Mass: Harvard University Press, 2002.

Horne, James. *Why We Sleep: The Functions of Sleep in Humans and Other Mammals.* New York: Oxford University Press, 1998.

———. *Sleepfaring: A Journey Through the Science of Sleep.* Oxford University Press, 2006.

Idzikowski, Chris. *Learn to Sleep Well.* San Francisco: Chronicle Books, 2000.

Jacobs, Gregg D. *Say Good Night to Insomnia.* New York: Henry Holt, 1998.

Jacobson, Edmund. *You Must Relax.* New York: McGraw-Hill, 1957.

Jahnke, Roger. *The Healing Promise of Qi: Creating Extraordinary Wellness Through Qigong and Tai Chi.* New York: McGraw-Hill, 2002.

Jouvet, Michel. *The Paradox of Sleep: The Story of Dreaming.* Cambridge, Mass: MIT Press, 1999.

Jung, C. G. *Memories, Dreams, Reflections.* Recorded and edited by Aniela Jaffé. New York: Vintage, 1965.

Kroker, Kenton. *The Sleep of Others and the Transformation of Sleep Research.* Toronto: University of Toronto Press, 2006.

Maas, James B. *Power Sleep: The Revolutionary Program That Prepares Your Mind for Peak Performance.* New York: Villard, 1998.

Martin, Paul. *Counting Sheep: The Science and Pleasures of Sleep and Dreams.* New York: Thomas Dunne Books, 2002.

Max, D. T. *The Family That Couldn't Sleep.* New York: Random House, 2006.

Mednick, Sara C., with Mark Ehrman. *Take a Nap! Change Your Life.* New York: Workman, 2006.

Moore-Ede, Martin. *The Twenty Four Hour Society: Understanding Human Limits in a World That Never Stops.* Reading, Mass: Addison-Wesley, 1993.

Moyers, Bill. *Healing and the Mind.* New York: Doubleday, 1993.

Moynihan, Ray, and Alan Cassels. *Selling Sickness: How the World's Biggest Pharmaceutical Companies Are Turning Us All into Patients.* New York: Nation, 2005.

Myrone, Martin. *Gothic Nightmares: Fuseli, Blake and the Romantic Imagination.* London: Tate Publishing, 2006.

Petersen, Melody. *Our Daily Meds: How the Pharmaceutical Companies Transformed Themselves into Slick Marketing Machines and Hooked the Nation on Prescription Drugs.* New York: Farrar, Straus and Giroux, 2008.

Rothman, Hal. *Neon Metropolis: How Las Vegas Started the Twenty-First Century.* New York: Routledge, 2003.

Sanders, Shirley. *Clinical Self-Hypnosis: The Power of Words and Image.* New York: Guilford Press, 1991.

Schwartz, Tony. *What Really Matters: Searching for Wisdom in America.* New York: Bantam, 1995.

Solms, Mark. *The Neuropsychology of Dreams: A Clinico-Anatomical Study.* Mahwah, N.J.: Lawrence Erlbaum, 1997.

Spaar, Lisa Russ, ed. *Acquainted with the Night: Insomnia Poems.* New York: Columbia University Press, 1999.

Styron, William. *Darkness Visible: A Memoir of Madness.* New York: Random House, 1990.

Summers-Bremner, Eluned. *Insomnia: A Cultural History.* London: Reaktion, 2008.

Taylor, Jeremy. *The Living Labyrinth: Exploring Universal Themes in Myths, Dreams, and the Symbolism of Waking Life.* Mahwah, N.J.: Paulist Press, 1998.

Van de Castle, Robert L. *Our Dreaming Mind.* New York: Ballantine, 1994.

Von Furstenberg, Diane. *Beds.* New York: Bantam, 1991.

Walsleben, Joyce A., and Rita Baron-Faust. *A Woman's Guide to Sleep.* New York: Three Rivers Press, 2000.

Waugh, Evelyn. *The Ordeal of Gilbert Pinfold.* Boston: Back Bay, 1957.

Williams, Simon J. *Sleep and Society.* Abingdon, U.K.: Routledge, 2005.

Wright, Lawrence. *Warm & Snug: The History of the Bed.* Gloucestershire, U.K.: Sutton, 2004.

INDEX

ABOUT THE AUTHOR

PATRICIA MORRISROE received a B.A. from Tufts University and an M.A. from New York University. She is the author of *Mapplethorpe: A Biography* and was for many years a contributing editor to *New York* magazine. She has written for numerous other publications, including *Vanity Fair* and *Vogue*. She lives in New York City.

ABOUT THE TYPE

This book was set in Monotype Dante, a typeface designed by Giovanni Mardersteig (1892–1977). Conceived as a private type for the Officina Bodoni in Verona, Italy, Dante was originally cut only for hand composition by Charles Malin, the famous Parisian punch cutter, between 1946 and 1952. Its first use was in an edition of Boccaccio's *Trattatello in laude di Dante* that appeared in 1954. The Monotype Corporation's version of Dante followed in 1957. Though modeled on the Aldine type used for Pietro Cardinal Bembo's treatise *De Aetna* in 1495, Dante is a thoroughly modern interpretation of that venerable face.